The Naked Path of Prophet series

Ecstatic Prophets, Compulsive Fascists

A study of how ecstatic-experience can transform each other's fascisms into love with 1 Samuel 18-31

translation & commentaries by
Brian J. Shircliff

VITALITY
buzz, bliss + books

Ecstatic Prophets, Compulsive Fascists:
A study of how ecstastic-experience can transform
each other's fascisms into love with 1 Samuel 18 - 31
vol 2 of The Naked Path of Prophet *series*
Copyright © 2025 by Brian J. Shircliff

Published by VITALITY buzz, bliss + books LLC
vitalitybuzz.org

VITALITY buzz, bliss + books LLC publishes original creations to grow the mission of VITALITY Cincinnati Inc, a 501(c)3 education-based nonprofit: sharing holistic self-care from neighborhood to neighborhood, person to person, and breath by breath since 2010.

The opinions and ideas expressed herein are those of the author and do not necessarily represent the opinions of the VATRONS of VITALITY buzz, bliss + books LLC or the Board of Trustees of VITALITY Cincinnati. Any errors, of course, are solely the author's.

Every effort has been made to give credit to other people's original ideas through the text itself and the recommended resources that follow this text. If you feel something should be credited to someone and is not, please get in touch through our website and every effort will be made to correct this text for future printings. Thank you!

We invite you to honor your mind, your body, your whole self. Do only what you know to be right for you. While the invitations offered here in this book, on our websites and social media, and in our classes are geared to be gentle and easily modified by the participant to fit the participants' needs, please consult your medical doctor or health professional before undertaking any practices.

Artists Sean Long and Julie Lucas contributed their work to this edition. Thank you!

ISBN: 978-1-954688-27-8
Library of Congress Control Number: applied for

This volume is dedicated
to the toddler in each one of us adults —

this 'inner-toddler' who knows so well both

freedom's playful curiosity
&
fascism's compulsive control.

May we be wise(r) adults who discern the significant differences between freedom and fascism...

adults who choose wisely for the good of all on Earth and in the Universe...

that more and more delight becomes possible for us humans figuring out together how to get along compassionately with each other and all creatures of Earth...something eventually even the most unruly toddler figures out...maybe with some compassionate help.

in gratitude

to the VATRONS
who breathed life into this volume
by pre-ordering their copy

Cynthia Allen & Larry Wells, Mark Brockman, Helen Buswinka,
Roma Cusimano, Mary Duennes, Paula & Mark Dunson,
Denise & Mike Eck, Pat Kreider, Mary Maxwell, David Meredith,
Eric Nichols, Krista Powers, Bob Reineke, Jodi & Wayne Shircliff,
Bill Tonnis, and anonymous friends

I'm very grateful to Helen Buswinka for reading and improving early versions of *The Naked Path of Prophet* and *Ecstatic Prophets* with her deep wisdom. Thank you, Helen!

CONTENTS

Inner-Styles & After-Styles

Resources for Further Discovery

An Invitation to This Volume
The Naked Path of Prophet volume 2

We are quick to forget that when one one group decides for another what is best and who is better and why and clothes such decisions in having been spoken by 'God'/divinity...that is fascism.

Fascisms raise and rear us. They permeate our 21st century organized religions, governments, businesses, teams, and even the most loving adult families — though children change the dynamic as I'll invite us to wonder about together soon.

Even my once-beloved yoga is steeped in fascist thinking if we think, as teachers, we always know what's best for a student/ fellow-discover instead of reminding each other that each one of us can sense and feel and then choose what's best for oneself.

And that's just it, isn't it? As full-grown adults, we want to decide for ourselves, right? We want to live self-determined lives that do not infringe on anyone else's self-determination. Fascism does not allow people to choose for themselves — fascism dictates. How often we inflict fascism upon one another...in small ways, sometimes in lethal ways, in ways that keep that tragic game of one-better-than-another going.

How quickly we cry out when someone blocks our path to a self-determined life and just as quickly then turn around and block someone else's livelihood — and even sometimes seek to destroy them — people who want to live self-determined lives just as much as you and I do. And often we seem stunned why someone would act this way — and why we act this way.

I suspect more and more senseless atrocities and genocides will continue to happen and we will all play our part, even unknowingly, until we come to know the taproot and millennia-old mindset from which they emerge.

What troubling taproot?

In my area of the world, it's the Bible, that 2500+ years old archive of writings from hundreds of writers through nearly a thousand years of writing — all these writers with very different agendas and viewpoints — all these writers often writing at each other.

So much imagination, language, and ideology — religious or not — comes to the 21st century — consciously or not — through the Bible. It's a book about the most tender love and a book about the most atrocious violence in the name of 'God' — both of these opposing forces coiled together into one big book. So many, yesterday and today, continue to think the whole book is "God's way" without evaluating much of it.

And do we ever need to evaluate it....

Judaism's Torah and the larger Hebrew Bible in which it is housed are filled with fascist elements. Using this same Hebrew Bible, Christianity steeped itself in '*Christ*' — the title Jesus rejected and sought to undermine. Christianity as an organized religion with its many branches and the "New Testament" (sic) animating those branches are riddled with fascist elements too. Islam finds its roots from this same Bible as well.

It appears to me that followers of these three religions — Judaism and Christianity and Islam— rarely notice the fascist elements in their/our own religion. They/We often celebrate these fascist elements. Even their/our so-called wise leaders rarely call out and even less rarely remove these fascist elements from daily worship or prayer or sermon/

instruction. I went along with it all too in my own Roman Catholic Christianity...until I started paying attention.

Why should we be surprised when the three Biblically-inspired religions' followers formed by fascism erupt with terrible violence, often against each other, century after century after century?

> Christian & Nazi Germany against the Jews of Europe in World War 2 and long before that

> Israel against Palestine, Hamas-with-others against Israel ...all too often and for decades

> on and on and on...each committing atrocities and attempting to eradicate the other in the name of their 'God' and in the name of their religious tradition.

It doesn't need to be this way. There are things we can do.

But it's trickier than we anticipated, isn't it? That taproot invites a tongue-twisting doublespeak, a one hand doing one good thing and the other harming, even killing. Love and sweetness intertwined with hate and terrible violence — all in the name of 'God.'

It's time we pause a bit and then begin untangling this messy Bible — and the taproots twining within our own guts — to become clearer on what it is we are doing personally and collectively, and in that paused space, discover we have very different choices before us between self-determination and control/fascism.

For those of us who follow an organized religion, we often sense/feel one thing within our skin and then seek out what's best to do with that feeling by appealing to the religion's code and cult/code-directed-community — not by doing the hard and messy work in the pause of sensing what might be best for oneself and the world, of working it out within oneself. And sure, we might appeal to old codes and stories for wisdom — but we'll need to bring that wisdom into oneself to decide if it is indeed wise for this moment.

Organized religion offers its own problems, for sure. But it's not just with those of us steeped in organized religion who have problems.

That taproot of biblical proportions sprouting everywhere...

Some of us today espouse democracy and its self-determined ideals in one grand speech and then minutes later want to control others and their choices through a fascism that arrives within us, from where we do not usually seem to know.

We're always surprised when it comes around again — this fascism, this need to control. It erupts out of nowhere and then avalanches into some tragedy again for all involved, whether it's a few people or millions.

And we act surprised. "I didn't see that coming!"

But that's an entirely ignorant response, we must admit, if we really know ourselves well. As Moshe Feldenkrais reminds us adults in *The Potent Self*, we are responsible for our ignorance as much as our bliss.

Nazi Germany began an absolute catastrophe through what became World War 2. As many as 75 million people or more died from Nazi Germany's plans to dominate the world through war and through deliberate genocide. You'd think today we'd all have enough historical memory of that disaster to say that fascism is not a wise, life-giving choice.

When church/religion marries or dates or hooks-up with state...

The ethos and mythos perpetuating my own religion of upbringing has been permitted to continue its wreckage without much cost through the millennia...the indigenous children of Canada being the most recent victims of the church-state domination of indigenous peoples...all the while the Vatican continues emboldening its adherents toward an ethic of life, an ethic that seems to apply to everyone but themselves.

Whether it's 20th century Canada or medieval Europe or long before, the Roman Catholic Church and local governments often collude together. The Church's Vatican-driven Albigensian Crusade — a tragedy rarely discussed by Catholics — is an early Holocaust, for sure, with thousands upon thousands of anyone who would not respect the Vatican being thrown into the flames. Jews. Christians who saw no need for the Vatican. People who just wanted to live a non-church life. People who recognized the dangers of statecraft. Men. Women. Children. Innocents.

The Vatican called these people "heretics" — and they were. Look up what "heretic" means. It's an Ancient Greek word: 'someone who chooses for oneself.' What was the crime of these heretics killed by the Vatican? They simply chose their own self-determined path instead of bowing down to the Vatican. These martyrs wanted to live self-determined lives. That's it.

The Inquisition was a torturing result of that Crusade, all in the name of 'God' and of *'Christ.'* And from the Albigensian Crusade and the Inquisition all these massive churches and seminaries were built. How? Who funded them? All of them funded through the property and land taken/stolen from these people killed because they would not bow down to the Vatican. All these *bons hommes*/"good people" were cleared out of the way, forced into the flames. France became a larger, more present-day-sized nation from that collusion with the Vatican. When deciding how to attack these cities full of 'friend' and 'enemy' alike, the Vatican-directed-Papal-legate-monk Arnaud Amalric said, "Kill them all, God knows His own." After the monk and his men returned to the Vatican genocidally-victorius from the French Holocaust known as the Albigensian Crusade, the monk was given a promotion as archbishop of Narbonne, France.

Some historians question whether Amalric actually said this terrible thing...but he did brag in a letter to the Pope (Aug 1209) that he and his men killed 20,000 people — men, women, anyone and everyone.

Look carefully and you'll often find that government-systems rely on organized religion, and for more than values or a vision/story. Royal-systems are steeped in this fascist religion-government collusion, where organized religion often blesses the head royal with their "divine right of kings" or "mandate of heaven." What kind of thinking is at the heart of those philosophies? Of some being better than others, some being worth less than others, and some being forced to die for the 'good' of the system. Our 21st century royalties are not so forceful and not so violent, and this is probably why they still stand. (Barely.)

The "divine right of kings" or "mandate of heaven" ideologies even show up in democracies like my own that have tried to separate church/religion and state...just look at our desires for celebrity-presidents and celebrity-leaders-too-big-to-fail upon whose words (doublespeak?) we all too often hang. The Supreme Court of my country recently affirmed that essentially any and every action of the US President is legal. Imagine! The very same nation who fought against a king who legally could do no wrong!

And no wonder...our early and recent visions of US leadership are steeped in the same *Christ*-myth that created modern

Judaism and Christianity, both of these religions intertwining deathly fascist elements with absolutely freeing and beautiful, all-serving elements. The taproot is dangerous...the Bible is dangerous...hierarchical thinking is dangerous...for anyone not awake, for anyone not bringing a flashlight or lamp, for anyone not willing to shine their own inner light into shadowy corners, personal or institutional.

In this "land of the free" a democratic President for whom I voted and upon whose every word I once celebrated also dropped 26,171 bombs in a single year on the untried 'guilty' and their children and aged parents and neighbors — all in the name of freedom for the few (me). This same President was awarded the Nobel Peace Prize (!). The following President for whom I didn't vote dropped even more bombs the next year, and then they stopped counting or at least stopped letting us know the count. It rarely makes the news, and when it does it's often doublespeak: "freedom for all!" said in the same speech as "fuck with us and we'll destroy you and your children and your children's children..." though often masked with nicer rhetoric like "we will defend our people and assets" even within another sovereign nation's borders. (2016 bombs: *NBC News*, Jan. 9, 2017, F. Brinley Bruton, reporting on a Council on Foreign Relations report...2017 bombs: *Newsweek*, September 19, 2017, John Haltiwanger...according to this article, by Sept 2017, the number of bombs dropped had already surpassed 2016 totals)

Control feels so very much differently from self-determination, ecstasy, & relationship

It would be quite easy to continue pointing out the significant faults of all these hierarchically minded institutions that we/I have all too often cheered on with my voice and my dollars and my pledges — but that's entirely myopic. I commit these same one-human-is-better-than-another games in my own relationships, even and especially the ones who matter the most to me. Even when I try so hard to live a life that does not infringe upon other people's self-determination and personal choices, how quickly I find myself reducing their choices or leaving them no choice at all but the thing I determine is 'right' for them.

From where does that desire to control come? Is it only from that devious strand of the Bible that seeks control...that strand so starkly different from Jesus and the Hebrew prophets?

What is it within me that wants to hold power over others, that must get the upper hand...instead of living out of relationship, our equality as humans — life! — together?

There's something else....

You've had some experience that clues you into the infinity of life, right? Some dream, daydream or nightdream. Some sensation that gave you an inkling of the vastness and depth of life and equal-value of all living creatures. Right? Yes? You have been delighted?

Such experiences are often ecstasy-inducing. They cannot be created, but they do seem available to each one of us in every second — if we let ourselves notice. And that's a sticky point for many of us adults, isn't it...letting ourselves delight and letting ourselves stay with delight amidst our adult responsibilities...?

But if we're honest, we'd admit: we are made for ecstasy. Yes. We are made for ecstasy. You knew this as a small child, right? You can still feel it within your body, at least every now and then? And maybe life is all about trying to live within that ecstatic-knowing — and steering clear of blocking others from their own ecstatic-knowing. Toddlers eventually figure this out — they can gaze into another creature's eyes and respond with compassion. Maybe with a little help along the way. Maybe after a few failures first. Even the same toddler who punched you in the face once and then again just to see what you'd do about it. There's hope for us all.

Ecstasy. Breathe in and feel It.

Breathe out and feel It.

Bliss is possible with every breath, especially when we simply let one's breath come and go. Can you sense that? Sense the difference between controlling when/how you breathe and simply feel yourself being breathed? It can be delightful....

But all too often instead of staying with that evolving ecstatic-feeling that clues me into the nature of the Universe, something compels my choosing to control others. You too?

Why? From where do these compulsive feelings arise? Might it indeed be from the assumptions of that control-oriented strand of the Biblical taproot we've inherited from our (great+) grandparents who passed along ideas that are — if we are honest — sometimes poison?

They did their best. We must do better.

That old taproot needs untangling...but maybe there's more....

One strand of the taproot could help...? 1 & 2 Samuel!

If we really wanted to make a difference in the world, it would probably be a lot easier to write some new epic fiction for the screen/streaming to awaken today's 8 billion humans to the very real hierarchically minded threats of our time...instead of trying to unravel what is happening in 1 & 2 Samuel. And yet — even then our 21st century epic would be influenced by 1 & 2 Samuel, whether we immediately recognize it or not. David and Goliath, the whole *christ/messiah* business — perhaps even lampooning the whole 'origin story' of *christ/messiah* — David and Jonathan lusting after each other while Jonathan's father-the-king lusts after David too, David seeing naked Bathsheba on the roof and lusting after her and later killing her husband to cover over their misdeeds, *Christ* Saul and *Christ* David committing genocide to grow their personal powers...it's all right there in 1 & 2 Samuel.

A band of fiction-writers crafted 1 & 2 Samuel as a warning to awaken hearers of their tales to the problems of royalty, of organized religion, and of having a *messiah/christ* of any sort — likely the problems of their time, or the roots of the problems that continued to haunt them years after royalty failed while the temple-cult was gaining power again.

Those same things haunting people ~2500 years ago continue to haunt us today — the hierarchical imagination continues to kill us and encourages even more murders in the name of 'God.'

Early Jesus-followers and gospel-writers latched onto that much older notion of *messiah/christ* without evaluating it and without hearing/heeding the warning in 1 & 2 Samuel and projected *messiah/christ* onto Jesus. How tragically ironic that during his lifetime Jesus was pointing out through his clever wisdom that we are all the salt of the earth and the light of the world — each and every one of us, not just *messiahs/christs*. Such a message of all-equal-under-God got Jesus killed by the hands and demands of those preferring hierarchy and organized religion over of a human being's life.

As this *Naked Path of Prophet series* points out, 1 & 2 Samuel written centuries before Jesus reveals the ridiculousness of following these bloodthirsty, genocidal, mafia-boss-like *messiahs/christs*...Saul, David, Solomon...just to name three *messiahs/christs*. The gospel writers likely never read 1 & 2 Samuel. It's possible the writer of the Gospel of Matthew did as he was a Pharisee writing to fellow Pharisees — the group who championed reading the whole Hebrew Bible for wisdom and not just the Torah. But the writer of the Gospel of Matthew and the other gospel-writers were likely blinded by Chronicles' and Psalms' poisonous paradigm of the character David being a leader — a *messiah/christ* — to emulate.

All of 1 & 2 Samuel likely came before Psalms and Chronicles. Read 1 & 2 Samuel carefully, especially in Ancient Hebrew, and no one in their right mind would want to emulate David or put his star on anything important.

The writers of 1 & 2 Samuel reveal the idiocies of following *messiahs/christs* of any sort — even handsome ones like Saul and David and Solomon — when following YAHWEH is far wiser and more life-giving and more dependable.

If we're going to be able to face the significant challenges of the 21st century — and there are many! — so that we might give birth to another generation of human life on Earth, then we would be wise to notice the roots from which so many of our assumptions grow. For my Christian brothers and sisters, I suggest that identifying with *christ/messiah* is the problem and Jesus' wisdom/lifestyle could be a solution. For my Jewish brothers and sisters, perhaps it's worth asking if Jacob-becoming-Israel is the wiser symbol than *Messiah/Christ* David.

Why do we continue to latch onto these ancient ideas without evaluating the wisdom of their roots, generation after generation?

Could it be that we never really outgrew our penchants for saviors or *messiahs/christs* or fascist minded leaders?

Are we really stuck with needing some kind of 'parent' to protect us? Is there a reason we do not want to grow up and be personally potent adults together?

Maybe it's time now to be the leaders — together, with one another — who get curious about solutions for our 21st century challenges, pause and delight in life together, playfully hash out new possibilities together, and enact together what works for all on Earth. It could be delightful.

How to begin?

Perhaps it's wise to go back to (a) beginning...to understand how we got here and then move forward

What do you remember/imagine your first breath was like after being born from the ocean-bath of your mother's womb?

It might have been wonderful, it might have been terrifying, it might have been disorienting...like the slightly older baby who later flips from back to belly and cries because the feeling is new and therefore threatening to them. Their ever-aware nervous system and mine and yours has been honed for millennia to keep us all safe and knows that newness is a threat. New paradigms and orientations are threatening to any human — in this infant's situation, the ceiling and floor are now flipped. It doesn't get any easier when we are adults unless we cultivate a sense of newness — and new choices, new possibilities — <u>every day</u>. Even when newness makes us a little squeamish, as safe and palatable as we try to make it.

With something seeming new to us every day as infants and toddlers, we had at least some inkling of finding safe ways to explore newness when we were very young. We figured out that slowing every move down somehow can make things less scary, and making the move or the newness smaller and more bite-sized probably helped too. And whenever we did that back then or do it now, we realize we always have a choice...to continue with the experience if we like it, to do it slightly differently in a way that maybe feels more safe, to do something else entirely, or to do nothing at all. But even in doing "nothing" we are doing plenty if we're alive...all of it seemingly in the background.

That first breath outside the womb that might have been jarring eventually gets easier — at least if we are to remain alive. That full-body movement that is breathing is constantly going on, often without even being aware of it happening. And we get used to one's massively powerful heart continuing to pump blood with such an enormous thump, at such an enormous continual rate. And we get used to being able to digest our food in the background and clear out wastes and attacks to our immune/relational system and build and repair muscle and bone and skin and every inch of oneself, all the while growing and exploring and eventually learning through seemingly a million attempts to sit up on one's own and stand up on one's own and walk on one's own. Neuroplasticity pioneer Moshe Feldenkrais wisely called these attempts "approximations." Each slightly new/different approximation listened to within oneself can help each creature to learn an easier way...a learning path that is never complete and never perfected under the greatest force of our Earthly lives: gravity. Thanks to gravity and these approximations that many of us took toward sitting up and eventually standing up and walking, we grow bone, our human ability to evolve, to adapt to the gravity-rich planet on which we live.

How novel!

Each move we make and each breath we take can be novel, new, and not so threatening to one's ever fragile and ever strong nervous system that learns through all these approximations how to stand tall and with ease and move on a planet where gravity stops for no one. We figure out ways to outsmart gravity — to sit up, to stand, to move on and with our bones — all of it driven by a curiosity and need to get somewhere... to that toy, to that sibling/loved one, to a snack, to something new and curious but not overly threatening. Each move involves risk — and yet our curiosity outweighs that risk...if we really want to get to what it is that we want.

Learning — exploring these possibilities, one approximation at a time — can be an absolute pleasure if we're curious. Sure, there are moments we might feel threatened and back away, and maybe for wise and good reason to keep oneself safe. I reach over here for the shiny toy. Hmm. That didn't get me there. I roll onto my side and I can reach a little further. Hmm. Still not there. Ouch, I reach this way and it hurts. I change it up and roll onto my other side and dig my toes into the ground and — whoah! — I have that toy in my hands. I taste it. I smash it into the ground. It gets away from me. Do I still want it? Hmm. Yeah, there's nothing else that looks all that interesting. Hmm. How do I get there this time? Oh wait — my fingers look tasty.

Babies can be more fascinated with their fingers and toes than the most expensive toy. I love watching babies discovering more and more of themselves without any inhibition, without any guilt, without any embarrassment, without any need to rush to the next toy or appointment or social-media-post or thrill outside themselves. Fingers, toes, their whole selves. Over and over again, though in some new way each time. Delight. Ecstasy in this very moment.

And so can we.

How and why did we fall away from such satisfying pleasure and such safety in being alive in one's own skin, even in the face of newness?

Well, we had to, at least to a certain extent, to get on with life. Freud and Feldenkrais both point to it too, even though their philosophies usually disagree with each other: one's delight of life gets socialized out of us by 'bigger people'...authorities, adults upon whom we depend to stay alive and navigate Earth and the human-made systems that very well could preserve our life or kill us or call us to kill.

As babies, of course, we cannot walk away from danger, at least not easily — whether that danger is a storm or an animal or a car or whatever. As babies, we can't feed ourselves, we can't care for ourselves when we're sick. In that first year of life, we can do so little for ourselves besides breathe and suck milk and follow our curiosity and seek dependability, all of which keeps us alive and growing in one's unique way. The bigger people take care of the rest.

As babies we know the bliss of life. Ecstasy. Often. Without doing much of anything but sensing it. It's luscious, this ecstasy, these fingers, these toes, this breath, the curiosity they invoke and the ecstasy that seems to magnify itself with that curiosity, the way the light dances around us, the way these bigger people sometimes smile and touch us and look into our eyes and make just-right soothing sounds and keep us nourished. Such moments calm and grow one's nervous system and sense of safety, expand one's whole sense of self and sense of the world — it's incredible.

How did we ever forget?

All the while, the bigger people are taking care of things for us, deciding what's right and what's wrong for us, sometimes even ordaining that it's their will or even God's will, often for our own safety. We don't usually think of parenting as fascism, but it is.

And we as infants figure out quickly how to exert our own control over those caring for us and often necessarily controlling us: scream and some bigger person does something for me.

In those early years, all those helpful responses to our screams and all those decisions made for us — that keep us alive when we're basically helpless — those decisions are love, or at least loving. But with each growing year of maturity, we don't want those bigger people making all those decisions, if any decisions, for us. Especially in our teen years. And such a feeling is healthy, mature, moving into self-sufficiency and personal potency, at least as self-sufficient and ethically potent as we humans can be in polite/civilized society.

But when we are younger, every time a bigger person makes a decision for us that is not what we want or when we want it — whoah — do we ever let the world know!

Toddlerisms

The two-year toddler over there at the train station cannot rest easy, won't be held, won't stand on his own or hold anyone's hand for safety's sake — all this as his family awaits the train — and he's about to melt down no matter what mom or dad or guardian do and — there you go, he's now ruined for life just like the rest of us. One of the adults sits him in his stroller despite his very loud and squirmy protests while the adult places the straps around his arms. Once again the little boy is not allowed to do what he wants and he screams and tries in vain to free himself and he comes to distrust that that adult is dependable as he has his tantrum in the stroller. Even though most of the time the adult gives the toddler what he wants — and even with obvious love and affection — maybe this time feels different to the toddler and from now on the toddler has a shade of doubt that that adult has his/toddler's best interests in mind, forever from this moment forward. Maybe to this toddler, all adults become just a shade more suspect too.

Never mind that had this stroller-strapped toddler squirmed too much at the wrong moment just before he was confined, he could have plunged to his great injury or death off the platform as the train whooshed by.

But the toddler doesn't know that: from his perspective, not only did he not get what he wanted, he was punished for it and made to be strapped into his stroller where no one would listen to his cries — no one would give him what he wanted. And forever his nervous system was shaped by this instance and every time before and after too.

This is a pivotal moment. We all go through something similar, where what we want is thwarted. Really, there is no way around it — it's the journey to adulthood in a world where we are first forced to conform and then gradually agree to conform just enough to get along with the larger flow of societal life, at least as much as we choose to participate in that flow each day.

Tantrums. Something like this happens to each one of us as children — on the train platform, in the grocery cereal aisle, playing with our siblings or neighbors, anywhere and everywhere where what 'I want' gets thwarted and 'I cry' and 'I scream' and no one does anything about it.... And such things can continue to mess with us with any conflict or any experience that threatens us after that. Tantrums can even happen in adolescence — which can last well past our 20s if we are not careful.

That is until we are mature adults with some sense of reflection — until each of us discovers these authorities raising us when we were toddlers (or older) did their best for us, even with such stroller-incidents on the train platform. Whether the toddler-become-adult remembers such incidences or not, every adult's nervous system is imprinted with such things that gave us reason for temper tantrums. Without a pause for reflection, without one's deliberate personal growth, sometimes those early tantrum-instigators rear their ugly heads long afterwards, as adults, when something triggers our anger even decades later when we feel confined — our choices feel reduced — and then we try to assume control over others to grow our choices (at least we think that will do it). But throwing a hissy fit or tantrum in the cereal aisle at the grocery store or a bar or at work as an adult is not exactly a way to grow one's long-term personal potency.

All the way back to our times as infants and toddlers, we adults have known ecstasy/delight and we have known control/fascism — and we learn quickly how to use both to one's personal advantage.

The long, compulsive road to maturity

In growing up from those toddler days, there are so many bumps along the way. Even in loving ways, those authorities raising us can block our way to ecstasy and to a self-determined life as we grow older....

Sometimes when we delight in our ecstatic experiences at the 'wrong time' or in the 'wrong way' or in the 'wrong place' according to the (probably/usually) loving authorities who care for us, we get all tied up inside. And we let the world know it. True if we are two months or two years or twelve years or even twenty years old.

When that shiny toy is so far away we can't yet figure out a way to get there.

When we're hungry or thirsty. When a sibling jumps on us. When the bigger people don't get us from our nap in time. When we're one degree too hot or cold.

When the toddler boy who knows little more than sensation begins fondling himself into an erection and the mother gets uncomfortable and prevents him from continuing. The toddler boy has no idea why his mother is uncomfortable when he's experiencing something nice — but that toddler boy learns and learns a lot in that moment. Though I can't find the reference anywhere, I heard a student of Jung once claim that this very experience enacts "patriarchy" in the boy's psyche as something in the boy plots to get back at his mother and later all women by putting them below him for making him feel uncomfortable about his erection that was only delightful and curiosity-inducing before that encounter, his nature.

As far as I know, Jung never said anything about a father's discomfort with his young daughter exploring her genitals in front of him though I think it would be fair to say that a parent's/authority's perceived discomfort no matter the genders of the child or of the parent will affect the child's ever growing more and more complex nature with sensation around their own genitals or anyone else's. Taboos arise from the reactions we internalize from the bigger people, really about anything.

When our desires to explore ourselves and know ourselves and the simple ecstasy of sensation within one's body get blocked

Ecstatic Prophets, Compulsive Fascists

by anyone and anything outside one's own self, compulsions arise, our need to assert some sense of control arises. Life gets complex. We get complex. We know what is pleasurable and we know we'd be happier fulfilling that desire right here and right now but we also know our fulfilling such desire might make us less in society, less in the eyes of the bigger people. And if we are hierarchically minded as adults, those 'bigger people' can be one's boss, someone we admire like a celebrity, anyone we feel is better than us. But being hierarchically minded as an adult is not the only way one can be — personal authenticity and potency are possible too.

Such societally-induced complexities shape our nervous systems, whether we are young or old. And if we haven't outgrown the hierarchical mindset — no matter one's age — we will likely inflict our perceived hierarchical privilege on someone we perceive to be below us in the hierarchy when we feel those feelings of compulsion arise within us, when we feel thwarted in some arena of one's life. Whenever we don't get what it is that we desire, how quickly we then sort our thwarters and really everyone into people I can control and people I cannot control (or need to be very clever to control), people who are lesser than me and people are worth more than me. If we live with a hierarchical mindset and come up against someone with their own hierarchy of who they think is worth more or worth less, there are now competing fascisms...war.

Of course, we are born into hierarchies — the bigger people take care of us so that we survive. Adolescence, for many, is the struggle to discover more of a relationship — a sharing in decision-making — between adolescent and adult-authorities...parents, teachers, coaches, bosses, and more. If we navigate that passage well, healthily and holistically minded, adolescents and adult-authorities (re)discover their equality and live out of it and make decisions — at least at some point — more circularly and less hierarchically. Peace ensues. Ecstasy becomes more and more available to both adolescents and authorities when this 'social contract' gets worked out well with and among each other. We do not war quite as much when we get closer and closer to letting adult-people and almost-adult-people live 'self-determined lives'...a more circular view of life.

And the opposite is true too. The more we put someone above or below us and the more we fail to recognize we breathe the same air and are equally alive in the wind we all share to stay alive — the more we enact hierarchy's insidious ways toward a fascism that, most often, exists underneath the surface of many of our dealings. Hierarchy breeds order within a family where adults care for children until the children can fully care for themselves; hierarchy breeds war within a society where people are seen as less and more than each other.

How quickly as 'adults' we all too often forget our gains from adolescence — our moves toward power-sharing with the most important authorities of our lives (parents/guardians) — and dispense with our newfound freedom by then giving over our thinking and decision-making to a new set of parents/guardians who might love us less than the parents who actually gave us life. What new parents? Father So-and-So, Sister So-and-So, President So-and-So, Pope, Bishop, Rabbi, Imam, Priest, Minister, Reverend...all these So-and-So's who maybe do care for us but who cannot parent us if we are to be adults. We might have watched our parents/guardians give over their power and thinking to similar authorities. And we foolishly do the same and play the hierarchical game instead of choosing love, potency, self-determination, and shared communal power among adults.

Again, as Feldenkrais wisely warned us, as mature and potent people we are responsible for our own ignorance, for those places where we could shine some light, realize our personal power and responsibility and live out of it with joy, with delight.

All too often we choose fascism over freedom. Most of us are never really aware of the subtle ways that we enact fascism in our relationships and memberships and participations in institutions built with assumptions about some people being worth less and some people being worth more. Maybe such fascisms are just in our peripheral vision — just in the shadows we can't quite catch, our areas of not-knowing completely, maturely, wholly...unless we have a strong desire to see and hear and feel and grow.

What to do? What do we do especially as we continue to flirt with disaster with each other and our attempts at fascism over a planet much larger than human-life, a planet that will win as humans lose, lose, lose?

What to do?

Well, our character Samuel in the fictional saga of 1 & 2 Samuel bearing his name seems to offer a way.

He and his fellow ecstatic-misfits (read: prophets) purposefully unplugged from hierarchies...as best they could...and they seem to gather on the mountaintops in out-of-the-way places where empire's insidious ways often choose not to reach because it's too much of a bother.

Even when the top-symbol of the empire/hierarchy — the king — shows up to kill, the bloodthirsty King Saul falls into ecstasy with Samuel and the other ecstatics and Saul loses interest in killing. At least for the time he's there.

It might seem strange...to have a king so ecstatically moved to fall to the ground, to take off his royal-robes willingly, to strip himself completely naked in his ecstasy with the wind... as King Saul indeed does in 1 Samuel. We'll hear the tale here very soon.

Such ecstasy is available to all of us, of course, not just Samuel, not just so-thought divine-kings, *christs*, *messiahs*.

And not only does such ecstasy with the wind free kings to be human again, it loosens those complexes that we all had to go through to live into adulthood, those compulsive feelings that drive us to try to control and hinder one's ability to enjoy ecstasy and appreciate ecstasy's abundance. Those complexes we created and inherited to keep us alive in those early years often wreak havoc within us as adults until ecstasy breaks through again as it/It did when we were so young and vulnerable. Ecstasy helps us realize we adults are potent and have choices and can invent even more choices, that we do not have to be locked in patterns of control. Ecstasy freely given and freely received flattens hierarchies, leads to love. Nonviolence is the creative act of awakening in the oppressor an experience of ecstasy — surprise! — of our sharing in life in an infinite, unbounded, non-hierarchical way. Indeed, the only hierarchy in ecstasy is YAHWEH — the ALL of us existing within, well, the whole.

Ecstasy with the wind restores us to who we are, to all we can be. Ecstasy offers a glimpse into our infinite reality, one's infinite potential within THE ALL. The miraculous and extra-ordinary can become the every-day, 1 Samuel reminds.

What's required?

Well...breathe and feel. Sense. Stay with It. Feel the comings and goings of the wind on your skin, and come to know there are big gusts and subtle breaths and little swells and stirrings. We swim in a constant atmosphere that keeps us alive, that is dependable and yet flowing/changing. And even with climate change, this atmosphere is far more dependable than any institution we've inherited from our grandparents. The atmosphere of THE ALL is more dependable than any 'leader' or institution demanding that you feel one way about anything and that you respond to that sensation in their prescribed way.

What do you feel? Would you like to sit with that feeling awhile and discover that it probably changes? Such a pause-rich process with the constant-and-yet-flowing atmosphere leads to knowing, and such knowing is unique to you and unique to me. We learn to move and walk in our own styles, one's own unique way to be in relationship with gravity and the atmosphere surrounding us and penetrating us into life.

Soon, you'll probably want to have more and more of your skin in contact with this atmosphere, to want to have no barriers between you and this atmosphere. Of course your clothes are penetrated by this atmosphere...but there's something about being naked with this atmosphere, as 1 Samuel reminds, and it's something to want to share, with a circle of friends choosing and being chosen through an ethic of 'self-determination' — a deep respect for each other to discover what's right for oneself that also respects everyone else's 'self-determination,' that respects one's own path of growth as a human.

We knew something of the spirit of 1 Samuel as babies too, the ecstasy of the wind at that delicious temperature licking our naked baby-skin. It's what we can know and be known by at any time in one's life.

After all, this big wind — YAHWEH — is being naked with you and me right now...entirely revealing Itself and feeding you and me life whether you notice It or not, like It or not... inviting you and me to share in this more circular view of life...

but to notice It —

to appreciate It —

ah! — now that's living!

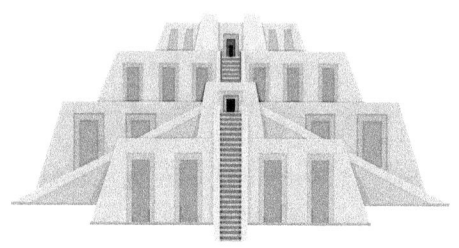

CHOOSE WELL!

An Intention
for *The Naked Path of Prophet* Series
(included in every volume)

This series has interest in the questions of the various scholarly theories about the origins and redactions (assembling + editing) of the Bible...

but this series will not try to solve those riddles.

Biblical scholar Thomas Römer's books offer excellent summaries of many of the most current theories about the origins of the Hebrew scriptures, especially *The Invention of God* and the *L'Ancien Testament*; biblical scholars of the Westar Institute/Jesus Seminar have done much to help unravel the Christian traditions' layers to reveal the ecstatic roots of Jesus and the world-resounding message of Paul about this peasant Jesus and what God did for him. Maybe you've checked out *The Gospel of Jesus* by Robert W. Funk, Arthur J. Dewey & the Jesus Seminar or *The Authentic Letters of Paul* by Arthur J. Dewey, Roy W. Hoover, Lane C. McGaughy, & Daryl Schmidt.

Inspired by these and other scholars' excavations of the Bible, this *Naked Path of Prophet* series aims:

first, to reveal more of the cleverness of the Hebrew puns in the biblical texts and then bring forward this cleverly-styled wordplay/poetry into a clearer English translation

  ...so that more people can identify such style running through much of the Bible and, if they find such style helpful for our 21st century world, then bring it forward in new ways;

and second, to reveal a significant idea for our time and all time, which continually gets passed over by scholars and by religious leaders and the faithful of any and all traditions, namely, that the Bible being a collection of many differing imaginations and writers could be divided into two competing camps: **the hierarchically-minded** and **the circularly-inspired**

...so that more people can identify which imagination is used within their own family, classroom, workplace, religion, and governments and that, by knowing the differences between circular-imagination and hierarchical imagination, have the ability to choose which is most life-giving and helpful in any moment.

Hierarchical Imagination

A hierarchy has a human-leader over various strata of minor leaders over various sub-classes of humans. A hierarchy is a system where some humans have more value and more power than others. Often there is even a non-class of humans... untouchables who have no value or enslaved-people of all sorts, sex-slaves of all genders or eunuchs or maid-slaves or wet-nurses, each of whom might be valued/valuable but having very few if any rights to their own human personhood. This is what hierarchies do — they sort and place people based on their value to the system that those with power create and those without power accept until revolution boils over and there is a paradigm shift with some people losing and/ or gaining power and privilege within the new hierarchical system...unless an entirely different and more circularly-minded system is chosen.

The hierarchical imagination often uses a podium from which one person addresses the masses who follow. There is little conversation in such a system, even when the group is small. The speaker stands over and above the followers who hear and obey. Perhaps the followers take issue with some of the speaker's announcements so the followers find ways to safely communicate their disagreements through channels long after the speech. Often such 'communication' is made passive-aggressively because it's the only safe way to 'communicate' in such a system. The speaker/leader then either takes those communications into account or delivers another speech that clamps down even more on the communicators or changes the system entirely so that the system becomes more circular than before and people have more influence in decision-making. In a hierarchical system, it is impossible to commune with the leader who ranks above all unless there is revolution or unless the top-dog leader changes the rules of the system to make the system more circular. But even then, the people that top-dog leader rules might not want or might not accept a more circularly-inspired system.

The hierarchical imagination plays out in royal-slave systems, in despot-follower systems, in guru-follower systems, in organized religion's leader-follower systems, in celebrity-follower systems...each and all of any era.

With the hierarchical imagination, people can and often do awful things to each other. The hierarchical system depends on it. And when people know no other option besides the hierarchical system, desperation can settle in quickly...tragic motivation to want to climb a rung higher and then another rung higher...moves that see people in the way or people down below as enemies or problems to solve. With a hierarchical mindset, it's easy to point out that a person is evil or bad or wrong.

Someone with a circularly-inspired imagination realizes instead that people are not bad or wrong but instead are stuck inside hierarchical systems, ways of imagining that have limited who they are and all that is.

All too often, hierarchical imagination limits one's map of the Infinite, what we're all too often tempted to call 'reality.' As we keep growing and have more experiences in life, 'reality' keeps changing doesn't it?

Circularly-Inspired Imagination

A circularly-inspired imagination is much different, of course. With this imagination, each human recognizes the equal-value of all humans and sometimes even of all life, of every living thing. Such a circular imagination perfects itself as an entirely holistic imagination…where participants recognize on their own — often through very different experiences — that there is no separation between creatures…where it is readily recognized that we all exist within a larger and highly interdependent whole, as a Universe, the One-Verse, the Infinite, THE ALL. That is to say, we all exist in 'God.' When we recognize we participate in such a Whole, it's a lot easier to live more harmoniously with every creature, with all inside that ever-expanding circle.

The circular imagination often invites everyone to sit in a circle, with no one person any higher or more valued than another. A circle invites speakers and hearers and co-hearers alike to use all senses in communicating…even a deep look into someone's eyes or listening carefully to the subtle sounds someone makes or getting a wisp of the feeling in the air communicates a great deal. A circle breeds a sense of equality, a sense that we're all in this together and that we all will be needed in some diverse and equally-valued way to move forward in our shared life together on the planet. Could there be a leader or moderator or convener of the circle? Of course. But such leaders of a circle try to be very mindful not to interject their opinions or will upon the circle; instead, circularly-inspired leaders ensure that all ideas are heard, that everyone who desires to speak gets to speak, that those with information share what they know and invite ideas and people to evaluate information openly and wisely and to grow information's usefulness through deliberation and discernment. There is equal access to knowledge and opportunity in a circular system, even if knowledge and opportunity are not 'free,' even if they must be merited through effort and growth.

Circularly-inspired imaginers know well that some experience inspired them to a larger vision of THE ALL. Someone with a circularly-inspired imagination knows that an experience can free anyone stuck in a hierarchical imagination — an experience as simple as a breath or a gasp from an ecstatic's clever rap or wild story or a deep look into someone's eyes. A circular-imaginer knows too that the awakening that comes from an experience must happen within each person and unfold within each person in that person's own time and in its own original way. It's not possible to make someone know THE ALL. Such an awakening erupts out of nowhere — is ecstatic in that way. Mentoring relationships can help, of course, especially when a mentor invites the mentee to spend some time in some activity, some study, so that some awakening might happen in the mentee's own time. Sensible mentors know too that what awakened themselves might not be the same thing that will awaken their mentees. Indeed, no two experiences are ever the same, right?

Beyond these mentor-mentee relationships, there have been glimpses of the circular imagination being lived out today or in times past, though they all too often either get snuffed out by hierarchs or the hierarchically minded or devolve to a hierarchical system because some who once perceived something of THE ALL can no longer stay with that vision and imagination, for whatever reason.

Sometimes, too, we live and act more circularly in one arena of our lives but think and act more hierarchically in others. For example, what a gift it is to be pro-LGBTQ+ and you and I invite to the round-table all people who feel different in terms of their sexual identity and their gender identity...but what good is that if we still think that people of our own ethnicity or skin-tone are better (or worse) than others? What a gift it is to be antiracist...but what good is it if you and I hate women or nonbinary humans? Or what good is it to greet everyone we meet as an equal but then buy our t-shirts or shoes made in sweatshops owned by millionaire CEO's or buy coffee or chocolate grown and picked by slaves?

We need to get to the root issue — and it's not racism, it's not homophobia or the patriarchy or transphobia or anything like that. Those are all nasty symptoms of the hierarchical imagination killing us all.

Democracy...
circularly-inspired or hierarchically-motivated?

Perhaps you're wondering where democracy rests between these camps?

Democracy — or rule by the people — attempts to break free from the hierarchical imagination with democracy's more circular attempts to allow all voices — at least those of a certain age — to be heard and with every person of age getting an equal vote. But all too often democracy devolves into hierarchy when celebrity-presidents of every party — and even the parties themselves — are followed at every word by their followers, all too often with little discernment as to the value or wisdom of what the leader or party offer. In smaller groups in a more local place, of course, circular-democracies can thrive. In larger groups, it can be quite difficult...unless there is a common appreciation for what ultimately gives life.

Some roots of circularly-inspired imaginations

So...hopefully you're becoming curious about how a circular imagination actually works or could be helpful in the 21st century, and how it has been lived out in past eras. Well, my friends, that's the very heart-intention of *The Naked Path of Prophet* series with its devoted interest in YAHWEH's wild and sexy wind. All are called by the wind/breath, we've been reminded by the wise ones through the centuries, few choose themselves or allow themselves to notice the sensations of the wind.

Jesus was interested in the circular imagination...his authentic parables and wisdom sayings and table-fellowship reveal that...but he lost first to the hierarchs of the religion of his region's day and then after his death to those wanting a more hierarchically minded church.

Paul was interested in the circular imagination...the very rhetoric of his authentic letters to early Jesus-interested communities call for a more circular approach to governance where God rules and all people are valued equally below and because of God who raised up even a peasant (Jesus)...but Paul lost first to Rome and then to Peter's hierarchically minded camp which projected Rome's sense of order and destruction onto Jesus-interested communities, and still does.

And where and how did Jesus and Paul get interested in a more circular imagination?

Perhaps they were inspired by the wandering ecstatics and their little quips of wordplay and poetry, clever parables or episodes of story, and exceedingly bizarre actions for, perhaps, nearly 1000 years before Jesus and Paul ever set foot on Earth. Those little ecstatic bits were becoming the Bible, at least the first half of it. It's a circular-style and circularly-minded imagination that seeps out in the poems of the likes of Amos and the Isaiahs and Jeremiah and more, in the stories of 1 & 2 Samuel and much of 1 & 2 Kings, in large portions of Genesis once called "J/Yahwist" because of these storytellers' penchant for calling the divine "YAHWEH." Likely a band of multiple storycrafters through the generations, I've chosen to call this group 'the band of YAH.' Much later after their first tellings of these stories, the ancient Levitical priests (possibly with some later help from the Deuteronomic scribes) assembled these stories into what today we call Genesis, the first book of the Bible. The band of YAH is expert at flattening triangles/ hierarchies into circles, often with humor.

Rather interestingly, this circular-style and imagination seems to seep out during the most difficult and oppressive times in history both before Jesus' time, during Jesus' lifetime, and long after.

Perhaps you've caught a wisp of It?

Perhaps you've had an experience of YAHWEH brought on by Its life-giving, inspiring, encircling wind? Such an experience is starkly different from the institutions we humans have built century after century to try to honor such wind....

Do we take the time to discern the differences?

As collision after collision happens in our world — as hierarchs assert power over hierarchically minded and circularly minded — it concerns me how challenging it seems to be for us humans to distinguish a hierarchically minded imagination from a circularly-minded imagination. It's not easy. Everything gets so murky swimming in the midst of the shipwreck — not to mention the traumatic experiences that led to the collisions that got us swimming in those dangerous waters in the first place.

How often we try to swim away to safety...but....

I've watched friends leave church-communities — led by pastors who openly proclaimed their status as hierarchs — immediately jump right into the next church-community or even an entirely different religious tradition, both being led by friendlier hierarchs of the same hierarchical system/ imagination that still aggravates my friends, though they're not entirely clear why. The very person upon whom their original church was founded — Jesus — was up-ending the hierarchical imagination of his day with his clever parables and wisdom sayings, and with being present and loving with those he is said to share meals/time...women, tax collectors, children, the ill...people who were not regarded as people in Jesus' time. Sadly, so few of my own Christian tradition cannot discern the differences between what Jesus was saying and doing and what Peter or Pilate or the Sanhedrin-leaders were said to be saying and doing in the gospel stories we've inherited. This inability to discern hierarchical mindedness from circular-mindedness happens in every religious tradition, not just my own Christianity. It's even present in yoga...tragically, it's nearly everywhere and we are the ones who pass on this hierarchical imagination unwittingly.

I too went right along with and even invested in the hierarchical system within my own religious tradition...for far, far too long...hoping it would change and thinking my queer outside-on-the-edges life/teaching would change things someday and somehow...until I realized my staying within my low place in the massive hierarchy as a lay religious educator was still giving power and credence to the hierarchical system. Finally I realized I had to swim away from my position and even my local parish to preserve my own life. I too often found the same hierarchical imagination in so much of yoga and have sought out other styles of movement as well.

And so I hope that my church-going and religious friends of all traditions and yoga-friends swim away from the shipwrecks of all hierarchical imaginations before it's too late to even notice what's in the breeze and always has been — life! Such a realization of the wind of life is precisely what welcomed every awakening and 'miracle' that gave birth to a religion in the first place...and all too often just a short time later the circular, spiral-rich experience concretized in messy hierarchies that stifle the original experience that was so rich and life-giving and able to be accessed by anyone living on the planet. Such access to that circular, spiral-rich experience is always available...for anyone who breathes and can sense such breath.

Organized religion of any sort cannot bear the circular imagination that must wait on YAHWEH alone — the very breeze of life — and not anyone directing or liturgizing, not anyone creating formulas or potions or laws or concert-sets to cull their divinities to act.

As we'll soon discover, the ecstatic/prophetic imagination of the Bible's prophets does indeed call on YAHWEH to act...but it's the very experience of sitting, breathing, contemplating, perhaps even spitting just-created-in-the-moment stylish rhymes and rhythms and stories or gasping or laughing with them that stirs the breeze to act. Could it perhaps even be as simple as uttering 'YAHWEH'? When you open your mouth or nostrils, in pours that wildness of YAHWEH. Dare you let YAHWEH have Its sexy, ecstasy-inducing way with you?

In a world undergoing such vast changes from day to day, in a world where the old orders no longer satisfy, might we have the courage today to play with such an open, circular style? Might we do so because we've had an ecstatic experience that makes us suspicious of the dangerous hierarchical systems of today and yesteryear? Might we do so because we'd like to let such an ecstatic-style expand and discover if it has something new to offer human life on the planet? Or just because it's fun and feels good, in YAHWEH's surprising ways?

No matter —

 play.

Play is the very style of YAHWEH as these circular-styled biblical texts mentioned above point out again and again...after all, within a circle, we can be pleasantly surprised together, we can see deeply into each other's eyes, hear more clearly each other's sounds and make meaning from them, taste the possibilities of life's abundance together, smell each other's scents that drift to us in the breeze, touch gently and lovingly the open hands of one another...

circle around!

let the breeze blow!

play!

open yourself to a refreshing surprise!

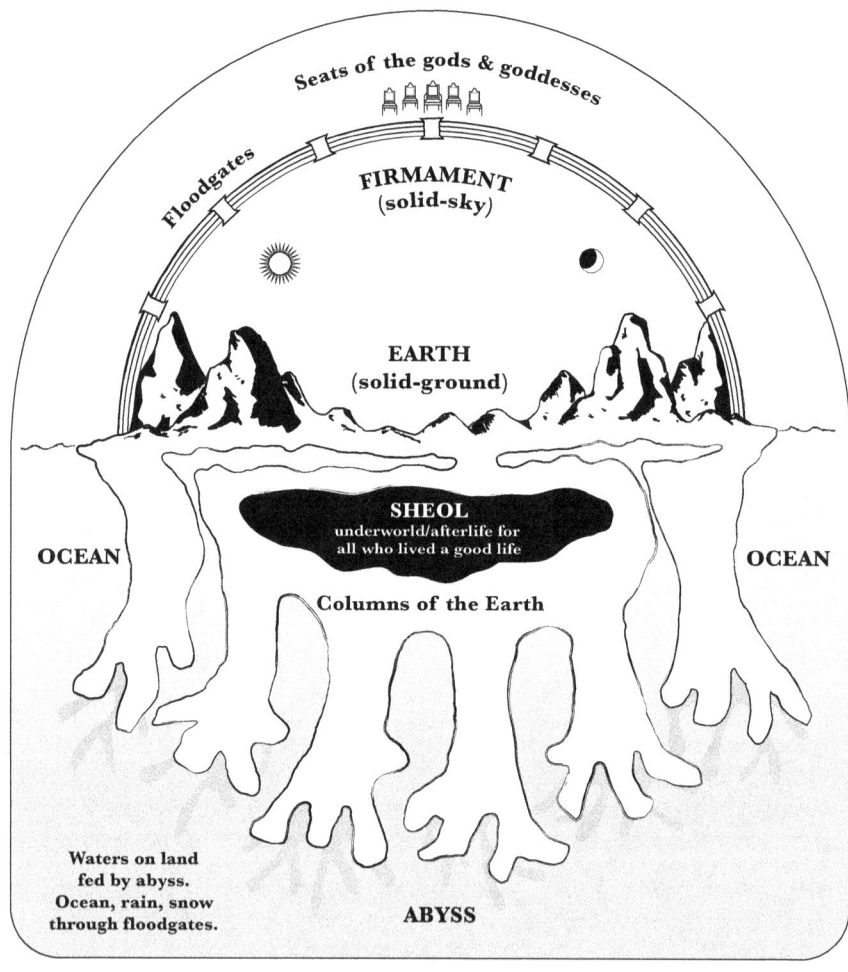

A decent translator knows something of the context of the world from which a text comes...and here is a glimpse of that very different world(view) of the ancient world...a world where no one had yet stepped off Earth or out of its atmosphere to view the world/planet as they knew it!

What is a translation?

It's one person's or one group of people's best guesses about bringing an idea from one language into another.

The key word here is <u>guesses</u>. We never can know for sure if our guesses are accurate — especially when translating something that is thousands of years old.

Any translator worth their salt and light must defend their reasoning for choosing the words they do for a translation.

Many people have read my translations of portions of Genesis in *A Wildly Sensual YAHWEH* and of 1 Samuel 1 - 17 in *The Naked Path of Prophet* and have been sure that I must be using different Hebrew texts than what their favorite Bible must have used to create their translation. But that's not the case — we all tend to use *Biblia Hebraica Stuttgartensia*, a received and continually improved text of the Hebrew Bible.

Some scholars will look to some of the more ancient fragments/portions of texts found at Qumran or elsewhere. I honor and appreciate and welcome that.

But those fragments/portions do not change the fact that the Ancient Hebrew word for 'prophet' is actually closer in meaning to 'ecstatic'

that the Ancient Hebrew word for 'Hebrew person' is actually closer to 'bordercrosser'

that the Ancient Hebrew word for 'knowing' can mean 'knowing' and it can mean 'sex'...depending on the context... and sometimes it can mean both at the same time...

that most Bible translators will choose only one word and I will give you most of the possible meanings of a word so that you can let all of them swim in your imagination.

Why would I do that? Because it's likely this is what a Hebrew hearer would do when hearing a story. A good Hebrew story is forked — which to say it has at least two story-trains running at the same time on parallel and intersecting tracks. Sometimes those story-trains collide, sometimes they miss each other.

When a story is forked like this, something happens in one's imagination. One's inner-container opens up and as the hearer you are flowing free and no longer so damned boring or depressed or serious and you've got life and you're even letting life be made through you, through every cell of your loins and your imagination and by golly that's damned sexy — because you know! you are being known! — and you too begin creating new versions of forked stories to awaken another person and another person and another. A forked story invites you to join the band.

Try it out. Go find your favorite translation of the Bible and read the Eden Story — the so called Adam and Eve story (Genesis 2.4 - 3.24). Every time you come to the word 'know/knowing/knowledge' read the sentence once as 'know/knowing/knowledge' and another time as 'sex/sexy.'

You'll notice quickly, I think, that both versions of the story — this fork — work.

That's the beauty of an Ancient Hebrew story or poem — the Ancient Hebrew language is always forking and making you wonder which fork is intended. Maybe both forks are. Especially if you are an ecstatic, if you know something of ecstasy...no drugs needed.

I hope this translation of 1 Samuel 18 - 31 invites you to notice the forks and to play with them, as any Ancient Hebrew hearer would.

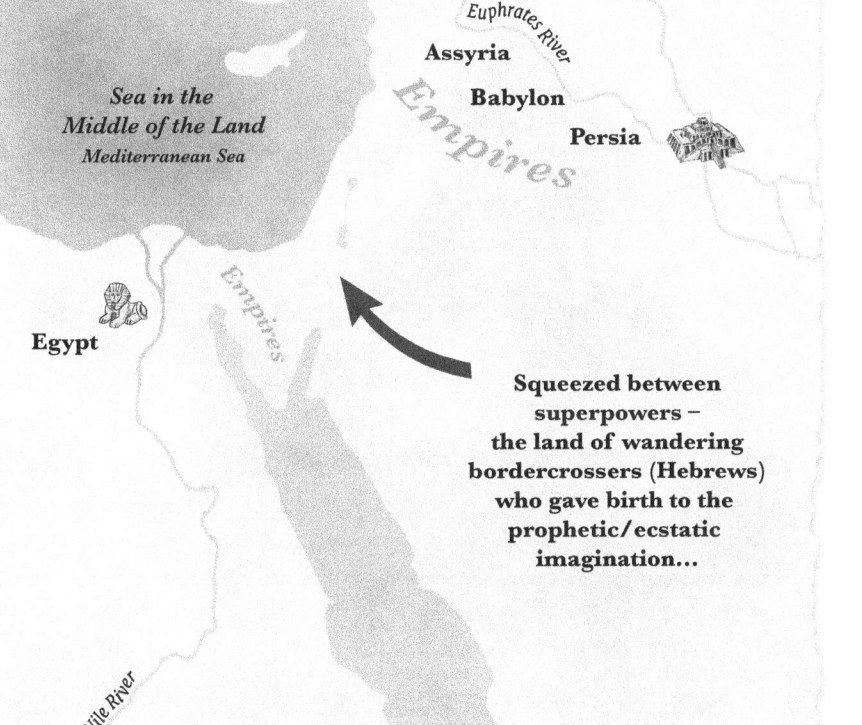

Tigris River

Euphrates River

Assyria

Babylon

Persia

Empires

*Sea in the
Middle of the Land*
Mediterranean Sea

Empires

Egypt

Nile River

Red Sea

**Squeezed between
superpowers –
the land of wandering
bordercrossers (Hebrews)
who gave birth to the
prophetic/ecstatic
imagination...**

Catching up on the plot,
our side-splitting fiction of 1 Samuel

In the first 17 chapters of 1 Samuel...

a woman who hadn't given birth to any children cries out her desires for a child in a wild style never before heard...her name is Hannah-Bend-Down...and she speaks in a 'style'/DBR — with honest emotion and a pun-rich poetry that would surprise anyone in the ancient world — even though the priest Eli-Climb-Up overhearing her thinks she must be drunk...

in her elation at the birth of her son — a birth that validates her value as a woman in the ancient world — a son she names after EL/divine — Hannah-Bend-Down gives her baby-son Samuel over to the priest Eli-Climb-Up so her son could be a young priest-in-training in front of the ark in a big tent... the boy wears the special strangly-yarned-underwear (*ephod*) for YAHWEH, 'clothing' which must be so threadbare and revealing that Samuel's mother makes for him a little robe to wear when she visits him so that his genitals don't leak out...

YAHWEH speaks to this young boy Samuel as the wind inflates the tent at night, as the candle before the ark flickers in the breeze and dances shadows and light all over the place, where Samuel sleeps in his *ephod*-underwear, and YAHWEH tells young Samuel about a new style It (YAHWEH) is bringing forth...where YAHWEH 'strips Itself naked'/GLH for young Samuel as if It were a slave, as if It were captured by Samuel in war...as if Samuel were YAHWEH's boss...

while Samuel's bosses, the head priest and his sons, die from their foolishness and the ark they'd served and protected and taken into battle is stolen by the enemy Philistines, the young priest-in-training Samuel runs off to The Heights — the mountaintops of Ancient Israel & Palestine not all that far from his ancestral home...

Samuel emerges twenty years later clearly changed from the boyish-priest-in-training that he was undergoing....now more mature and seemingly out of nowhere Samuel reminds the people to trust YAHWEH alone...a style of thinking where all humans are equal under YAHWEH with only YAHWEH topping anyone and any creation...Samuel even reminds people to get rid of their ASHTAROTHS, the goddess some YAHWEH-worshippers at one time had YAHWEH marry, just like BAAL had married ASHTAROTH to consummate fertility for oneself and the land...but the ecstatics-prophets like Samuel didn't buy into the ASHTAROTH-as-YAHWEH's-wife narrative because from an ecstatic's viewpoint the only bride for YAHWEH was human beings who breathed in YAHWEH...

and this YAHWEH is one sexy divinity...once the ark is captured by the Dust-Rolling-Philistines and placed in their holy temple of DAGON (BAAL's father), YAHWEH knocks DAGON face-down on the ground and DAGON's hands and feet are broken off...just like the fish DAGON is...DG/'fish or grain, food'...

and YAHWEH's YD/'hand or penis' then gives sore-assholes to the Philistines who urge their mayors and priests to do something through their confederacy of towns...and eventually they send the ark back to Israel by a couple of milking cows with a box filled with things to remove YAHWEH's curse on/in their sore-asses...a box of golden mice and golden ruptured assholes...

and even though the ark is back in Israel, the former priest-in-training Samuel has nothing to do with the ark anymore... instead Samuel only serves YAHWEH...

Ecstatic Prophets, Compulsive Fascists

despite the Israelites knowing that the Dust-Rolling-Philistines' system of government was powerful and effective with its people-mayor confederacy, the people of Ancient Israel in 1 Samuel prefer the ways of hierarchy and demand to be ruled by a king like 'all the other nations,' no matter how much Samuel reminds them that a king would take their children and their most prized possessions and anything and everything that matters to them — even their 'choice young men'/BCRYM — all for the king's self and his own kingly/selfish desires...

meanwhile YAHWEH only desires people — even Ancient Israel/Judah — YAHWEH only desires their attention, their love, their naked-sex with It...their ecstatic-relationship...

and Samuel accedes to the people's wishes because YAHWEH tells him to do so because from YAHWEH's perspective the people reject YAHWEH and not Samuel...so YAHWEH selects a king, Saul, anoints him privately, and then has this king selected by lot in front of all the people...YAHWEH gives the people their MSHYCH/'*messiah*, oil-smeared commander, anointed one'...but not without a little 'ecstasy'/NBYAH for the young king first, ecstasy that Samuel points out for Saul to notice on his way back home...

and does he ever have an ecstatic experience — enough that even other people notice!

and Saul is only a boy when he's chosen by lot as king, though a handsome boy standing head and shoulders above everyone else but he hides among the baggage when the lot fell upon him to be king...and what was he doing as he hid among the baggage? he was 'loving himself, masturbating himself, hiding himself within himself'/CHBAH...

why? how could that be?

...maybe that's what ecstasy does...it grows if one lets It...if you really know what YAHWEH is all about...

and for awhile young King Saul unites the people — well, most of the people — to protect the most vulnerable of Ancient Israel against the supposed enemies of Ancient Israel, including Philistines...

and yet the ecstatics-prophets on the mountaintops hang out near the Philistine garrison...and they seem to get along with whomever...just like the wind gets along with most breathers... It comes, It goes...It's constant and dependable...It enters all who want to live...

and Saul quickly becomes corrupt and entrenched in his role as King and builds penis-monuments to honor himself — all the while his son Jonathan and Jonathan's gear-carrier are the only two in Ancient Israel showing courage in battle, even with a clever strategy of getting naked to entice the enemy to desire them as Jonathan and naked-assistant attack the Philistines...

and where do most of the rest of the warriors of Ancient Israel have a habit of hiding out when they get scared? they do as Saul did when he was publicly selected as king...they CHBAH with one another...they 'enfold themselves within one another, make love with one another, hide within each other'...

and Samuel is so unhappy about Saul's ongoing selfish foolishnesses that he performs funeral rites for Saul — while Saul is still alive...

and YAHWEH too grows to despise and reject Saul as ruler and sends Samuel to anoint another king — and find him in another nation (!) — while the current King Saul is still alive...

and Samuel is afraid to do such a thing but goes as YAHWEH orders and has this man Jesse-There-He-Is pass each of his sons in front of Samuel — all of them exceedingly attractive and with patriotic and hierarchy-loving names — but YAHWEH does not like any of them even though Samuel sure does...

so Samuel asks if that's it and the father says the youngest (and least valuable in the ancient world) is outside tending to the little animals — a job reserved for slaves or not-yet-of-age-for-marriage children to see if they can handle the responsibility of caring for the family's smaller-wealth/animals...

and YAHWEH falls for this youngest son David — the one whose name means 'boiling over with love, affection' — and Samuel anoints this youngster king at YAHWEH's direction...

and King Saul becomes paranoid about his power and sensing that his subjects are becoming less and less loyal to him and has fits of rage and his own servants/slaves suggest they fetch a young musician to soothe his rage — who will strum the king's musical-strings with his YD/'hand or penis' — to being 'relief'/RUCH to the King whenever the raging 'bad-wind'/RUCH bothers the king...

and young David boils over with affection so much and King Saul likes this youngster David so much that he sends a letter to David's father that David is to stay with the King...that David has charmed him and now the king bows down to David...ahem...

and time passes and David eventually ends up back home, perhaps because the enemy-Philistines attack...maybe David was old enough for the king's soothing (!) but too young for battle...

and the Philistines' lead-warrior Goliath challenges Ancient Israel to send out one person to fight with him, that the winner and his country lives, the loser and his country becomes slaves to the winner's country...

Goliath's name means Stripper...and all the coins he wears as his chain-mail were most likely taken as he strips those he slays on the battlefield of anything valuable...

...and his weapons and even his own size are legendary — Goliath's massive...

and no one among Ancient Israel steps up — not even King Saul, though he should have because in a hierarchy the buck stops with him...and in a honor-culture like theirs, if you say 'no' to the challenge, you lose...

and Jesse-There-He-Is sends off young David to check on his brothers at the battleline and to deliver goodies to them and their officers, and while David's there he hears the banter about Goliath's offer and how if some brave soul among Ancient Israel steps up and wins that this brave soul would be enriched so greatly for life and get to marry the King's daughter...become royalty...

...and David joins the battleline banter much to the upset of his brothers who accuse their much younger brother of all kinds of things...

...and David steps up and says he'll fight and everyone shouts their approval and there he is before King Saul who offers his own armor and weapons to young David instead of King Saul actually doing the honorable and adult thing and fighting the massive Stripper-Goliath himself...

...but the armor and weapons of a grown man are much too big for a young teenager...so David removes them and chooses instead a few rocks and his slingshot and walks towards Goliath and they insult one another and David loads his shot and hurls a rock at Goliath's forehead and down Goliath goes...

...a kid kills a seasoned hero — a giant — with a rock and a sling...

and Ancient Israel attacks their enemy-Philistines as David uses Goliath's sword to chop off Goliath's head as King Saul looks on...and Saul still does not seem to recognize David, the young handsome boy who used to strum his strings and soothe his rage...perhaps the King has so many 'choice young men' at his war-disposal and every whim that as much as David had pleased him before so many other 'choice young men' also please him...

and King Saul asks his general whose son this boy is — this 'ripe virgin youngster'/AYLM — yes, Saul lets this slip from his mouth — and the general does not know the boy but will find out for the lusting King...

and perhaps these Samuel-tales share some similar spirit with the Ancient Greeks' tales of the same era...the Greek dramas of warrior-valor & warrior-PTSD...the Samuel-tales a warning about the dangers of kings and *christs/messiahs* and organized religion, all of which send innocents off to war often to often kill innocents...

and all the while in 1 Samuel 1 - 17 we are fed a steady diet of YAHWEH being the wind...YAHWEH whispers, hisses, thunders, strips naked, gets stirred and excited by Its ecstatics and, apparently, by young David...

the writing of 1 Samuel is exceedingly bawdy, funny, pun-rich, hilarious...a 'style'/DBR similar to the band of YAH who crafted much of Genesis, a style similar to Jeremiah and the Isaiahs and Amos and Jesus and Paul and other ecstatics, other prophets...and for this reason I call the unknown-writer of 1 & 2 Samuel by the name of X after the ecstatics...an 'ecstatic,' of course, in Ancient Hebrew is NBYAH, the word most translations of the Bible call 'prophets'...

and how could such writing as 1 & 2 Samuel ever be allowed into the emerging Bible that was being catalogued and edited by the royal-loving Deuteronomists — many generations of a political-party who gained their power from the king and even gave the power to the king and the royal-system? how could they let 1 & 2 Samuel slip through into the Bible they were assembling when this Samuel-saga makes Saul and David and eventually Solomon look like absolute fools?

well, let's hear the story unfold and see...and discover if the nuances of the wind — of the ecstatics' understanding of YAHWEH as the wind — seduces us along the way too....

A Few Notes on My Translation
of 1 Samuel from the Biblical Hebrew

...as it's my intent to avoid having to dance one's eyes all over the place with footnotes and to barge very little into the story unfurling itself in 1 Samuel so that the 21st century reader can catch the subtle differences that the band of X intends for us to catch...

(xx) indicates I've added this to explain an assumption that the band of X has about life in the ancient world of what is now called Ancient Israel/Palestine, the ancient trade routes of the eastern Mediterranean seaboard, the Levant

xxx xxx xxx...underlining indicates my efforts to highlight a clever pun that appears in the Ancient Hebrew text

x...a single italicized word indicates something that has been borrowed from Ancient Hebrew or Ancient Greek and brought into English...a word that might be wise to note its divergent roots

I have also capitalized divinities with their assumed vowels included for ease of reading — for instance, YAHWEH instead of YHWH and ELOHIM instead of AHLHYM. This whole business of ELOHIM in the Bible is tricky...could be translated as God, gods/goddesses, divine/divinity. These might be controversial choices for a number of reasons, though I believe you'll come to discover it makes for ease of reading for a wider audience. I have retained only the 'original' consonants-only versions of non-divinity words — for instance, GLH instead of GaLaH or GeLaH or something of that sort. More details on this system can be found in **Hebrew Alphabet - transliterated** and **Major Characters** in the *Resources* near the back of the book.

Trying to bring forward the flexible style of Ancient Hebrew verbs, English verbs like 'climb' and 'style' — for example — are used transitively and intransitively, even sometimes when not appropriate in modern English usage. Try it out. Play along, if you dare.

here continues
a translation
from the 'original' Ancient Hebrew
we have received through the ages
of the first scroll of Samuel...

chapter 18

And it was just as (David) had finished styling it out to Saul that the living, breathing body of Jonathan was <u>tied up</u> with the living, breathing body of David.

And Jonathan loved him as much as his own living, breathing body.

And Saul took him that day and wouldn't give him back to return to his father's house.

And Jonathan and David cut a covenant (made a serious promise to one another by walking in the blood between just-cut, valuable and now dead animals) — in one's love for the other as his own living, breathing body.

And Jonathan <u>stripped himself</u> of the valuable outer garment designating his rank that was on him — Jonathan stripped himself as if he had been invaded and conquered — and gave it to David —

and his clothing

and even his sword

and even his bow

and even his underwear, the belt that held his weaponry...

And David went out on everything (every campaign and lethal-errand) that Saul sent him —
<u>with devotion and success and careful caution</u>.

(More clever ambiguity in word choices from our band of X... their double/triple-entendre style...as the love-triangle plot thickens between Saul-David-Jonathan!

This business of being 'tied up with one another'/QSHR can have different meanings...'conspiring with one another, even in a treasonous way'...'tied up together as being in love with each other'...and even as simple as 'tying/knitting two or more things together'...as *Strong's Exhaustive Concordance* notes...

as Saul and Jonathan mirror one another very differently in their 'giving'/NTN...Saul can't give up his hold on David whom he likes so much, while Saul's son Jonathan gives up all his outward-facing power to David in his own love for David...

and Jonathan handing over his MAYYL/'coat-of-rank' and even ripping it off himself as conquered people would be forced to do also plays upon MAYL/'to act unfaithfully or treasonously'...which is precisely what Jonathan seems to be doing by ripping off all his royal-clothes and weapons and rank and giving them over to David, his king-father's AYLM...

remember in these stories that David is a young man — a 'ripe-and-ready-youngster'/AYLM somewhere on the cusp of puberty and thus marriageable in the ancient world, AYLM is what Saul called David just a few lines before these we just read — one who up until then had been 'concealed'/AYLM from public/adult life. Children, in the ancient world, weren't considered human until they were marriageable, until they were worth something in the economy. AYLM is what Saul lets slip from his mouth in describing David just after the young teen took down a giant, a hero, Stripper-Goliath, the one who was once so in control on the battlefield that he could strip the slain of their wealth/armor and pocket it for himself and his own weaponry. In that act of slaying Stripper-Goliath, our character David demonstrated his devotion to Ancient Israel and YAHWEH and even the king who didn't have the courage to fight Stripper-Goliath on his own. David steps into major success with hurling some insults and a single lethal rock… David, the one who boils over with affection and love, made the king boil over with affection at witnessing his young battlefield prowess…and now the king's son has demonstrated his naked affection for David too…oh my! It's quite a powerful triangle, these three…

and as for 'devotion and success and careful caution'/SCL can mean all of these…. which one is it? or all three? hmm…we'll have to see how this plays out with David acting both with 'devotion' to Saul and 'careful caution' as he, gulp, probably should be when Saul's bad winds get a hold of him…

there's a great deal of style in this and coming passages, style that an ancient hearer would surely catch and not be so sure which way the story leans….)

And Saul put (David) in charge of the men/people of war, who fight,
and it was good in the eyes of all the people
and even in the eyes of Saul's slaves.

And so it was —
when they were (fuck) arriving —
when David was returning from killing the Dust-Rolling-Philistine(s) —
that the women from all of Ancient Israel's cities went out singing and dancing —

to greet and announce Saul — the king! —
with tambourines
and with rejoicing
and with <u>triangles</u>
and the women <u>answered one another...sang...testified</u>
and laughed and mocked him
and said,

"Saul kills his thousand,
and David his many, many, many...millions!"

(Ouch! That's a slam! And not just that...

SHLSHYM sometimes means 'musical instruments, like triangles' or sometimes means 'thirty'...and while we might assume that in this case it would be 'musical instruments' because tambourines were just mentioned, any ancient hearer's ears might prick up, especially if only thirty people are showing up to announce the King. The King! Sure, King Saul can kill his thousand, but David is so much better than him — at least from a hierarchically motivated imagination — because David kills with impunity on these raids upon which the King sends him...David kills his 'many, many, many...millions'/BRBBTYU but the King gets so little credit when the love-boiling David is the victor...this King Saul that all the people 'asked for'...

...or...is the 'triangle' a ridiculously clever allusion to the love-triangle that maybe the whole nation knows about...Saul-David-Jonathan...something that would prick up the ears of any ancient hearer...

and perhaps so as the band of X does have these women SCHQ/'mocking' the king! The king!

And MCHLH can certainly mean 'dancing'...though *Strong's Exhaustive Concordance* notes that it is the feminine form of MCHSHBH, a use which always carries with it some forethought, even scheming forethought. Even the 'singing'/ SHYR — which some manuscripts have SHUR/'traveling, journeying' — offers some complexity to the story in that these women might have been traveling around with their singing and dancing and sharing their political opinions about and against the king and maybe even against David...all through the kingdom, it could seem...perhaps in the very spirit of the band of X who offers these very pointed tales to mock the system of royalty and mock the system of ark-religion-and-Law/Torah and mock the system that enacts genocide and amplify with curiosity the vibe of the ecstatics, the prophets who care little for kings or queens...

BOAH/'arrive, bring, come, go' can also mean 'fuck' as it often does in the band of YAH's Genesis stories...some of these BOAHs in 1 Samuel can go either way...some both ways...and that's half the fun in orally shared tales like the band of X's stories that became 1 Samuel and the band of YAH's stories that became most of Genesis likely were....)

And anger blazed up in Saul — very much so!

And it was bad in his eyes, this style.

And he said,
"They give David his many-many-many...millions
and to me they give thousands —
what more for him but the entire kingdom!"

(Note...Saul gives himself more than the women did...his 'thousands' vs. their 'thousand.')

And so it was —
Saul kept an eye on David from that day forward.

And so it was —
that very next day that it rushed onto Saul —
a wind of ELOHIM/God-or-the-gods-and-goddesses —
a bad/troubling one —
and he was driven into a prophetic-ecstatic-experience in the
middle of the house —
and David <u>strummed the strings with his hand/penis</u> that day
as he'd done on other days —
and there was a spear in Saul's <u>hand/penis</u> —
and Saul hurled the spear, and said,
"I'm sticking it right into David — to kill him —
and right into <u>the piss-trench</u>!"

And David circled around to avoid facing him two times.

(Here's young David in the house trying to soothe Saul when
Saul has his madnesses — maybe that damned jingle from the
women ringing through his head, that damned jingle about
David being exponentially better than himself. "I'm the king!
They should like me better..." perhaps Saul thinks....

And remember...Saul has had a thing for young David, his
AYLM, his 'ripe-and-ready-teenage-youngster' whom he
refuses to send back home to David's father.

And how does David soothe, ahem, the king during these fits
of madness? Well, ahem, that's not entirely clear. The phrase
is NGN BYDO. NGN can mean 'to strum the strings, to thrum
or tamp out a beat.' You'd think the BYDO would help but
that complicates it all even more. B means 'with' and YD can
mean 'hand'...and it could mean 'penis,' as we well know from
earlier stories of 1 Samuel.

So young David uses his hand or his penis or both to strum
the strings or to strum King Saul's strings whenever Saul goes
deeper into his ELOHIM-driven ecstatic-experiencing. But
this seems to be very different from the ecstatic-experience

Ecstatic Prophets, Compulsive Fascists

that Samuel told young Saul he'd encounter through YAHWEH after Saul left him to return back home in 1 Samuel 10. This time the ecstasy is inspired by a bad wind from ELOHIM — and the bad wind version sounds not too pleasant.

It's not so clear who this ELOHIM/'divinity' is — 'God' or 'the gods and goddesses' — the very problem the band of X seems to throw back into the faces of the Levitical priests. It's the priests through their Torah who try to diminish the influence of the prophets who so freely say 'YAHWEH' out loud; the priests declare that the Divine's name 'YAHWEH' should not be uttered freely, in vain, so they prefer to call the Divine One "ELOHIM" — the same name for 'all the gods and goddesses' of their Canaanite neighbors whose godhead EL ruled over all the ELOHIM.

And not only that, here with Saul, could it be that the same ELOHIM-wind that gives life can give madness — maybe depending on the intents of the breath-holder? Or is this ELOHIM signifying the ecstatic-madness that gods and goddesses like BAAL and ASHTAROTH or even EL would surely excite within oneself? such lust stirred up with ancient fertility concerns...very real concerns for food and for children/lineage...both needed to survive into another generation?

I suspect the band of X is playing with all those questions here in 1 Samuel.

Remember through our characters in this fictional-story... back in 1 Samuel 10, Samuel had pointed out to Saul what YAHWEH's wind felt like and what it did within someone... how Saul would get whipped up with the ecstasy of the wind with YAHWEH's wind-followers as they whooped it up — as It whooped them up — as they were coming down a mountain and running through a town...just after Samuel had anointed/ smeared with oil and kissed Saul and on Saul's way home to eventually, one day, be selected before all the people as first king of Ancient Israel...where Saul was found 'loving himself, hiding himself within himself' and perhaps still within his YAHWEH-given ecstasy — among the baggage.

Saul had that experience of getting whipped up into an ecstatic-frenzy with the prophets running down the mountain before becoming king. He knew 'ecstasy'/NBYAH. He tasted ecstasy, YAHWEH's love-potion available to all breathers. But he never went back for more.

And at least so far our character Saul has rarely/never lived out of that experience — even though he seemed to enjoy it before, found himself changed by It. Maybe he was filled with that ecstatic-experience in stirring his nation to defend themselves against Snake when he first heard the news of Snake's invasion...but since then? It's all been making penis-statues for himself and letting everyone else fight but himself. And now David strums the strings to soothe the king but the king goes deeper into his own blood-thirsty madness — enough to want to kill young David.

And that's just it...maybe that's what X is pointing out in their saga. Once you taste YAHWEH's love, you must continue to cultivate it, cultivate one's love for It. How? By feeling, sensing, luxuriating in the life-breath alone, even breathe life into others in our love-making, however that comes for you and me.

But our hierarchies/fascisms — governments, religions, and sometimes even our families — block that potent experience, that experience of knowing where power really comes from... from life Itself, from YAHWEH.

Perhaps one's life with YAHWEH is a bit like the Zen koan... "better to not begin, but once begun better finish!"

We will need to discern these experiences of ecstasy...Saul's experience with YAHWEH before becoming king and now this ELOHIM-driven experience that makes him go mad.

Perhaps it's different when one is at the pinnacle of hierarchical power as King...at least different from being just one of the guys/gals/nonbinaries in the band of ecstatics in their being whooped up together by the wind on top of mountains...far different when one sits on a throne as sovereign who must be called to mete out justice and some sense of safety (or terror)...

and as for the 'piss-trench'/QYR...most translations have it as 'wall' and that's fine until we get to some later stories — 1 Samuel 25 — where QYR is surely more than just a wall though maybe 'piss-wall' would be true too...I suspect our character Saul is not just bragging here about having — unsuccessfully — pinned David to any old wall though I can imagine his satisfaction at having pinned David into the wall that he pisses on and where it dribbles away from his house, the ancient latrine...this boy he once loved but now despises because everybody loves David — and even Jonathan — more than anyone loves the king. Talk about 'a bad air'!)

And Saul was afraid of <u>facing</u> David, time and time again, because YAHWEH was with him.

And from Saul, (It/YAHWEH) <u>had turned away — beheaded him.</u>

And Saul <u>turned</u> David <u>away</u> from himself — <u>tried to behead him</u> —
and put him <u>in-charge</u> of a thousand
and out he went (in battle)
and (fuck) he came back to <u>face</u> the people.

(Quite a style-rich couple of lines!

We hear three similar sounding phrases: the first two are SUR/'turned away or beheaded' + MAYM/'against or from'... the same SUR that Samuel had advised the people in his first adult speech on beheading the BAALS/ASHTAROTH among them. The third phrase sounds similar: SRR/'to be in charge' + AYM/'people.'

The juxtaposed PN/'facing' helps us to discern the differences between Saul and David even further. Just more stylish play by the band of X to tickle one's senses and imagination, to invite us to crave more and more style that comes from these sounds dancing in the wind...when the ear receiving the wind is not polluted by bad winds, or selfish desires....

The band of X is fond of playing games with their word choices, as we know well from the previous volume of *The Naked Path of Prophet*, with 1 Samuel 1 - 17. YD/'hand, penis' is one of those strange Ancient Hebrew words that in context becomes clear which one is intended...except in more band of X and band of YAH stories where YD/'hand' and YD/'penis' are usually interchangeable. Same goes for BOAH/'come, go, bring, enter, fuck'. Sometimes it seems obvious that BOAH is most definitely 'come, go' and definitely not 'fuck' but other times BOAH could be either and both or perhaps even our modern English way of saying 'oh fuck'. The same happens in the band of YAH's Genesis stories where BOAH for sure has to do with sex...less lovemaking, more like fucking.

You see, with the band of X and the band of YAH, we never quite know for sure which way they lean with their word choices. And I think that's their strength as storycrafters. Here comes that SCL again...with its triple-possibility of determining where one's devotions lie....)

And so it was —
David in all his ways was <u>devoted and successful and carefully cautious,</u>
and YAHWEH was with him.

And Saul saw that he was <u>devoted and successful and carefully</u>

cautious — very much so! — that he acted like a stranger to his face...that's how afraid he was.

And all of Ancient Israel and Judah loved David
because he went out (in battle)
and (fuck) he came back to face them.

And Saul said to David, the one who boils over with love and affection,
"Look there —
my daughter — the greater one — the older one —
Merab-From-Many...(as in 'all your millions') —
she is the one I'm giving you to be your wife —
— only — uh — be for me a son of power...of virtue, strength, wealth...of the upper-classes —
and purposely pick fights —
the fights of YAHWEH!"

(Remember what all the circling women said of David...that he'd killed his 'millions...many-many-many'/RBBH to Saul's thousands...and here Saul is offering to David his daughter who happens to be named 'From-Many'/MRB...she seems to be the furthest thing from our expression of 'one in a million' as she's just From-Many...and yes, the band of X seems to be highlighting the misogynistic assumptions in Saul's royal/ hierarchical imagination of giving his daughter away without any say from her, as is the custom in their ancient world...the band of YAH also challenges these traditions in the Rebekah story in Genesis...the women of the band of X will have their say in this story very soon...though if you listen carefully women are the ones who circled around and danced and sang out their truth — a truth that pisses off the king — and the Samuel-saga's women-characters continue to make the big moves over and over again....

Now this business of Saul asking David to be a 'son of power... of virtue, strength, wealth...of the upper-classes'/BN CHYL...

while not hailing from the same cities or even tribes — Saul's Gibeah of Benjamin and David's Bethlehem of Judah (though David's father was from Ephraim, like Samuel) — Saul's and David's hometowns are only 10 miles from each other — as if Saul is signaling, 'look, be a brother to me' while at the same time demanding that David climb up a notch on the social ladder toward his own now-top-perch...Saul's hierarchical way of staying on top of David who like Saul was from the middle of 'nowhere'...recall where young King Saul was when his country was being invaded...out in his family's field and not in any city...not in any so-seemed city of importance like a city housing the ark...

and all this at the same time that Saul asks David to 'pick fights'/LCHM — the *hiphil* version of the verb, often indicating some force — like any person hailing from Bethlehem/BT LCHM/'House of Feast-or-Fight'....quite clever style by our band of X to place David as being from the place where one must war for one's bread...where one must devour the enemies and then devour their animals/wealth...and David's older brothers have been doing just that as the king's army... and as for David's battles note too that Saul refers to these battles as YAHWEH's, not ELOHIM's...and we're never quite sure in the Samuel-saga just which ELOHIM — the One God or the multi-divinities of the region....)

And Saul said (to himself),
"Let it not be my hand/penis on/in him —
let it be on/in him the Dust-Rolling-Philistines' hand/penis!"

And David said to Saul,
"Who am I —
who am I getting my life from an <u>extended-family-including-maidslaves</u> of my father —
among (everyone in) Ancient Israel! —
that I could be son-in-law to the king?!"

And so it was —
when it was time to give Saul's daughter Merab-From-Many
to David
that she was given as a wife to Flock-of-EL from the region
where people did their dances in the grassy-meadow.

(Notice, Saul does not respond to David's questions and
concerns with words...a deafening silence to this love-boiling-
David who admits he's born from a maidslave/SHPCH — or
perhaps that his father is from a not-pure family/MSHPCHH
and not as worthy of marrying royalty as, say, David's older
brothers might be who, it's likely, were born of higher-
class wives than slave-wives. Let's recall when we first meet
David in 1 Samuel, David was the youngest, and out tending
the animals as his brothers were paraded before Samuel...
and merely an afterthought at that as YAHWEH through
Samuel finds no value in the older brothers, no matter their
pedigree. Note too that David's mother is never mentioned,
though his father Jesse-There-He-Is is mentioned and even
by name a few times in the earlier stories. Maybe David
indeed was born of a maidslave. All of these various pecking
orders and hierarchies of value would have been immediately
recognizable to an ancient person hearing this story — and
the band of X seems even to go to great lengths to make sure
any reader would notice them too with their careful choices of
words, their style, their not-so-subtle juxtaposition of words/
ideas next to contrasting words/ideas, and even their silences
on certain matters.

And what a strange juxtaposition we have here with these two
suitors for Merab-From-Many...

David...the one who boils over with affection...who admits
he's born into an extended-family/MSHPCHH instead of
the more hierarchically 'pure' family-that-has-roots-in-the-
ancestors/MOLDT — more on this key juxtaposition and
differentiation can be found throughout Genesis, *A Wildly*

Sensual YAHWEH — The Naked Path of Prophet vol 0 and with Hannah's story at the beginning of 1 Samuel in *The Naked Path of Prophet vol 1*....

and **Flock-of-EL**...a suitor who hails from a region where they do their dances in the meadow...not even a city! And again which EL are we talking about...EL as 'the One God' of Ancient Israel? or EL, the divine-head of all the ELOHIM: the whole host of heaven including BAAL, ASHTAROTH, DAGON, etc.?

Saul doesn't seek out an upper-class person worthy enough of his daughter's hand in marriage — he finds someone marginally better than the bottom-feeder, low-in-the-pecking-order David, the youngest in his family and a not-pure family at that — perhaps to humiliate David even more.

And notice again that Merab-From-Many seems to have no say in the matter — and the band of X makes that super clear, and will clarify it even more in short time.

All these pecking orders of royal life and priestly life — as we learned in *The Naked Path of Prophet vol 1* — are very different from the ecstatic-prophets on the mountaintops, like Samuel himself, those ecstatic-humans who get high on the wind of YAHWEH — the wind that is YAHWEH — and have no interest in pecking orders or hierarchies of any kind...these ecstatic-prophets who note and live out the inherent equality of all human beings, no matter what family, no matter their gender, no matter even if born of an enemy of Ancient Israel... the only exception so far is perhaps Agag whom Samuel killed because Saul refused to...Agag the reputed murderer of pregnant women in town after town, generation after generation.)

But Saul's daughter Michal-Who-Is-ALL —
she loved David.

And they reported it to Saul,
and the style of it all was smooth and straight and right in his eyes.

(Why was it 'smooth and straight and right'/YSHR to Saul?

Because the one — David — everyone thought was better than Saul was to have Saul's younger daughter as his wife and not the older daughter, a complete affront against David in the ancient world where Saul's first daughter should be given to the more honorable person...but Saul gave that older daughter — Merab-From-Many — to someone from the middle of nowhere with a bad name.

And not only this, note the clever juxtaposition of the daughter's names...

Merab-From-Many...a name hailing back to what was said of David with his many-millions more than Saul — Saul gives his older daughter to someone marginally better than David in the ancestor-valued and hometown-valued pecking orders though this bad-named fellow hadn't killed Goliath and, as far as we know, hadn't gone out on campaign to rout the enemies of Ancient Israel as David had been doing as a loyal follower of the royal-system that enriches the king...

Michal-Who-Is-ALL...Saul's younger daughter with quite a name

Listen like an ancient would to these names and their meanings — especially in an oral culture like theirs. Listen now to how these characters' names play out in the story. Think these names are merely a coincidence? Uh, more on that soon.)

And Saul said (to himself, or perhaps out loud among the royal court),
"I'll give her to him —

she'll be like bait in a trap — like a noose around his neck —
and may the Dust-Rolling-Philistines' hand/penis be on/in him!"

And Saul said to David a second time (...David...the love-
boiling, former ripe-and-ready-youngster who once soothed-
and-pleased Saul...),
"You'll be a son-in-law for me this very day!"

And Saul shouted out orders at his slaves,
"Style it out to David in secret — with an air of mystery — saying
'Listen here — he's delighted by you — the king is —
and all his slaves love you —
now be a son-in-law to the king!'"

And Saul's slaves styled it out into David's ears these very
styles,
and David said,
"Is it such a <u>low-valued — even a cursed thing</u> — in your eyes —
to be made son-in-law to the king?
<u>I am a man of poverty — and low-valued and cursed</u>!"

And Saul's slaves reported back to (Saul) saying,
"In these stylish ways of putting it, David styled it out."

(...'all the slaves love you, David'...this is a rather unusual thing
for a king to have spoken by his own slaves/royal-court to
David to try to convince David that it's okay for him to marry
Michal-Who-Is-ALL...and that's the very comedy that the
band of X brings forward in their fiction about the fool-rich
roots of monarchy...and the fools who even consider marrying
into its 'ring'...

note the differing styles between what King Saul says/has his
slaves say for him and the stylish ways David parses it out
to these slaves, even calling himself 'a man of poverty' or
'poor-man'...in Hebrew: AHYSH-RSH...say those sounds out
loud in their style...and then the character-David plays with

'low-valued, despised, accursed'/QLL referring in a stylish-double-entendre-way to the difficult matter at hand when all the people love him but the King wants to stab him dead into the piss-trench. Let's not forget what David has experienced with this Saul, while strumming his strings, ahem, and Saul's spear, ahem.

But did David speak accurately? That he himself is a 'man of poverty'? Maybe compared to the King. But recall what David was doing when we first met him, when Samuel came to his father's house so that YAHWEH could choose a new king...all these brothers were there and some of them — eventually— fought for Saul and thus were on the royal-payroll...and there was David out tending his family's flocks/wealth while the brothers are not at least then helping him...and then later David's father sent him to check on his brothers in battle and to deliver a basket of expensive food to David's brothers and to their captain. David's not exactly poor....)

And Saul said,
"Just like this, say it to David:
'There is no delight for the king in a bridal-purchase-price except...
100 foreskins (you are to cut) from the uncut-dicks of the Dust-Rolling-Philistines —
to take revenge on the king's enemies!'"

And Saul thought about the interpenetrating aspects of his plan — to make David fall into/onto the Dust-Rolling-Philistines' hand/penis.

(What an ask! And what clever style here....

'in a bridal-purchase-price except...100' = BMHR KY BMAHH...say the Hebrew out loud...how the sounds play with one another and then 'revenge'/NQM said by Saul sounds a bit similar to 'low-valued, and even cursed'/NQLH said earlier by David... all of this as if Saul is trying to match David's poetic/style-spitting wits.

One can quickly discover how such a foreskin-request by the king would indeed put David in great danger...first to go strike down 100 Philistine men into the dust, expose their genitals, cut off the tip of each one's penis, put that tip in a bag, and get away — 100 times — all the while a battle raged around him. Even if the battle had concluded and any Philistine alive saw David doing such a grotesque thing, that Philistine viewer would surely rumble up more support to go attack David as he performs such a vulnerable act as bending down and doing all of this, his own back exposed to potential danger from spear or sword or arrow or a rushing band of Philistines intent on getting revenge against David as he humiliates their dead.

And the verb choice about Saul 'thinking about the interpenetrating aspects of his plan' is actually just one rather strange word...CHSHB...which can mean lots of things...'value, consider, reckon, plan'...and *Strong's Exhaustive Concordance* notes that CHSHB seems to be derived from 'plaiting or interpenetrating or weaving things together'...and Saul has certainly been doing quite a bit of all of that, ever since he saw David the first time. It's what kings do — as Samuel first pointed out to the people demanding a royal-system. Kings exploit through their weavings. It's the very nature of such a hierarchical system.

And all the while these political games are being played by Saul and David, the ecstatics-prophets were on the mountaintops of Ancient Israel/Palestine getting high on the breeze, on YAHWEH, and loving only that...an experience that Saul has had a taste of before but so far has no interest in returning to...he's more interested in 'interpenetrating aspects of his plan' to watch David die and such sick hopes may be why he's haunted by 'a bad wind of ELOHIM'....)

And the slaves reported to David with these stylings-on —
and <u>the style of it was pleasing in David's eyes</u> —
to become the son-in-law of the king.

(This exact line about 'style being <u>pleasing</u>'/YSR was used
earlier for Saul, and now here for David. And here we can
see David making a significant choice in enmeshing himself,
interpenetrating and weaving himself, into the royal-family,
into the hierarchy.)

And the days (of campaigning/battle? of David's time to bring
the marriage-deal with Saul to fruition?) had not yet been
<u>completely accomplished</u>.

And David stood himself up tall
and went — he and his men —
and killed the Dust-Rolling-Philistines —
200 men —
and David (fuck) brought back the foreskins from their dicks
and <u>completely accomplished — as in counting them out</u> —
for the king —
to make himself son-in-law to the king,
and Saul gave him his daughter Michal-Who-Is-ALL to be his wife.

(Do you get a whiff of the mafia here? Do this dirty-work of killing
and you move up in the family's esteem and the family's pecking
order through marriage. This is how hierarchies work...royal,
corporate, political, religious, or otherwise — though thankfully
not all of them require killing, or foreskins. But hierarchies
often demand something twisted in their membership and
carrot-dangling possibilities for upward-mobility.

Quite stylish and tight storytelling with the two different uses
of 'completely accomplish, fulfill'/MLAH in just a few lines of
biblical text.

Keep in mind too — Saul might have had sex with David long before Saul married his daughter off to David...back before David was his twangy-harp-boy strumming his strings...David the ripe-and-ready youngster...the one who boils over with love and affection....)

And <u>Saul saw</u> and knew in every way
that YAHWEH was with David —
and his daughter <u>Michal-Who-Is-ALL</u> <u>loved</u> him —
and Saul added it all up, more and more —
<u>he was afraid</u> of facing David anymore.

(Saul 'saw'/YRAH and Saul 'was afraid'/RAH...and...

Saul's daughter 'loves'/AHHB David, while Saul is an 'enemy'/AHYB to David, which we'll hear in a moment. Such similar sounding words with such different meanings. Catching just how cleverly styled this storycrafting is? and how it would sound when styled out loud to a gathered audience?)

And so it was —
Saul was an <u>enemy</u> to David every day after that.

And those in-charge of the Dust-Rolling-Philistines were going out (on campaign/battle).

And so it was —
whenever they went out (on campaign/battle),
David acted with more <u>devotion and success and careful caution</u> <u>than all</u> of Saul's slaves,
and his name became highly valued and prized —
very much so.

(There's our old friend SCL/'devotion and success and careful caution' coming around again...and a clever little double-entendre with MYCL/'Michal' and MCL/'than all'…the difference of a *yod*, the tiniest of Hebrew letters, like a comma in shape and size and sound…enough to delight the ears of ancient hearers.)

chapter 19

And Saul styled it out to his son Jonathan and to all this slaves to murder David.

And Saul's son Jonathan was delighted by David —
very much so.

And Jonathan reported it to David saying
"He's seeking — Saul — my father — to murder you —
— now — protect yourself — please — until morning —
you'll stay in hiding/secrecy/disguise — hide yourself in lovemaking—"

(Why only until morning? Shouldn't he — Jonathan — be concerned about the daytime too?

Maybe not if they are sleeping together that night and can protect each other…in the same bed…with their arms wrapped around each other in their lovemaking…and with weapons out and drawn and always at the ready…

and with our old friend CHBAH/'hide yourself in lovemaking' used earlier in 1 Samuel and also in the Eden story of Genesis — CHBAH is a special kind of hiding, as in wrapping oneself inside of and around each other…the word to describe what Mud-Creature/Adam and Woman/Eve were doing in their particular kind of hiding from YAHWEH…*Strong's Exhaustive Concordance* notes CHBAH is surely related to CHBB/'to love'… and the 'love'/AHHB of Saul's daughter for David sounds similar when spoken out loud to CHBAH/Jonathan's desire to 'hide-by-lovemaking' David...Jonathan CHBB/'loving' David...

and just to make this lovemaking even clearer, rather curiously, in this particular warning from Jonathan to David about Saul's murderous plot, Jonathan uses <u>both</u> the usual form of 'hiding, secrecy'/STR and the kind of hiding that involves love and lovemaking, 'hiding around and inside another person'/CHBAH...

CHBAH has been used in the 1 Samuel saga — four times in fact — once to describe Saul hiding himself in the baggage while Samuel was announcing him as king in 1 Samuel 10 — and we're left to wonder if he's there 'loving' himself or wrapped up in 'loving' another human and likely a slave responsible for the baggage — Saul the just-then-selected-by-lot king! — and then three times in 1 Samuel 13-14 to describe Saul's men who had fled from battle in their fear of the Dust-Rolling-Philistines and they CHBAH'd themselves in and around each other in their, ahem, caves where they were hiding.

Yes. Three times it's said this way, that these soldiers — Saul's men — were hiding in their holes, in their 'caves'/MAYRH... and *Strong's Exhaustive Concordance* is not bashful in noting that the root of MAYRH is AYUR/'to be naked.'

Why these very clear references to man-on-man sex in the military and in the kingship with Saul's love for David...the one who'd make anyone boil over with affection for him...and with Israel's two great military-threats, David and Jonathan, in their love and even serious-agreement/covenant with one another?

I'll have a lot more to say about this later, but I suspect the band of X is making it quite clear in their fiction-perhaps-based-somehow-on-reality that the very roots of Ancient Israel's military and kingship had to do with man-on-man love, same-sex love...so why would the Levitical priests craft their Law/Torah around punishing by death men having sex with men as they do in Leviticus 18 & 20 when it was precisely what led Ancient Israel to its military strength and then the safety of the Levites? As biblical scholar Ted Jennings points out in *Jacob's Wound*, the pederastic coupling of older-warrior with younger-warrior could have begun in Ancient Israel, not Ancient Greece...and it very well might have been the strength of their militaries in that these men would fight to save each other, in their true love for each other...all by hiding themselves in the arms and caves — bodies — of the other.

The king seems to like such male-coupling too.

And it's likely the ecstatic-prophets also allowed and maybe even encouraged this kind of love, any kind of love, in their ecstatic-experiences on the mountaintops in their gatherings of misfits who fled from the merging and emerging hierarchies of their time. After all, it's such penetrative love as this that gives birth to prophets as the band of YAH professes in what became the core story of Genesis...YAHWEH planting Its seed of life in Jacob...the ultimate story in Genesis that gives birth to the very name of Israel...Jacob's nickname...the very name Israel that indeed means 'God-wrestler' or 'God-contender' or at its very root 'the one who is in-charge of God'...'the one who bossed God around'...

and so it is — here in our ongoing tale of the love-triangle of Saul-David-Jonathan, we see Jonathan recommending to David that he not only 'hide'/STR but 'hide-in-Jonathan's-wrapping-penetrating-embrace'/CHBAH....)

(Jonathan continued his warning:)
"—and I — I'll do it — I'll go out myself —
and stand at attention by/for my father's hand/penis —
in the open-field — which is where you'll be —
and I myself'll style it out about you — with my father —
I'll see what's-up —
and make a report to you!"

And Jonathan styled it out in a good way about David to his father Saul,
and he said to him,
"Do not make a serious mistake and then bear the blame, King, regarding your slave, David —
because he hasn't made a serious mistake and borne the blame regarding you —
because he's only done good by you —
very much so —
he put his living-breathing-body into his own palms —
he killed the Dust-Rolling-Philistine (Goliath) —
and YAHWEH then made a huge rescue —
for all of Ancient Israel —
you saw it —
you took great joy in it —
so why would you make a serious mistake and bear the blame —
with the blood of an innocent person —
to murder David —
for no reason...
<u>what with all that bowing down in front of him you used to do</u>?!"

(Our character Jonathan uses quite a choice of words here... CHNM/'bowing'...closely related to the word CHNN which is the very unusual word Saul used earlier in 1 Samuel in sending a message to David's father that King Saul would be keeping the boy David because David 'made me bow down, he's so charming and favorable'/CHNN. Jonathan appears to be reminding his father-the-king Saul of his previous fondness and attraction to David when he was a ripe-and-ready-teen. Jonathan could've stopped his argument at 'to kill an innocent person'...but he didn't. He let that word about 'being charmed' hang....)

And Saul heard the tone of Jonathan's voice,
and Saul swore,
"As YAHWEH lives, he will not be murdered!"

Ecstatic Prophets, Compulsive Fascists

And Jonathan called out for David,
and reported to him — Jonathan did himself — all these
stylings-on,
and Jonathan (fuck) <u>entered David — uh, Jonathan brought,
entered with David</u> —
to Saul...

and so it was —
he was in his presence — facing him —
just like before,
just like it was, what seemed like just three days ago.

And the war was growing again — for existence —
and David went out,
and he warred against the Dust-Rolling-Philistines,
and he killed them —
a huge kill —
and they fled from his face.

And a bad wind from YAHWEH was within Saul,
and he was in his house,
he was sitting there,
and <u>his spear was in his hand/penis/phallic-control</u>,
and David was <u>strumming the strings with his hand/penis</u>,
and Saul tried killing — with his spear —
right into David —
and into the piss-trench —
and (David) <u>let it shoot out — um, slipped away</u> — from Saul's face,
and he had struck-to-kill with the spear into the piss-trench,
but David <u>fled</u> and would <u>escape to safety</u> that night.

(Um, what a strange verb choice here...'let it burst through,
let it shoot out, emit, slip away'/PTR...used only four times in
the Bible...two references in Psalms 22 and Proverbs 17 have
to do with something 'separating' and 'something shooting
out'...so here in 1 Samuel we have to wonder what the band
of X was intending...perhaps they purposefully chose a verb

that gets messy with meaning, that shoots in different double-entendre directions.

Two sentences later we get the same verb that is ordinarily used to 'flee'/NUS which was also used a few paragraphs before to describe what the Philistines did in front of David — they fled. And just to make the scene even stranger, the band of X drives it home with David 'escaping to safety'/MLT. Three different ways of saying 'getting away.' Michal will use MLT shortly too.

And just before all of this, Jonathan BOAH/'entered, fucked' and we get the direct-object-identifier AHT attached to David as direct object but it can mean 'with' as well. So that means 'Jonathan fucked David' or 'Jonathan fucked with David, perhaps as in messed with him' or 'Jonathan entered in with David, as in arrived with David, brought David.' All of these are possible from that arrangement of Hebrew letters. This is the style of the band of X...the meanings can always go multiple ways...prophetic/ecstatic speech usually does...it bursts in multiple directions and plays with one's imagination which awakens the hearer to what is — ecstasy — the now and always. All that including the whole business of YD/'hand, penis, phallic-control.'

And there's that 'piss-trench'/QYR again and Saul wanting to stab/rape David into it as David strums his strings with his hand/penis to calm Saul with his panic/manic-bouts brought on by, gulp, YAHWEH. All this would've been damn funny in the ancient world...especially considering the fun the band of X is poking at the King. The band of X's intention with these fictional-origin stories of the Kingship in Ancient Israel often pokes fun at the whole system of monarchy and religion, with a King in love with a love-boiling-man-boy David and the King's son madly in love with the love-boiling-man-boy David and the King having issues with the wind and the King erecting his own religious penis-pole — and the damned jingle in the air from those women earlier, the jingle about

David being exponentially better than Saul — that jingle and its truth that seems to haunt Saul....)

And Saul sent ambassadors to David's house —
to guard him
and to murder him in the morning —
and she said to David — his wife Michal-Who-Is-ALL did —
"If there is no escaping to safety tonight with your living-breathing-body,
tomorrow you'll be murdered!"

And Michal-Who-Is-ALL lowered David down through the window-opening —
and he left —
he <u>bolted away</u> and escaped to safety.

(Again, more differentiation from what happened back there with NUS and MLT in the many forms of 'fleeing'...now here with 'bolting away'/BRCH...all these necessary ways of getting away from royalty, the system that allows such threats to one's personal safety all based on the whims and manic-bouts of a King given full power, the people thinking it's YAHWEH's desired system when they 'asked-for-it'...Saul's very name.)

And Michal-Who-Is-ALL took the household-god-action-figure, and put it in <u>the bed</u>,
and a weave of goats-hair she put on its head
and plumped it and dressed it in clothes.

And Saul sent (again) ambassadors to take David,
and she said,
"He's not well — exhausted and ill."

And Saul sent the ambassadors to see David,
"Climb him up to me in <u>the bed</u> —
to <u>murder</u> him!"

And the ambassadors (fuck) entered and —
what do ya know! —
the household-god-action-figure was in the bed
and a weave of goats-hair for his head!

And Saul said to Michal-Who-Is-ALL,
"How could you hurl this at me — betray me like this?!
You sent away my enemy!
And he escaped to safety!"

And Michal-Who-Is-ALL said to Saul,
"He said to me,
'Send me away — let me go —
why should I murder you?!'"

And David bolted away
and escaped to safety
and (fuck) arrived to Samuel
at The Heights.

(Lots of similar-sounding words here with MT and RMH...the
hiphil form of MUT/'to murder' used twice and MTH/'bed'...and
Saul accuses his daughter of RMYT-ing him, from RMH/'to hurl,
shoot, beguile, betray'...and David runs to RMH/'The Heights.'

Catching how the band of X plays on sounds? These tales
were most definitely performance pieces, these scraps of story
that were one day sewn together to become 1 Samuel in the
received text we have. And these similar sounds and puns all
play significantly into the meanings available to any hearer in
the ancient world and today, if we're careful readers/listeners
of what's there in the Hebrew.

The already paranoid King can't even trust his own family
because even his own family recognizes David's innocence
and on top of that two of the King's own children are in love
with David.

And note a woman in the ancient world not only with a speaking part but a key player in the plot of the story, a savior! This story would have been positively shocking in the ancient world, at least as we compare it to earlier epics like *Enuma Elish* where the evil woman sea-monster is killed for disobeying men/gods and like *Epic of Gilgamesh* where women-characters had small roles directed by always more powerful men. But here in 1 Samuel it's a woman who has a clever plot to save her beloved — the one who boils over with love and affection — from her father's jealous rages. Talk about style!)

And (David) reported to (Samuel) all that he did to him —
all that Saul had done —
and he and Samuel left and stayed in the shepherds' pen (the awe-inspiring home of the ecstatics, which can be any sheep-pen, anywhere and everywhere in the world for such wanderers, bordercrossers).

And it was reported to Saul:
"Listen here — David is in the shepherds' pen in The Heights."

And Saul sent ambassadors to take David,
and in seeing the band of ecstatic-prophets in their ecstasy —
and Samuel taking his stand (unbudging, at attention) as erect as a pillar — as leader over them (a pillar undeterred by the king's likely armed ambassadors) —
and it came upon Saul's ambassadors —
ELOHIM's wind did —
and they were in ecstasy too — even they were — doing what prophets/ecstatics do in their ecstasy.

And it was reported to Saul,
and he sent more ambassadors after them —
  and they became ecstatic too — even them!

And Saul added it all up, did it again —
he sent a third group of ambassadors —
  and they became ecstatic too — even them!

And so he went — even he did — to The Heights.

And when he (fuck) entered in —
  all the way to the great well
  which is at that sharp-place where only thorns grow, where
wild phenomena happen, where all can be observed it's so
high —
he asked — (Saul did...the king named Asked-For whom the
people asked-for from Samuel) —
and he said,
"Where are Samuel and David?"

And someone said,
"Listen here — in the shepherds' pen in The Heights."

And he went there — to the shepherds' pen in The Heights —
  and It was upon him — even him! —
  ELOHIM's wind was —

and he went, went, went —
  did he ever go —

and became ecstatic as prophets do —
  all the way until he (fuck) entered into the shepherds' pen in
The Heights —

and he stripped himself of his clothes — spread himself out
and flailed around —
  even he did! —
  and became ecstatic —
  even he did! —
  right there in front of Samuel's face —
  and he fell down naked-and-sly
  all that day
  and all night...

and that's why they say,
  "Is even Saul among the ecstatics?!"

(This is an incredibly clever and stylized piece in our tale...

the King that the people asked-for whose name is Asked-For/ Saul — he goes, goes, goes — doubled in the biblical Hebrew for playful attention, tripled here so you know it's not my mistake — and he 'strips himself'/PSHT...which can also mean 'spread himself out or flails around'...
and Saul falls down 'naked-and-sly'/AYRM...the very word used in the Eden story to describe the ever-wise snake and the ever-naked mud-creature and his woman...
and such naked-spreading-out is what YAHWEH seems to want to do to/with mud-creature/Adam...and in other campfire stories similar in spirit to the Eden story and to 1 Samuel, ELOHIM/YAHWEH one day pours Itself into Jacob, where YAHWEH/ELOHIM plants a special blast of life into Jacob that he might become Israel, the one who wrestles EL and wins, the one who is in-charge of EL and the old pantheon of gods-and-goddesses/ELOHIM with YAHWEH at the top, the one who gives life to all through the wind....

And here is the blood-thirsty King Saul who once fell in love with the affection-boiling youngster David when David had courage and success in taking down Goliath...this Saul who loved David...this Jonathan — Saul's son — who loved David as if they were the same body...this David who is loved by Saul's daughter Michal...this Saul who wants to nail David to the wall/piss-trench — perhaps in more ways than one — and now this Saul intent on killing David falls into the ecstatic trance of the prophets with Samuel standing up all erect in front of them all, erect and unbudging and not even flinching when the King's guard shows up. How Samuel trusts the wind — YAHWEH — fully!

Welcome to the Bible, my friends, especially the Bible of the prophets, these ecstatic-voices in the Bible that the priests and kings and any type of hierarchically minded authority will try to cover over again and again and again...

but YAHWEH rules all, even the-gods-and-goddesses of past, of present, and likely of future...at least here on Earth where breath is vital — is VITALITY — for any creature who wants to live...

YAHWEH...the wind...breath...life-force that imbues all and is ALL....)

chapter 20

And David <u>bolted</u> from the shepherds' pen in The Heights
and he (fuck) entered
and said right to Jonathan's face(s),
"What did I do —
what would make me so guilty that I should be punished with death?
What did I do to miss the mark and bear the blame before your father's face(s) —
that he would seek my living-breathing-body?!"

And he said to him,
"<u>How dare he — pierce/sully the situation</u> —
you won't be murdered —
listen up — it's for himself that my father does all this —
he doesn't do a single thing —
making <u>big-styles and little-styles</u> (talking such big-game...or little-game)—
without first within my ears <u>stripping himself naked like a slave or exile is forced to do</u> —
and why would my father hide from me this style (this plan to murder you) —
it can't be so!"

(The greatest of ironies is that Jonathan uses these words associated with the ecstatic-prophets just after David ran to him from the safety of the ecstatic-prophets' den...such

DBR/'style' in Jonathan's word choices...with GLH/'stripping naked like a slave or exile is forced to do'...earlier in 1 Samuel this GLH is what YAHWEH was doing for Its prophets, Its ecstatics. Did Jonathan perceive where David had been and used the prophets' style to communicate his intuition about David's whereabouts? Or did someone in the royal-court tip him off?

Jonathan also glosses the situation with Saul and David... CHLYLH/'how dare he do this' comes from its root in CHLL, that rather unusual word that has do with 'cursing, profaning, playing the pipe, prostituting, and piercing, wounding'...some things that lovers do with each other and therefore are often considered profane by unknowing others.

But Jonathan's advice and love and style and promises — does it measure up to what Samuel and the prophets can offer David? After all, David was safe there with Samuel, and YAHWEH's ecstasy — or at least ELOHIM's ecstasy, if indeed YAHWEH and ELOHIM are different from each other in 1 Samuel. YAHWEH seemed to penetrate and affect Saul as It seemed to do with anyone and everyone there with him. Enemies are paralyzed there naked at Samuel's feet when YAHWEH's wind blows...the impulse to kill disappears with YAHWEH's ecstasy-inducing wind....

David's big error here — and the continuing error of his life — is that he leaves Samuel...he 'bolts away'/BRCH...one more slightly stronger form of 'fleeing'...David leaves the place where he has been most protected...near Samuel but not just Samuel...any den of prophets who can allow YAHWEH's life-giving presence to permeate the space around them without getting all hierarchical about it because ecstasy does not allow hierarchies to live when YAHWEH is the only one and only thing more valuable than any human...David leaves the very place where the bloodthirsty Saul gets not only his bad-winds of rage cooled off but especially re-experiences the ecstasy of his youth, the 'good-winds' of YAHWEH that encourage a leaving-it-all-behind for the jarring and at-first-uncomfortable creature-comforts of the mountain, where the wind blows even more wildly, where only thorns seem to grow, where one is high enough to see it all, to feel it all, where life teems with abundance...not the limited-abundance of castles and weapons and economies of state....

Indeed, if Saul liked this ecstatic experience so much — Saul, the king, naked and sprawled out on the ground like everyone else, equal with everyone else in the throes of ecstasy — Saul could have stayed there too.

David could've stayed there — where he's safe — the first place where he seems to be safest from Saul's sexually violent mood swings, even with Saul right there with him. And David's beloved Jonathan could've joined them too. But as much as he seems to love David, Jonathan seems to be gaming up a game too, doesn't he? Is Jonathan using David as a pawn in his own pursuits of power, of one day ascending the throne himself with love-boiling David ever faithful by his side — or David dead at his/Jonathan's own hands or the hands of his father, the King?

They all could have left behind the kingly-game, the hierarchical game of trying to top each other and instead let YAHWEH continue topping them. Forever. Their wives could've joined them too. Their whole families could have swum away from the royal-shipwreck. But they didn't. None of them yet. And they probably won't.

The allure of power, wealth, slaves waiting on you, every citizen-slave offering the king's family and royal-court the best of what they have every day as part of the agreement to protect them and rule them...that's all quite alluring...especially if you like the idea that people are worse or better than you... the very hierarchical imagination that opposes the all-are-equally-valued ecstatic/prophetic-imagination that simply arrives once you've known ecstasy, once you've glimpsed the vastness, the infinite-nature of THE ALL, of YAHWEH.

Think such an idea of leaving behind the kingship and power is impossible? What did Gautama do, after all? He ran from the court and its comforts and settled under a tree and bliss was there (and everywhere). And if the gospel-stories about Jesus are accurate in some way, he too preferred the discomfort of the desert and living wherever — the wandering life, the bordercrossing life — to the life of being better than others. Jesus dines with prostitutes and tax collectors, the despised of his time. He allows children to be near him — children having no value in the ancient world until they are marriageable. He talks with women and foreigners and enemies of his nation.

Such is the ecstatic-prophetic imagination that disrupts the hierarchical lifestyle...be it religious, royal, political, familial, personal, whatever.)

And he swore again — David did —
and said,
"Know, know, know — does your father ever know everything —
you see — I've found enough favor in your eyes that you'd
bow down to me —
(which is to say, how would your father ever trust you
when you favor me and we are in love
and your father — King Saul — knows me, has known me in every
way that humans can know each other — including sexually —
and knows everything about our situation?)
and (what if King Saul, your father) has said,
'Do not let him know this — do not let Jonathan know —
otherwise it will carve him from the inside-out — such grief!'
and even then — (I swear) as YAHWEH lives —
and (I swear upon) the life of your living-breathing-body —
that there's only one step between me and murder!"

And Jonathan said to David,
"Whatever your living-breathing-body says —
I'll do it for you!"

And David said to Jonathan,
"Listen here —
tomorrow is the new moon — a holy day —
and I — I am to <u>stay, stay, stay with</u> the king
to eat with him —
but you must send me off —
and I'll hide myself in the open-country
until evening of the third day —
and if your father <u>musters, musters, musters me in my official
capacity,</u>
then you say,
'He <u>asked, asked, asked for a leave of absence</u> of me — David
did —
to run to House of Feast-or-Fight — his city —
because the annual slaughtering-animals-as-divine-sacrifices
event is there
for his whole extended-family-that-includes-those-born-of-
maidslaves.'

And if he says, 'Good,'
   there's peace and safety for your slave — for me —

but if <u>rage, rage, rage</u> comes to him,
   know in every way that a bad thing is about to be carried out
by him —

and then you are to make loyal-love with your slave — me —
because of YAHWEH's cutting a deal, making a serious promise
— you (fuck) entered into it with your slave, with me —
with yourself —

but if there's within me any guilt-punishable-by-death,
murder me yourself — even your father (should murder me
then too) —
whatever you have to (fuck) bring upon me—"

And Jonathan — the one whose name means YAHWEH's-Gift
— said,

"How dare this happen to you — you being pierced/sullied by the situation —
because, look —
if I knew, knew, knew in any way (including sexually)
that a bad thing is being carried out by my father —
to (fuck) enter into you — to go after you —
and I'd not report it to you directly—"

And David said to Jonathan,
"—who would report it to me — or what if your father answers harshly/stubbornly?"

And Jonathan said to David,
"Come on, let's go out into the open-country."

And they went out — the two of them — into the open-country, the field.

(Tripled words — in Hebrew they are doubled — intensify the meaning for sure. Almost as if to say, 'Damn it, I mean this!' And how many times over in this little dialogue!

Note how David expresses a bit of doubt about Jonathan and to Jonathan in the last few exchanges...and he should...because Jonathan promised before to tell David that Jonathan's father was about to murder him/David and that information hasn't always been provided, at least in a timely manner... once even Jonathan's sister/David's wife Michal saves David, not Jonathan...and where was Jonathan during the whole mountaintop thing with Samuel and Saul's ambassadors falling into a trance and even Saul himself?! Saul had sent two rounds of ambassadors to hunt down David at Samuel's before Saul went himself — and Jonathan provided no warning to David about any of them?! For David to go out into the open-field, the wild open-country, alone with Jonathan after all of that is more than an act of trust...it's where and how Abel was killed by his brother Cain in the legendary soap-opera campfire stories that any ancient would know and recognize, what we today call Genesis, assuming that story was conceived by the time of 1 Samuel.)

And Jonathan said to David,
"YAHWEH — Ancient Israel's ELOHIM — (witness what I say, I swear by It)...
I will penetrate deeply and intimately into my father — sound him out —
this time tomorrow — definitely in three days' time —
and listen here —
good will come to David —
and if not I'll send for you and I'll <u>strip myself naked like a slave or exile is forced to do</u> — reveal it —
directly to your ear —

it's true —
YAHWEH's going to do this for Jonathan
it's true —
and It will do even more —

because if it's good and pleasing for my father
to do bad things to you,
then I'm going to <u>strip myself naked like a slave or exile is forced to do</u> —
reveal it —
right into your ear —
and I'll send you away —
and you'll go to a safe and peaceful place —
and YAHWEH will be with you just as It's been with my father —

and (no way!) if I'm still alive
  ...you make YAHWEH's loyal-love with me

and (no way!) if dead...
  ...you will not <u>cut</u> off your loyal-love from my house/family forever

and (no way!) YAHWEH will <u>cut</u> off David's enemies — every single one of them — from the face of the earth...

and so Jonathan <u>cuts</u> (a covenant — a serious agreement) — with David's house

and so YAHWEH seeks it out from the hand/penis of David's enemies!"

So Jonathan added onto his swearing to David
in his love for him —
because his love for his own living-breathing-body —
that's how (Jonathan) loved him.

(Well...that was a mouthful! The specific ritual of covenant-making — 'cutting a covenant'/CRT — in the ancient world was serious business, a more-than-serious vow. It's nothing like our contracts in the 21st century that have 48-hour clauses where we can break them with no or little penalty...or even sue the other party after those 48-hours with some lawyer-discovered loophole to get out of the deal. As Jonathan makes clear, in the ancient world, this is a serious vow that lasts not just in this generation but for all future generations — break the deal and the dealbreaker dies.

Jonathan and David go out into a field because of what a covenant requires — literally cutting open an animal, naming one's promises to each other, and then walking through the blood and guts of the animal — quite a memorable experience, to say the least, and meant to be that way. It's what is assumed by an ancient hearer when they hear 'these two cut a deal.'

In ancient covenant-making, usually each party offers gifts to each other to show they mean it...which in this case only, with Jonathan and David, very well could be their offering their bodies to one another in love-making...'in their love for each other's living-breathing-body...as if they were one body'...as we've heard before about these two...and no other gifts are mentioned here with their covenant/agreement.

What's more than a little tricky here, though, is the language wrapped up in this covenant. And I suspect the band of X is playing some games that any ancient hearer would catch... more about this later, as the story rolls on.

In any case, note the key words used with this 'covenant'/BRT...how the band of X distinguishes between CHSD/'loyal-love' and AHHB/'love'...which is to say, this is no simple cut-and-blood-dried-on-your-feet covenant of neighbors. This is a deal made between lovers — at least that's what Jonathan seems to want to continue through this deal.

I also wonder if there's a vying for what exactly proper loyal-love looks like here in a broader sense...a war of word-meanings between the prophetic-imagination and the priestly-imagination. The Levitical priests and the Deuteronomist-royalists composed the Torah; the priests later took the band of X's writings and stripped all the sexuality from them and that priestly version of the Samuel-saga would become Chronicles...the very dry tales of David and the empire, all of it just as fictional as 1 & 2 Samuel. And guess what...all these love-rich stories of Jonathan with David that we are getting in 1 & 2 Samuel are not in Chronicles. No surprise! Jonathan is mentioned in a few Chronicles' genealogies as David's DOD — David's 'relative, uncle, lover.' And guess how translators usually translate DOD in 1 Chronicles 27.32? As 'uncle' — no surprise! But that same combination of letters can also mean 'lover' — as I noted back with Saul in 1 Samuel 10 in the previous volume.

And a bit more about the style in these last few paragraphs of our story here in 1 Samuel 20. It's more than a little unusual how Jonathan is using that wild phrase 'strip myself naked like a slave or exile is forced to do'/GLH...the verb that earlier in our 1 Samuel saga was used by YAHWEH to describe exactly how YAHWEH reveals Itself to the prophets/ecstatics. But here, Jonathan uses it to describe how he'll be with David — his devotion to pouring it all into David, everything he hears from his father, into David's ear.

And why? Why is Jonathan so stylish, trying to be clever? Though David doesn't anywhere in the 'on-screen' dialogue tell Jonathan that he'd just run to Samuel and watched Saul fall into a trance apparently like all the other prophets there on the mountaintops of Ramah/The Heights, maybe Jonathan knows either from David or from his father's ambassadors or however that David had just returned from the prophets... people who pride themselves on puns and turns of phrase and style. Maybe Jonathan knows he needs to up his game, use the stylish manner of speaking like the prophets to capture David's attention...because once you get a taste of that ecstasy in the wind and in a stylish phrase, it's hard to notice anything else as valuable...unless one is addicted to power/control, as Saul seems to be. Or maybe Jonathan realizes that he's screwed up so many times in his earlier promises to send word to David about his own father-the-king's making plans to murder David. Or what if that whole earlier Jonathan-taking-off-all-his weaponry and joining his body with David's is not about love on Jonathan's part but a ruse, a way of getting the very powerful and popular David on his side to secure his/Jonathan's own interests in the throne.

Quite honestly, we don't know. And with anyone who is hierarchically minded, we never know their full motivation... is this an act of love or a chess-move to elevate oneself in the hierarchy?

And here we have our old fuck-friends from the band of YAH's Genesis stories: 'know, have sex'/YDAY and 'enter, fuck'/BOAH...sexual pun-play with their double/triple-entendre meanings, not to mention YD/'hand, penis, phallic-control.' All within this stylishly rich love-triangle of Saul-David-Jonathan spinning out of control!

Now note before this little commentary I've inserted here, Jonathan was the last to speak. And as you'll see shortly, Jonathan speaks again...which is to say that David did not have anything to say about that long promise of Jonathan. Why? Maybe Jonathan left David speechless. Maybe David still doubts Jonathan's faithfulness, his loyal-love...even with the covenant. Maybe he's madly hungering for Jonathan, at their love for one another out in the wild open-country, out in an open field. In the ancient world, in our biblical narrative, when one person talks and the quotation ends and then the same person talks, it's usually a sign that the listener has some issue with the words first spoken.)

And Jonathan said to David,
"Tomorrow is the new moon — the holy day —
and you will be <u>mustered-and-missed</u> in your official capacity —
because your chair will be <u>empty</u> —
and on your third day, go down —
very much so — quickly —
and (fuck) enter the place where you hid
— on the day <u>of the deed</u> —
and stay <u>near the stone where things slip through and disappear</u> —
and I — three of them — splitters (arrows) — to the side —
I'll fire them off — send them off — by me — <u>to the mark — to the prison</u> —
and listen here — I'll send a slave/boy toward you — to find the splitters —
and if I say, say, say to the slave/boy,
'Look there, the splitters — over there! Go fetch them!' —
then you're to (fuck) come back — because there's peace and safety for you and no style (no plot by my father) —
(I swear) on the life of YAHWEH!

But if there is (a plot to kill you), I'll say to the <u>youngster</u>,
'Look there — the splitters — over there — further out there!'
— then go —
because YAHWEH is sending you away.

Ecstatic Prophets, Compulsive Fascists

The style that we're styling out —
me and you —
look here —
YAHWEH is between me and you — forever!"

(Big words again from Jonathan, YAHWEH's-Gift. Maybe 'the deed' referred to is where earlier in the story they made love when Jonathan had David CHBAH/'hide-by-lovemaking' inside his embrace?

The sound-rich style of the rest of the speech is even more slippery...AHTSL HAHBN HAHZL...with 'near'/AHTSL and 'slip through, disappear'/AHZL sounding nearly identical and pun-rich in Ancient Hebrew.

And as for the 'slave/boy'/NAYR...we don't know if he's a slave or a boy until later when Jonathan describes him by the word Saul let slip from his mouth earlier in 1 Samuel 17 when looking at the young David who had just cut off Goliath's head with Goliath's own sword — 'youngster or virgin-boy'/AYLM.

And all that 'missing' and 'mustering' and 'empty (chair)' is our old friend PQD...the strangest verb that always leaves me wondering and used so freely here and in different ways, each with a slightly different meaning but all of them with PQD at its root. The band of YAH plays with this verb very cleverly in the Joseph story of Genesis...each time PQD gets more peculiar.

And remember, remember, remember...as David continues to fear for his life, David left the very place where he was safest... with Samuel...the one place Saul could never get him...the place where when Saul showed up he became overwhelmed with YAHWEH's ecstasy, the trance that comes around any naked-with-the-wind ecstatic-prophet....)

And David hid in the open-country,
and it was the new moon — the holy day —
and the king sat down <u>to fight or to feast</u> —
to eat.

> (Recall that the verb LCHM, rather strangely, has two very
> different meanings in Ancient Hebrew: 'to fight in war' and 'to
> eat, feast, devour.' LCHM as a noun is 'bread' or 'grain for bread.'
> And the character David, of course, is from Bethlehem/'House
> of Feast-or-Fight.' X clarifies in this particular instance with
> LCHM here by adding AHCOL/'to eat.')

And the king sat down upon his <u>chair</u>
just as he had time and time again
on the chair by the <u>piss-trench</u>,
and Jonathan was standing up tall,
and (Saul's general) Abner-Patriarchy's-Lamplight was
by Saul's side,
and David's place was <u>empty</u>,
and Saul didn't style out anything about it that day
because he said (perhaps to himself),
'Something might've befallen him — crossed his path —
something not clean-and-pure
(as one must be clean-and-pure for any priestly/hierarchically
minded ceremonies, especially for the new moon)
but he himself for sure is not clean-and-pure!'

> (The king sits on a regular 'chair'/MOSHB like David
> apparently would — no king on a 'throne'/CSAH here! — and
> the king's seat is by the 'piss-trench'/QYR, perhaps some band
> of X humor here...while David's chair is 'empty' with that ever-
> weird verb PQD again. Being located by the convenient piss-
> trench makes one wonder if this was what caused the bad-air
> rages that came upon Saul — or maybe he was just so pissed
> off all the time that he conveniently sat near the piss-wall to
> try to get it all out so often...

Ecstatic Prophets, Compulsive Fascists

or is the band of X making fun of the king's purity concerns with his sitting right by where he and maybe others piss?)

And so it was —
the next day of the new moon ceremony — the second day of the moon/month —
and David's place was <u>empty</u>,
and Saul said to his son Jonathan,
"<u>Know in any and every way</u> why
the son of Jesse-There-He-Is has not (fuck) arrived —
neither yesterday nor today —
to the <u>feast/fight</u>?"

(Quite styled here in that Saul uses the two words that are sexual puns through the Bible — M+YDAY/'know, often sexually' and BOAH/'enter a place or a body, as in penetration, fucking' — perhaps as a way to remind Jonathan that he knows what David and Jonathan are up to. And I'd say the character Saul's choice of words is quite purposeful in that he uses MDUAY/'why or know why?' when he could have used LMH/'why' but he clearly wanted the sexual connotation of MDUAY to linger in the air with the 'entering, penetrating'/ BOAH for his son Jonathan to consider...that he as king is well aware of what Jonathan and David do together...just as Jonathan is surely aware of what his father-the-king has done with David in the past when David was sitting and making music there with his hand/penis, music sometimes pleasing — and apparently — sometimes enraging for Saul's ears when Saul needed calming down, to provide the king with some soothing pleasure. Ahem.

Note that Saul does not use David's name but refers to him via his relationship to his father, a father that David is not conspiring against behind his back as Jonathan is against his father-the-king. And to say David's name reveals too both of their longings for 'the one who makes you boil over with affection'...precisely what 'David' means, David being love-boiler for <u>both</u> Jonathan and King Saul/'Asked-For' and the beloved-husband to Michal...Jonathan's sister and King Saul's daughter. Yes, royal life here seems quite complicated romantically!

And there's our LCHM/'feast or fight' again. Style...for sure! And meant to awaken its hearer in every way....)

And Jonathan answered Saul,
"David had <u>asked, asked, asked</u> —
<u>from within me</u> —
<u>all the way</u> to the <u>House-of-Feast-or-Fight</u> —
and he said,
'Please send me off —
because the slaughtering-animals-as-divine-sacrifices event
of the extended-family-that-includes-those-born-of-maidslaves —
ours —
it's <u>in the city</u>!
And he did this — he shouted out orders at me —
my brother did —
now if I've found favor in your eyes — if you as superior
bowed down to me because I charmed you —
let me slip away, please,
and I'll see my brothers (possibly sisters included in this too)—'

— and that's why he has not (fuck) come <u>to the king's table</u>."

(Jonathan is playing with some style here...maybe caught off guard at first by the king's style/rhetoric but then recovering with rephrasing David's message as if David is a po-dunk hillbilly bragging about the event taking place in 'the city' without even naming it...a city known for its 'feast-or-fight' reputation...and Jonathan does indeed center in on the same word-choice for family that David wanted delivered, the one that shows his family is lower-class and 'impure' or at least not

Ecstatic Prophets, Compulsive Fascists

as pure as Saul thinks his own family to be...purity requiring no/few children through maidslaves because more wives could be had instead of having to use slaves to create children. And note the flourish that Jonathan adds at the end...not only reinforcing the '(fuck) entering-arriving'/BOAH that Saul has maybe enjoyed with David and even more so the power that Saul has as king...his table...and not anyone else's...his table — the king's table — from whom everyone here at this 'holy' feast-day eats the very best food so, ahem, generously given to the king and royal-court from the citizens who SHAHL/ asked-asked-asked-for King Saul/SHAHL.)

And Saul blazed with red-in-the-face anger at Jonathan, and said to him,
"Son of a perverted, rebellious woman!
Don't I know in every way including sexually
that you've chosen the son of Jesse-There-He-Is —
to your shame
and to the shame of your naked mother!!
You see — for every day
that the son of Jesse-There-He-Is lives on the earth
you will not be erect — firmed up —
nor your kingdom — your reign as king —
so now send for him
and fetch him for me
because a son of death-by-murder — that's what he'll be!"

(Note Saul's style with all of these 'son' references...including Saul's ancient-cussing to begin his tirade, which is probably akin to shouting out 'son of a bitch!' either at his son Jonathan or about the missing David. And as for the 'naked' reference regarding Jonathan's mother — surely she's not naked now, she's the queen after all! But Saul is painting a very dark picture for Jonathan that he will never reign as king — he will never be 'erect'/CUN and ready — and Jonathan's own mother risks nakedness if David is allowed to live. Why?

Because all the people of Ancient Israel seem to like David and ready themselves for his kingship — he took on Goliath, he wages battles with Ancient Israel's enemies, he acts like a king should...not like Saul who luxuriates under pomegranate trees while the battle rages on and then proclaims himself the cause of victory in 1 Samuel 14. Ancient kings fought in battle — but not Saul. Not since that first battle of his kingship — ever since then, Jonathan and David have been fighting the kingdom's battles for Saul.

And 'naked'/AYRUT is interesting here in a number of ways... in that Saul just returned from his own 'naked-and-sly'/AYRM experiences with the ecstatic-prophets when he was chasing after David....but from the standpoint of the king, one who wears the royal-robes of earth-dominating-power, nakedness is something about which to be embarrassed, ashamed...as it all too often is for anyone hierarchically minded. We compare our clothes to measure our status against someone else. Can we do this when we are naked — who looks more appealing, etc? Of course...but quickly we realize we both have skin and limbs and genitalia of some sort. In nakedness, we discover our similarities, the common humanity we share...where royalty and hierarchical mindedness break down.)

And Jonathan answered his father Saul,
and said to him,
"Why should he be murdered —
what has he done?"

And Saul hurled his spear at him — to strike him down, kill him —
and Jonathan knew in every way (including sexually)
how it would end with his father —
(that he would) murder David.

And Jonathan stood up tall from the table —
blazed in red-in-the-face anger —

Ecstatic Prophets, Compulsive Fascists

and he did not eat any bread/food that second day of the new
moon — the holy day —
because he was carved — his insides were hurting — for David —
because his father had made him feel humiliated and
dishonored.

(Note that Jonathan asks the same question of his father about
David's life/death as the king's soldiers asked of Jonathan's
father-the-king regarding the life/death of Jonathan in 1
Samuel 14. And Saul was right — Jonathan's insides would hurt
for David if Jonathan knew King Saul's intentions regarding
David. Kings have a way of putting to death the innocent to
firm up their own power when their own power is far from
firm. It's their hierarchical privilege.)

And so it was —
in the morning, Jonathan went out into the open-country
to make David know in every way (including sexually) —
and a little slave/boy was with him.

And he said to his slave/boy,
"Run! Find the splitters (arrows) that I'm shooting!"
The slave/boy ran,
and he shot off a splitter past him,
and the slave/boy (fuck) arrived to the splitter's place where
Jonathan had shot one off,
and Jonathan called out after the slave/boy,
and said,
"Isn't the splitter beyond you?
Further on!"

(More YDAH/'knowing, having sex' weirdness...and then this
clever HLOAH/'isn't' next to HLAHH/'further on'...as Jonathan
speaks stylishly and enacts the style that has been part of their
agreement with each other.)

And Jonathan called out after the slave/boy,
"Speed it up! Hurry! Don't stand still!"

And Jonathan's slave/boy gathered up the splitters,
and he (fuck) returned to his boss.

And the slave/boy didn't <u>know</u> anything at all —
only Jonathan and David <u>knew</u> in every way (including sexually) the style.

And <u>Jonathan...YAHWEH-gives gave</u> his gear to the slave/boy who was his,
and he said,
"Go on! (Fuck) Return to the city!"
And the slave/boy (fuck) left,
and David stood up tall from near the south
and fell on his nose/face toward the ground
and bowed down three times
and they <u>kissed</u> —
>passionately?
>in a firmed up way?
>as if fastening themselves to one another?
>delightedly and lovingly? —
<u>a man with his friend</u> —
and they wept —
<u>a man with his friend</u> —
as far as David <u>making it/himself bigger</u>.

And Jonathan said to David,
"Go — in peace and health and safety —
which we swore — the two of us did —
in the name of YAHWEH, saying,
'<u>YAHWEH! May It be</u> between me and you!
Between my seed/descendants and your seed/descendants!
Forever!"

> ('YAHWEH! May It be...'/YHVH YHYH. Such style that's been emanating from character-Jonathan's lips recently!

Ecstatic Prophets, Compulsive Fascists

And by the band of X's narration too...the clever punning on Jonathan's name...YHONTN/'Jonathan' and NTN/'gives'... the bands of YAH and X often tease proper names and their meanings, as we'll soon explore in more depth. The people 'asked for'/SHAHL a king and got 'Saul'/SHAHOL, right? And their asking for it is what spun out this whole plot.

'a man with his friend'...'friend'/RAY is actually the more neutral meaning of that word, and here are the others: 'lover' or 'full-brother' or 'lesser-brother' or 'neighbor' or 'associate.'

And the verb choice 'made to be bigger'/GDL is a clear choice by the band of X here — there are plenty of ways to say something like 'David wept even more so' or something like that...but X chose 'David made himself larger' or 'David making the whole thing larger.' Perhaps this is noting that David was making himself or had been making himself the bigger of he and Jonathan — perhaps more worthy of succeeding to the crown. And to make it even stranger, *Strong's Exhaustive Concordance* notes that GDL can also have to do with 'twisting threads' around each other — as if here to say David went as far as twisting himself around Jonathan. Or it could mean David's love for Jonathan grew, and it was evident in his clothes.

As for that kiss, *Strong's Exhaustive Concordance* notes all the different directions such a 'kiss'/NSHQ could go...with very similar sounding forms of CHZQ and CHSHQ that would dance through an ancient hearer's mind as they heard about this particular kiss, especially as David 'stood up tall'/QUM before 'bowing down'/SHCHH just before that kiss.

And with character-Jonathan calling his slave/boy a 'youngster, virgin-boy'/AYLM earlier in 1 Samuel 20 — just as Jonathan's father-the-king Saul called David AYLM in 1 Samuel 17 as young slave/boy David stood there holding Goliath's dripping head — we're circled back to Dr. Ted Jennings' thesis in *Jacob's Wound* about 1 Samuel revealing Ancient Israel's military-roots in military-pederasty...an older-warrior taking on a younger-warrior to train him in war, in the style of being a warrior, in love, in philosophy and the discernments of power, in lots of things that 'men' most likely needed to learn and know to become men, especially in their hierarchical society. This arrangement is famous in Ancient Greece, some see it as the reason for their military strength. Maybe why Ancient Israel was able to last as long as it did with such strong forces of empire pushing in on them.

When Jonathan took off his weapons and gave them to David in 1 Samuel 18, the beginning of this volume, Jonathan was doing something quite profound. Jonathan was most assuredly older than David — Jonathan had been leading successful battles against the Philistines long before David is even mentioned as a youngest brother and out shepherding small animals on the family-farm. But in that scene just after that, after no one steps up to take on Goliath, and the AYLM/'youngster, young virgin' David does and wins, Jonathan strips himself of all of his weapons — and even the clothes that held that weaponry — and gives it all to David as if to say that David is the 'older/greater' of the two, the one who would train Jonathan and be 'over' Jonathan. The younger of the pair in 1 Samuel is usually called 'gear-lifter, shield-bearer'/NSAH. But Jonathan reverses those roles with David early on. Is Jonathan a good 'shield'/protector/defense for David against Jonathan's father-the-king Saul? We'll see....

In the scene with the splitters/arrows, Jonathan now has a younger charge to care for as 'boss'/AHDNAY: his own 'youngster, virgin-boy'/AYLM, his 'slave/boy'/NRH who fetches his arrows. Both possibilities — AYLM and NRH — reveal the sickness of this royal government that either inculcates war into its youngest or has children as slaves

...all the while the misfits on the mountaintops of Ancient Israel — the ecstatics-prophets like Samuel though existing before Samuel — are welcoming YAHWEH into a new way, a circular way, where all are equal.)

What's with these epic names, You-Ask?

The Bible from which I taught high school Scriptures — *The New American Bible*, 1991 — includes a note for 1 Samuel 1.20 regarding the naming of the character Samuel:

"*Since she had asked*: the explanation would be more directly appropriate for the name Saul, which means 'asked'; Samuel means 'name of God.'"

While I always appreciated that this translation included some references to the deeper nuances of the Ancient Hebrew text — for instance, that the names held meaning for the story, something high schoolers I taught appreciated too — I now see this note wanting...and needing updating.

The Hebrew text in question goes like this:

VTQRAH AHT SHMO SHMUAHL CY MYHVH SHAHLTYV

I translate it as:

And she called out his name,
"Samuel!
(which means 'named for EL/the divine')
because it was from YAHWEH that I <u>asked for</u> him!"

Saul's name indeed does mean 'Asked' or 'They-Asked' with perhaps 'they' being 'the people.' And this section of the text has nothing to do with Saul, of course. Saul does not make his appearance in the story until 1 Samuel 9. But I have found a number of places where a character's name gets mentioned earlier in the story simply as the larger story unfolds:

> Saul has a DOD/'relative, lover' to whom he won't confess

the whole ecstatic-experience on the way back from Samuel's home in Chapter 10; David/DVD first appears in Chapter 16. Note: DVD, DUD, and DOD are all the same Hebrew characters without the Masoretic markings.

> Saul is concerned his father will be 'anxious'/DAHG in Chapter 9; Anxious/DAHG will soon appear in Chapter 21 as an ally to Saul.

> Merab-From-Many/MRB perhaps recalls the jingle said about her father's prowess in killing a thousand while David kills his RBB/'many, many, many...millions'

> The whole Nabal & Abigail story coming up will play hilariously on the meaning of Nabal's name too...and quite cleverly hers.

> We could also say something about the whole Hannah-Bend-Down and Eli-Climb-Up bit in 1 Samuel 1 and how they dance around each other in the story and how knowing what their names mean adds much to the story's playfulness, humor, and significance.

And that's the whole point I think — that the characters' names were not mere coincidences in these 1 & 2 Samuel stories. They were purposefully chosen to enhance the plot, especially when these stories were performed. I suspect this was the case with the names of the cities too.

Imagine sitting around a campfire and some member of the band of X has come to your town and tells this wild story and every time Saul's name is mentioned the crowd cries out in playful laughter "they asked for it!" And that's the point of this fiction that is 1 & 2 Samuel and much of 1 Kings — for people to wake up and realize that the hierarchical system of monarchy is deadly and the people asked for it once and got it and it ruined everything.

We must remember that in such a system the king serves at the pleasure of those in a ring around him — a king is easy to kill if 20 or 40 top-crust royalists want him dead. But if the royalists benefit from the king's presence and decisions, there's no reason to kill him and every reason to protect him and the system that raises him up as close to God as one can get — because the royalists get enriched and stabilized by protecting the king. Same goes for religion — raise up the high priest or pope until he no longer creates benefits for the upper-crust religionists; once he no longer enriches or provides stability for them, they will kill him.

Put yourself in the crowd hearing the Samuel-saga spun out night after night...

"They asked for it!" the lower-crust crowd cries out hearing the band of X enacting this drama about the dangers of monarchy and organized religion. "They asked for it!"

And every time the young, sexy — and later old, sexy — David is mentioned, the crowd cries out "love boiling!" And does it ever when he's around so far — Samuel fell in love at first sight and Saul and Jonathan and Michal and apparently the women singing the jingle did too — at least they announce that David kills more than Saul. If indeed that's a good thing....

Imagine being around the campfire and hearing the story unfurl for the first time and the second time and the third time — especially with the cat-calls from the crowd and the laughter and the 'hmm' every now and then, or even often! How this tale would get into your skin, into your dreams, as empires grew bigger and bigger around you. You could give yourself over to empire and hierarchical thinking and live happily ever after — as long as you conformed to your place in the hierarchy, as long as you stayed in your lane and paid your tax by coin or slave-labor and worshipped the emperor/king/high-priest as the lords of life — or at the very least the arbiters of life necessary for God to provide benefits through them to you and me, citizen-slaves.

Or you could wander away, cross borders that the empire never allows but also where they care little to control — up on mountains in far away places, where misfits shunned by the empire are free to be themselves, free to be caressed by the wind and free to shout out into It as one's true savior, one's true lifegiver. YAHWEH!

Say Its name and be freed within!

Feel the rush of life — ecstasy —
that comes in and out!

YAHWEH! Say It!

chapter 21

And Jonathan stood up tall and left and (fuck) entered the city,
and David (fuck) entered (the city called) Fruitful —
home of the priest Ahimelech-My-Brother-the-King.

(So David runs to a guy with 'King'/MLCH in his name?! If
he's concerned with his safety, why doesn't David run to the
one place he's been safest — to Samuel?! Or is David after
something more precious to him than his safety...something
which for him is worth risking his life...to get the prize...the
crown...all the while the prophets are on the mountaintops
of Ancient Israel safe and sound — even living right next to
Israel's enemies — these prophets/ecstatics getting high on
YAHWEH's breezes....)

And Ahimelech-My-Brother-the-King shuddered with terror
to call out to and meet David,
and he said to him,
"Why, <u>knowing you in every way</u> —
alone, separated from the rest of them —
one single man —
there's no one with you?!?"

(The band of X could have had the priest use LMH/'why', but
they put MDUAH/'why' from YDAY/'to know, in every way
including sexually' into the priest's mouth, who stutters and
stammers out a greeting to David, the one man who seems to
rival Saul, the one man known to at least some in the royal-
court as the one who could, ahem, soothe Saul. And note the
priest's name...he has good reason to keep his support for King
Saul quite clear and be suspicious of David being on a solo
mission of some sort, David this love-boiling leader of men....)

And David said to the priest Ahimelech-My-Brother-the-King, "The King — he shouted out orders to me for this particular style (my traveling alone, apart from the group),
and he said to me,
'Not one single person — do not let anyone know anything of this style
about which I'm sending you —
about which I'm shouting out orders to you' —
and as for the slave/boys I know (in every way including sexually) —
they're in such and such place.
So now what's that there under your hand/penis/phallic-control — five loaves of bread?
Give them over into my hand/penis/phallic-control —
or whatever can be found—"

And the priest answered David and said,
"There is no <u>common bread</u> under my hand/penis/phallic-control, you see —
only <u>holy bread</u> here
(and you can have it) if the slave/boys have protected themselves —
protected themselves — at least from any woman."

(Oh my — such a loaded response that gives us a window into the band of X's view of the priestly imagination. Many words that can go either way — and that's likely X's point. 'Common'/CHL or CHLL has been used before in our saga, usually as a swear word that has to do with 'piercing' — and it can mean 'playing the flute' and 'making a beginning as if by wedging oneself between two things' and 'gathering grapes' and all kinds of things that are recognized as 'common or profane or unholy' in the priestly-imagination. Note that all of them have to do with penetration or something phallic/male-genitalia, like a flute...or grapes/partying. All this overlaid upon the YD/'hands or phalluses' also mentioned... though in these recent instances here in Chapter 21, it seems that 'hand' is meant by YD — instead of 'penis'/YD — though the whole choice of 'knowing'/YDAY complicates that a bit. And priests in this 1 Samuel saga were known, ahem, for some strange things for sure...like making the young Samuel wear straggly-yarned-underwear in serving YAHWEH before the ark and like making the women-servers have sex with the priest's sons behind the so-called sacred-tent.

How would ancient hearers understand the dynamics of this scene? if they were royalists? if they were priestly/religious? if they were commoners...as common as the unblessed bread? if they were any of them sitting around a campfire after their dinner wine?

Whether the character-priest knew the Torah or not, whether the Torah existed and was popularly known before 1 Samuel or not (though it very likely did), the priest-character goes to some lengths to lay out some of the understandings certainly reflected in the Torah — for instance, who is pure enough to eat the stale bread that once was offered to YAHWEH before the ark — perhaps to be sure to lay out for any non-Torah-knowing hearer how the plot twists in this play-drama.

The laws of the Torah delineate for priestly/hierarchical types what is holy from what is unholy — indeed that's the whole point of Leviticus, to help leaders and followers discern how to access God through the way of 'holiness'/QDSH. The Deuteronomist-royalist party had their version of law in their ever-growing Deuteronomy. At some point in actual history, the Levitical priests and the Deuteronomist-royalists make a pact and what we call 'Leviticus' gets joined to 'Deuteronomy' to form much of the 'Torah' under the written-direction and editorial-direction of the Deuteronomists...this Torah possibly at one time including the Book of Joshua. Did that all occur — and at what stage of construction — before 1 Samuel was first composed? No one knows...though 1 Samuel seems to slam some of the Torah-understandings and makes both priests and royalists look like fools.

And as for women — the priest-crafted Leviticus does not look kindly upon women, especially regarding the mysteries of menstruation. Human blood, from a priest's holy-unholy perspective is unclean and therefore unholy/profane. And in a hierarchical imagination that has priests doing everything they can to maintain their system/religion where women are less than men, common men are less than priests, priests are less than God, though the high priest and the king are closer to God than any random priest or royalist. God is the holy of all holies, and from a priest's perspective, God is swirling around the ark when visiting from the heavens, whether that ark is encased in a tent or temple and at the service of a specially-trained kind of priest who knows how to maintain this holy order of specially-blessed bread and candlelight and animal-sacrifice at the right time and for the right payment...the priestly ways Samuel was raised to serve and continue before Eli-Climb-Up and his nasty-named sons died and the ark disappeared long enough for Samuel to feel no responsibility for the ark and its cult anymore.

The character Ahimelech-My-Brother-the-King says what he says because priestly and royal holiness demand order and a steering clear of all that is profane and common.

But not from a prophet's perspective — it's all holy — everything — all of it imbued with YAHWEH, everything alive through YAHWEH, the wind.

Can you pollute the wind, give off a bad-air with your ways of using the wind? Apparently so — as Saul has in his jealousy of David, of how the love-boiling David is loved by the people more than Saul. And note how David does indeed seem to 'boil over with love and affection'...makes you want to love him by his courageous deeds. Jonathan was enamored — enough to make political alliances in his love for the love-boiler (!).

And note the need for these slaveboys at war to be 'protected'/ SHMR from women, as this priest-character Ahimelech-My-

Brother-the-King requires in order for David to take the bread for himself and to share with the slaveboys — the ruse/lie David invents to get bread for himself and only himself as he runs away from Saul.

In ordinary/common situations, the Law/Torah's Leviticus 20 forbids men having sex with men — or as Leviticus more strangely says "males with males" — to the point of killing men who have sex with men. But here the priest agrees to give the holy bread to David to share with the boys/warriors as long as they have protected themselves 'at least'/AHK from women — never mind each other. Apparently, in the course of battle and being on campaign and on the king's errands, it's okay if the boys/warriors are together and doing whatever they do at killing in war, at training, at sex with one another, at sex with their older-warriors...if indeed this fictional-or-actual organization is military-pederasty, or even if it is not... boys at war do what boys at war do. None of that is 'unholy' from the priest's perspective...as long as they didn't get mixed up with any woman — another slam on the Torah delivered by the band of X.

All of this is to say, from the priestly perspective offered here by the character Ahimelech-My-Brother-the-King, male-with-male sex is fine in the military, but not apart from the military. And male-with-male sex will one day be fine in the priestly-directed temple with the QDSHYM/'holy prostitutes' as we hear in 2 Kings 23 — but apparently not fine apart from the temple and priestly oversight. Ahem. This 1 Samuel text thrives on juxtapositions to reveal the ridiculousness of laws of just about every sort...and instead the wisdom/morality based in the wild, life-giving wind.

Are you catching onto the band of X's clever style...their juxtaposition of things to reveal the idiocies of any kind of hierarchical imagination, be it priestly or royalist or even familial? ...and the wisdom of the ecstatics-prophets who just go on living their wild lives with the wind, up on the mountains.)

And David answered the priest and said to him,
"You see, every single woman <u>has kept herself back</u> from us —
these past three days —
ever since I went out (on campaign) —
and the gear of the slave/boys — it's been holy (perhaps
blessed before battle?) —
even though it's been journeying in a common way —
for sure it was made holy today with it being gear (war
implements sent on special-mission by the king)."

And the priest gave him the holy (bread)
because there was no other bread there
except the bread that had been facing —
the stuff that had soured, spoiled, turned —
the stuff that had been facing YAHWEH (near the ark, we must
suppose) —
and replaced with the warm (freshly-baked) bread on the day
(the old bread) was taken away.

<u>And there was</u> a certain man —
one of Saul's slaves —
on that particular day
<u>who had kept himself back</u> before YAHWEH's face (ark) —
<u>and his name</u> was Anxious-Doeg — of the the Red-Mud people
(cousins of the Ancient Israelites whose name descends from
Adam, 'mud-red-human-creature') —
Anxious-Doeg, the valiant/chief shepherd who was for Saul —
who was Saul's.

(The 'mud-red-human-creature'/AHDM/Adam or 'Red-Mud
people'/AHDMY/Edomite will circle around again...rather
curiously....

Note the clever two-time use of 'kept back from or restrain'/
AYTSR regarding the women restraining themselves from
the men and now Anxious-Doeg restraining himself before
YAHWEH.

Ecstatic Prophets, Compulsive Fascists

And the similar-sounding VSHM/'and there was' paralleled in the next line with VSHMO/'and his name was'...nice storycrafting for any audience hearing the story being performed right there in front of them.

And we are to assume that the priest Ahimelech-My-Brother-the-King is doing his priestly duty before the ark with the holy bread placed there daily — while it's hot — and all of this holy-show that the priest Eli-Climb-Up once did and that Samuel the prophet was once trained in at the very beginning of our 1 Samuel story...where Samuel wore the straggly-yarned-*ephod*-underwear in his priest-in-training service before YAHWEH's ark, such peculiar service and garb that his mother had to weave a special coat for him to wear when she visited her young son Samuel, most probably so that his genitals didn't fall out of his straggly-yarned priestly *ephod* and embarrass himself before his mother.

Based on his name, the priest here — Ahimelech-My-Brother-the-King — indeed might have gotten his special priestly appointment as ark-caretaker from King Saul based upon his blood-relation to the King.)

And David said to Ahimelech-My-Brother-the-King,
"Isn't there here — under your hand/penis/phallic-control — a spear or a sword —
you see, my sword and even my gear — I couldn't fetch them — with my own hand/penis/phallic-control
because the <u>king</u>'s style required urgency."

And the priest said,
"Goliath-the-Stripper's sword — the Dust-Rolling-Philistine — the one you struck down and killed in the valley with the big drunk tree —
look here — it's wrapped up in a special-cloth behind the strangly-yarned *ephod*-underwear —
if you can take it for yourself, then take it —

because <u>there's nothing else except it — nothing else so lavish-or-despised</u> here—"

And David said,
"—<u>there's nothing else like it</u> — give it to me!"

(There's some style emerging here in the way the priest-related-to-the-king and David parse it out with each other. The priest says AHYN AHCHRT ZULTH/'there's nothing else except it — nothing else so lavish-or-despised'...one of those phrases that can go either way depending; David interrupts and says AHYN CMOH/'there's nothing else like it' and with his different choice of words clarifies the priest's ambiguous statement.

In our 1 Samuel tale, this very Dust-Roller's sword once was the trophy for a deed well done by David — so lavish and at the same time such a despised/notorious trophy — it was once owned and wielded by Goliath, who before his death stripped slain Israelites and pocketed their wealth — this lavish and, at the same time, despised trophy kept near the ark. Recall that the ark was the lavish/despised prize of the Dust-Rolling-Philistines earlier in our saga and housed in their own ELOHIM/gods' temple...until that YAHWEH-trophy began raping their gods and giving sore-assholes to all the Dust-Rollers.

And the phallic-sword is wrapped in the priestly-underwear. Ahem. Catch the comedy....

Recall how young David was when he struck down Goliath and then chopped off Goliath's head with Goliath's own sword — this very sword. David was then a 'youngster'/AYLM — at least in the eyes of Saul. David tried to wear Saul's armor/gear, recall, but it was way too big for David then. Goliath's sword was surely too big for him then — at least too big to carry but not too big for David to dispatch Goliath's head from his torso

with David's virgin/first-time battle-passion and a rock...and
then Goliath's own weapon that had stripped so many people
of their lives. Will he be able now to not only wield Goliath's
sword but also travel with it on the run from Saul?)

And David stood up tall
and bolted away that day from Saul's face
and (fuck) arrived to Sure-There-Achish — king of the Dust-
Roller city with the wine-press and their drunken concerts.

And Sure-There-Achish's slaves said to him,
"Isn't this David, king of the earth, the land?!
Isn't it for this one they answer — shout in song to one another
— in their circle-dances saying
'Saul kills his thousand,
and David his many, many, many...millions!'"

And David took these stylings-on into his heart —
and he was afraid — very much so — of Sure-There-Achish'
face —
he was king of the Dust-Roller city with the wine-press and
their drunken concerts.

(David had killed the Dust-Rolling-Philistines' prize warrior
Goliath — and here is David face to face with one of the kings
of the land! Why? David feels safer here with an enemy-king
than with the king of his own land, his own home-country?
But even here — just how safe is he? As safe as he was with
Samuel and the other ecstatics, where Saul's hate for David
was transformed into ecstasy?)

And (David) transformed his taste — his intelligence and
behavior — right there before their eyes —
and he lit up like a madman — ran around into their hands/
penises —

and he scratched at the doors of the city-gate —
and his spit dripped down into the sign of his age—his beard.

(Well, David is clearly no longer a 'ripe-and-ready-teenager'/
AYLM as he was when, ahem, Saul first met him...now he has
the mark of male adulthood in the ancient world, a beard.)

And Sure-There-Achish said to his slaves,
"Look here —
you see the man is raving like he's insane —
why did you (fuck) make him come here to me?!
Am I lacking insane people that you've (fuck) made this one
come here to demonstrate his insanity for me —
this one you've (fuck) made come right into my house?!"

chapter 22

And David left from there
and escaped to safety in Adullam's cave (a naked and exposed
place in a nearby city not controlled by Ancient Israel or the
Dust-Rolling-Philistines, maybe 20 miles away from Sure-
There-Achish's city)
and (David's) brothers and his father's whole house/family
heard,
and they went down to him there.

And they gathered around him there —
every single man/person in a tight-space — in distress, in
dire-straits about their lives —
and every single man/person who was indebted to him —
and every single man/person with a bitter life —

and so it was —
over them he was in-charge —
and they were with him — 400 hundred men/people.

Ecstatic Prophets, Compulsive Fascists

('Over them'/AYLYHM...quite a hierarchical way of phrasing it in that all of these people who come to him form a band, a group, with David to be 'in-charge'/SR over them all.

What's different about David's band from Samuel's band or those wandering bands of ecstatics that Samuel sends young Saul into to have an experience?

Each of these groups includes misfits from the current hierarchical order. None of these groups fits — at least currently — into the royal design or, for that matter, into the priestly/ark design. That is, unless they pay their taxes to the king or pay a priest to offer animal-sacrifice in front of the ark.

But that's a very different kind of belonging than falling into ecstasy in Samuel's band.

Samuel's band of misfits gets high on the breeze, the wind, YAHWEH. YAHWEH is their leader, though we are told that Samuel was presiding/standing at attention over the group when Saul came to kill David and even the bloodthirsty Saul fell into the ecstatic-trance of the prophets. How does Samuel 'preside'? We are not told. Maybe he's the hospitality director, the one who makes sure all is well. There seems to be an equal-feeling of everyone in ecstasy and everyone fed this ecstasy by YAHWEH's breath — the only place yet that David has been completely safe, among this group of ecstatic-misfits.

Something different, we are told, feeds the band-around-David...certainly a familial love of David but also those with bitterness about their situations and, most likely, a wanting to get back at those who've wronged them — maybe Saul, the king. And here is David allowing this band to form with him 'in-charge' — not YAHWEH. Once the hierarchical imagination seeps into you, it's quite alluring...to find one's way to the top...to be important...to get somewhere...to be sought out to lead campaigns, of all sorts. All the while David could've gone back to Samuel and the prophets and been safe and lived an ecstatic life...but apparently the strings of power tug too greatly at him...to be 'in-charge' in his own right...

we'll have to see how these bands play on....)

And David left from there for the watch-tower of the From-My-Father-people...cousins of Ancient Israel,
and he said to From-My-Father-people's king,
"Please let my father and my mother come here to you
until I know in every way what ELOHIM/God-or-the-gods-and-goddesses will do for me!"

And he <u>guided</u> them there before the face of the From-My-Father-people's king,
and they stayed with him all the days that David was in the fortress.

(Note that the band of X has David 'guide'/NCHH his parents — David does not BOAH/'bring or fuck' his parents. Many of the times earlier in the saga, the band of X could have used NCHH instead of BOAH...but they didn't use BOAH here or NCHH earlier. And each time, the whole idea of 'fuck' seems to work with those BOAH incidents — whether someone potentially fucking someone or fucking with someone or feeling the whole fucked-upness of the situation. Fucking wild.

Note too that the From-My-Father-people's king never responds — but apparently allows David's request. In ancient storytelling, this is the storycrafter's way of conveying that the person who heard the request must have been dumbfounded by it or completely taken off his guard, unsure of how to respond.)

And the ecstatic-prophet Gad-Attack-by-Penetration said to David,
"Don't stay in the fortress —
go — (fuck) go by yourself to the land of Ancient Judah, the

tribe known for throwing up their hands/penises in praise!"

(Yes, these names do indeed point in this direction...Judah/
YHUDH from YDH has that YD/'hand/penis' thing in it and
the whole point of Genesis 38 plays on that double-entendre...
see *A Wildly Sensual YAHWEH*'s new edition. And Gad is from
GDD/'to invade, attack, penetrate, cut.')

And David left
and (fuck) entered the honeycomb-like forest that's so thick it
looks engraved, carved up, and thus full of hiding spots.

And Saul heard that David was in the know in every way
including sexually — and that there were men/people with him.

(So David has men/people with him, the king discovers...
where are these men/people from, the king must wonder?
And there's that haunting jingle in his head again sung by
the circling women...Saul with his thousand, David with his
millions...the king begins to realize that people of his kingdom
are or could be slipping away to join David...and not staying
with the king/him any longer....)

And Saul stayed in The Hill (which he'd had named Saul's Hill
earlier in our saga),
underneath an evergreen tree on a high spot,
and his spear was in his hand/penis/phallic-control,
and all of his slaves were standing at attention around him.

And <u>Saul</u> said to his slaves standing at attention around him,
"Hear me now, my <u>sons</u> of power and right-mindedness —
(which sounds like 'fellow <u>Benj</u>aminites!' but is *not* that)
for every single one of you — has the <u>son</u> of Jesse-There-He-
Is (Jesse's son of course is David) given you rolling-fields and
vineyards?
for every single one of you — has he put you in-charge of

thousands and in-charge of hundreds?

look — every single one of you — all of you are bound up together in a conspiracy against me —

no one has <u>stripped themselves naked like slaves or exiles are forced to do</u> to reveal right into my ears the covenant — the serious agreement — made between my <u>son</u> and the <u>son</u> of Jesse-There-He-Is —

and no one among you will pierce and weaken themselves in front me

and <u>strip themselves naked like slaves or exiles are forced to do</u> to reveal right into my ears that my <u>son</u> — with my slave (David) — has stood himself up tall against me to ambush me — today!"

('Whose <u>son</u> are you? Who has taken care of you all this time? And who is failing at their sonship and have given themselves over to be someone else's son? And which son of you all here will get us all killed today because you failed to reveal that David and Jonathan are out to get us — <u>us</u>!' But Saul never mentions 'us' — he's only worried for himself.

And Saul never mentions David's actual name again — maybe saying it out loud gets him all flustered inside, brings on those urges to fuck or kill, those bad winds.

Catching Saul's style — and hang-ups?

BNY YMYNY...this very clever speech here. It's easy to read it as BNYMYM, the usual 'Benjamin'...but there are extra Y's there that play on what Saul delivers with his stylish speech to his men...though he can't be sure they are <u>his</u> men anymore, not with the report that men are defecting to David, though Saul can't be sure who these defectors are for sure — at least not until he sees them with his own eyes.

BNY YMYNY literally means 'my sons of the right hand'... 'right hand' in the ancient world of the Levant has to do with justice, with power, with doing the right thing, with right-mindedness, as I've translated it here. One must know their rights from their lefts in the ancient world, and we modern readers must do the same if we are to understand the Bible, for sure.

So just before Saul gives this big speech, he addresses them as BNY YMYNY, which sounds so much like his own home-tribe from whom we can assume many of his men come and where they are currently standing, in Benjamin's tribal territory, under an evergreen tree, arial protection from David's or any enemies' potential arrows. Defense. Saul appeals for defense and rightmindedness from his men/people — the same people he fears are about to betray him. Are his fears rational? irrational?

And there's our old friend GLH/'stripped themselves naked like slaves or exiles readily do or are forced to do before their owners/captors'...once used by the prophets-ecstatics as a way of YAHWEH and now being used by the king, quite graphically. There are plenty of other words character-Saul could've used — 'told'/AHMR or even 'styled it out'/DBR or 'make someone see or recognize something'/the *hiphil* version of RAHH.

Recall too that the Dust-Rollers' prized warrior Goliath taken down by David is GLYT...from GLH...Goliath, the warrior who stripped the slain to take from them all their metal/wealth/protection to create his own legendary instruments of death. And now David has grown to wield Goliath's heavy sword as his own, and not just to chop off Goliath's head as a prize — now David runs from Saul and angry empire misfits come join him in their beef against Saul, head of the empire.

Perhaps Saul is toying with his men with the use of GLH, to see who will rat out what the priest gave to David, the sword of GLYT.)

And Anxious-Doeg of the the Red-Mud people (named for 'Adam' the mud-creature, these people being Ancient Israel's cousins) answered,
and he was standing at attention over (!) Saul's slaves,
and he said,
"I saw the son of Jesse-There-He-Is (fuck) enter the city known for being Fruitful —
to (see the priest) Ahimelech-My-Brother-the-King, son of Good-Brother —
he asked for himself to YAHWEH —
and he gave him meat/food —
and the sword of Goliath — the Dust-Rolling-Stripper — he gave it to him!"

(The King's stirring up his men with stylish speech worked — though it took a non-Israelite to tell him anything. Maybe none of his Israelite soldiers knew anything...which doesn't say much about their national security operation. Or perhaps an Israelite soldier did know something but held it back because they were more faithful to David than to the King they serve... or more afraid of what King Saul would do to anyone who knew and didn't report it immediately.

It begs the question though...why indeed would a cousin of the Israelites be allowed to stand guard there among Saul's soldiers — and so close to the King? What kind of royalty is this?

The band of X is surely here lampooning this royal government of Ancient Israel — and plenty of places elsewhere in our saga. If you read 1 & 2 Samuel and think Ancient Israel's royal government is wonderful, you most certainly haven't read carefully...or you're reading the sanitized Chronicles version onto these 1 & 2 Samuel tales. I mean, Goliath challenged all of Ancient Israel to send out one person to fight him — and no one would — no one except a young boy, David. A boy. An AYLM/'ripe-and-ready-teen.' In that situation before David shows up, it's the King's responsibility to put someone forward — if not even his own self. Goliath's challenge was about pride...and a lot more than pride. And where was Saul again? Hiding himself doing god-knows-what in the baggage? Luxuriating himself beneath a pomegranate tree?

The band of X has their character Anxious-Doeg use the word 'asked for'/SHAHL when describing David's visit to Ahimelech-My-Brother-the-King...and Saul's name means exactly that, from the same SHAHL.

Why Anxious-Doeg chooses 'meat or food or provisions'/TSYDH instead of using 'bread or war'/LCHM...who knows? Maybe to make the priest Ahimelech-My-Brother-the-King look worse in the situation in having him give David meat which would most likely be more substantial than some day-old bread?

And regarding this priest whose father earlier was Good-Brother and is now My-Good-Brother...it's a difference of a Y/*yod*...single comma-like letter...and likely some early text-copyist accidentally left it out earlier...or Anxious-Doeg is playing with some style here too in distancing himself from the priest's seemingly treasonous act of weaponizing David, though Ahimelech-My-Brother-the-King did it seemingly innocently in his dedication to the Crown through David's self-created crown-sent mission.)

And the King sent (soldiers) to call out after Ahimelech-My-Brother-the-King, son of My-Good-Brother, the priest — and the entire house/family of his father — the priests who were in the city of Fruitful — and they (fuck) came to the king — all of them.

And Saul said,
"Please hear me, My-Good-Brother's son."

And he said,
"I'm here, my boss."

And he said to him — Saul...Asked-For-It did,
"Why have you bound yourself up in a conspiracy against me —
you and the son of Jesse-There-He-Is —
in your giving to him bread and a sword
and asking for him in regards to ELOHIM/God-or-the gods-
and-goddesses —
to stand up tall against me —
to ambush (me) — today?!"

And Ahimelech-My-Brother-the-King answered the king,
and said,
"Who among all of your slaves is as right and trustworthy as
David?! He's the son-in-law of the king — (of you) —
he turns — changes course — at whatever he hears from you —
he is honored in your house/family!
The day I dared pierce — to ask for him of ELOHIM/God-or-
the-gods-and-goddesses?) —
how dare it be pierced by me —
that I'd set up the king to any kind of style with his slave (me!)
and with my father's whole house/family —
because your slave (me!) didn't know in any way about any of
this style — small or big!"

And the king said,
"Die, die, die, Ahimelech-My-Brother-the-King!
You and your whole father's house/family!"

And the king said to the runners standing at attention by him,
"Surround and murder YAHWEH's priests —
because even their hands/penises/phallic-control are with
David —
and because they knew in every way that he was bolting away
and they didn't strip themselves naked like slaves or exiles must
do before their bosses and reveal themselves into my ears!"

But the king's slaves would not consent to reach out their
hands/penises/phallic-control to happen upon YAHWEH's
priests.

And the king said to <u>Anxious-Doeg</u>,
"You alone — surround and <u>happen upon</u> the priests!"

And Anxious-Doeg of the the Red-Mud people (named for mud-creature-Adam) surrounded —
and he alone — he happened upon the priests —
he murdered that day 85 men who lifted up — er, wore — the straggly-yarned-underwear-*ephod* (that priests wore before YAHWEH's ark).

(The priest's use of AHMN/'right and trustworthy' hearkens back to the meaningful way that Saul used to address his men and accuse them all of conspiring with David. Recall he called them BNY YMYNY/'my sons of power and right-mindedness.' Was the priest tipped off that Saul was coming, tipped off by someone who heard Anxious-Doeg throw him/ Ahimelech-My-Brother-the-King under the bus/wagon for weaponizing David so he used a similar style?

It's a rather strange word to use here...PGAY/'happen upon' or 'encounter' or 'befall.' It's the word used in Genesis when Jacob happens upon a certain place and YAHWEH comes to him in a dream about YAHWEH being above all-the-other-gods-and-goddesses. Perhaps it's Saul choice of words here not wanting to take the blame for killing the priests of YAHWEH's ark — priests who are likely related to him by royal-marriage if not by blood. But Saul is so paranoid about David and the anti-Saul public sentiment that Saul thinks David has been stirring up — and Jonathan with him — that he will stop at anything to protect himself.

Just as My-Good-Brother/AHCHYTOB is likely misspelled earlier as Good-Brother/AHCHTOB, Anxious-Doeg's name is spelled two very different ways as well — DAHG and DOIG. Either these are copyist's errors, or possibly different traditions sewn together in this received text, or X is up to something clever here that I can't perceive.

Note all the plays with 'Saul'/'asked for'/SHAHL through the dialogue and narration. "They asked for it!"

Ahimelech-My-Brother-the-King has some stylish plays on words here too...'pierced' or 'profaned' or 'flute-playing' or 'grape gathering'/CHLL and the curse often translated as 'how dare I' or 'far be it from me'/CHLYL...note well what the band of X is playing with, with sound and meaning...its double-entendre...as Anxious-Doeg does this horrible thing of murdering these men, likely by piercing them through....)

And as for Fruitful — the city of the priests —
(Anxious-Doeg) killed with the edge of a sword
from man to woman to children —
even babies still young enough to be nursing —
and oxen and donkeys and sheep
— with the edge of a sword.

And one son of Ahimelech-My-Brother-the-King, Good-Brother's son, escaped to safety —
and his name is Abiathar-My-Patriarchy-Remains —
and he bolted away behind David.

And Abiathar-My-Patriarchy-Remains reported to David
that Saul had slaughtered YAHWEH's priests.

And David said to Abiathar-My-Patriarchy-Remains,
"I knew it in every way that day
when Anxious-Doeg of the the Red-Mud people was there —
that he'd report, report, report it to Saul —
I've caused this turn in events — I've caused this surrounding (death) —
with all the life (and death) of your father's house/family —
stay with me —
do not fear —
the one seeking my life (and death) seeks your life (and death) —
for sure, you'll be protected by me."

chapter 23

And they reported to David:
"Listen up —
the Dust-Rolling-Philistines are making war at the Citadel (in Ancient Judah, in David's home-country, in the hill country bordering Ancient Philistia) —
and they're robbing from the threshing floor...the center of commerce, where grain is readied for use and then sold."

(It's important to note that in our fiction here, Judah and Israel are not one nation yet. And as seasoned archaeologists like Israel Finkelstein point out, it's likely they never were in actuality a united monarchy, unless you count the many Israelites migrating to Judah/Jerusalem before and after Assyria attacked Samaria/Israel in 722 BCE. Ancient Israel was a vast and powerful nation before Assyria attacked; Ancient Judah was small, and not much of anything but a bunch of scattered and not very united family-groups until after Assyria began threatening Israel, and then much later Judah just to the south of Israel.

And who gets this briefing about Ancient Philistia attacking Ancient Judah's central-bank? David. Who hails from Ancient Judah.

Interesting, isn't it, that our David, our character-on-the-run-from-Israel's-king, is getting national/regional security briefings...?)

And David asked of YAHWEH:
"Should I go kill these Dust-Rolling-Philistines?"

And YAHWEH said to David,
"Go kill the Dust-Rolling-Philistines —
rescue the Citadel!"

And David's people said to him,
"Listen here —
we are here — afraid —
in Ancient Judah — the land known for throwing up their hands/penises in praise (and your home country) —
how more (afraid) if we go to the Citadel
against the very ordered battlelines of the Dust-Rolling-Philistines?!"

(After all, all of these bandits who joined David are probably excellent one-on-one in a fight — it's how they've survived against their hierarchically royal-minded government as subjugated citizenry for years...probably made easier for them to slide by with Saul's ineffective rule. But against a well-organized army like the Philistines...? But for these bandits with David to fight together against an organized power like the Philistines?! Especially when it's not really even their fight to fight — it's the people of the Judean leader's fight — a person whose name we do not know in the text — and David is intent on getting involved to win the allegiance of his home-country Judah in his future bid to become king of not only Israel but Judah...and then some. As these bandits remind David here, good luck....

A mob of people 'asked-for'/SHAHL Saul and got 'Saul'/SHAHL as their leader, their king...but it probably wasn't *everyone* doing the asking.)

And David asked of YAHWEH again,
and YAHWEH answered and said,
"Stand up tall! Go down to the Citadel! I will give the Dust-Rolling-Philistines into your hand/penis/phallic-control!"

Ecstatic Prophets, Compulsive Fascists

And David went — and his men too — to the Citadel,
and they warred with the Dust-Rolling-Philistines
and lead away their livestock/wealth
and struck them — killed them — with a great knock-out
punch/plague,
and David rescued those staying in the Citadel.

And so this is how it all happened —
when Abiathar-My-Patriarchy-Remains — (priest) Ahimelech-
My-Brother-the-King's son — had <u>bolted away</u> to David at the
Citadel,
he'd brought down with him the the straggly-yarned-
underwear-*ephod* in his hand/penis/phallic-control.

(This *'ephod'*/AHPOD — as most biblical translations leave it —
was used by the priests for divination, to know what YAHWEH
or ELOHIM ordained as the right way for future events...likely
with two answers inside — a rock saying 'yes' on it and one
saying 'no.' You ask a yes/no question of the Divine and pull
out a rock to decide your future. Magic 8-ball, priestly — and
now, warrior — style. It might appear that this is wisdom, a
wise way to go with one's life. Try it out for a night with your
every decision and see what happens....

And do note that the band of X describes the *'ephod'* far
differently from his priestly writing-competitors who crafted
the Torah. *The Naked Path of Prophet vol 1* describes those
differences in much more depth...see the essay on *'ephod'* in
either the first or second/revised edition.

I suspect that someone from the ancient ecstatic-prophetic
camp hearing this story of how the *ephod* came into David's
camp is laughing — and hysterically — at the ridiculousness
of this life...the see-through priestly undies, the Magic-8-ball
life, the fighting against one nation to help another nation so
that — perhaps — you can secure the thrones of both one day,
the running from King Saul, the getting bandits on your side
to stage a rebellion...all these things David is doing.

A whole theology of casting lots or flipping a coin to decide one's fate seems far from YAHWEH's lively breath....)

And it was reported to Saul that David (fuck) had entered the Citadel,
and Saul said,
"ELOHIM/God-or-the-gods-and-goddesses has delivered him into my hand/penis/phallic control —
(David) has shut himself in —
by (fuck) entering into a city with doors and <u>bolts</u>.

(A clever little turn of phrase...

David has 'bolted away'/BRCH a number of times and most recently so did the priest Abiathar-My-Patriarchy-Remains... and now Saul from whom they run is excited to learn that these two who bolted are now in the Citadel of a foreign power — Judah, a tribe not yet united under his Israel kingship — the Citadel being a city with doors and 'bolts'/BRYCH.

I suspect too that Saul has within himself that winning at the Citadel would be a two-fer...killing David and conquering a tribe that had been a nation on its own, albeit a nation that sometimes came to Israel's aid as it did for him in 1 Samuel 11.8.

Ever wonder where Jonathan is? Is he simply in hiding trying to stay alive — this warrior who had no fears about taking on anyone in battle, no matter how outnumbered?! Even with the strategy of getting naked to do it by climbing dick-and-balls with his fellow-naked-gear-lifter up to his well-armed enemies....

Or is Jonathan lying in wait for his father-the-king to make a strategic misstep and fall on his own sword? And what would be the strategy in that for Jonathan? To crown himself king? He's the oldest son of the king, after all.... Or to get behind

David being king, as the people would probably demand? Wild saga...!)

And Saul <u>heard</u> all the people — (gathered them all together as a way of hearing them and their war-cries for conquering more land/wealth?) —
for war,
for going down to the Citadel,
for cramping and confining the adversaries, David and his men/people.

And David knew in every way that Saul was scratching in upon him — in bad ways,
and he said to the priest Abiathar-My-Patriarchy-Remains, "Make the priestly-underwear <u>come nearer</u>!"

And David said,
"YAHWEH! ELOHIM/God-or-the-gods-and-goddesses of Ancient Israel—
<u>hear, hear, hear</u> your slave (me!)
because Saul is trying to (fuck) enter into the Citadel
to destroy the city
because of me —
will the <u>bosses</u> of the Citadel shut me into (Saul's) hand/penis/phallic-control?
will Saul go down just as your slave (me!) has heard?
YAHWEH! ELOHIM/God-or-the-gods-and-goddesses of Ancient Israel, please tell your slave (me!)!"

And YAHWEH said,
"He's going down there."

(A few gasp-worthy lines...

The band of X puts 'come nearer'/NGSH into their character-David's mouth requesting the priestly-*ephod*-Magic-8-ball-underwear — perhaps a bit comically. He couldn't have the *ephod* '<u>brought</u> nearer'/BOAH — which can also mean 'enter/ penetration, fuck,' let's remember — because Abiathar-My- Patriarchy-Remains is wearing the *ephod*. NGSH is also used euphemistically 'to lie with a woman,' *Strong's Exhaustive Concordance* notes. Curious choices of words here....

And 'bosses'/BAYL is an interesting choice of words too in that the last time it was used in 1 Samuel 12 when Samuel had come out from his decades of hiding to call the people to YAHWEH and away from BAAL/BAYL and ASHSTAROTH, the fertility god(dess) of the regions. BAAL is the traditional transliteration of this word in most Bibles, BAYL in my transliteration system. BAAL/BAYL — whether as verb or proper name for a god — always has to do with control, with bossing someone around. BAAL/BAYL often is used to refer to a young virgin boy taking a young virgin girl in marriage, with the boy replacing the girl's father as her 'boss'/BAYL... perhaps just one more reason the ecstatics-prophets seek to distance themselves from this whole system of BAAL/BAYL oppression.

And notice the juxtaposed differences in the story with 'hear, listen'/SHMAY with David and Saul...two men chess-moving around each other in their lusts for power...far different from the ways prophets SHMAY to YAHWEH's whisper.)

And David said,
"Will the Citadel's bosses shut in me and my men— into Saul's hand/penis/phallic-control?"

And YAHWEH said,
"They'll shut (you) in."

And David stood up tall — and his men/people too — like 600 men/people —
and they left the Citadel

and walked around — wandered around —
wherever they could walk and wander around —
and to Saul, it was reported that David had escaped to safety from the Citadel,
and (Saul) stopped everyone from going out (on campaign to invade the Citadel, perhaps the reason Saul's men were so excited, to invade and conquer another land and have more wealth then come their way).

And David stayed in the wilderness — in hunting-forts —
and he stayed in the mountains — the wilderness of tar liquifying in the hot sun — (about 10 miles south and east from the Citadel and even deeper into Ancient Judah) —
and Saul searched for him every day
but ELOHIM/God-or-the-gods-and-goddesses didn't give him into his hand/penis/phallic-control.

And David <u>saw — or was afraid?</u> — that Saul would go out (on campaign) to search for his living-breathing-body —
David had been in the wilderness of tar liquifying in the hot sun —
in the woody forest —
and Jonathan stood up tall — Saul's son! —
and went to David — toward the woody forest —
<u>he firmed up</u> his hand/penis with ELOHIM/God-or-the-gods-and-goddesses.

(Yes, you read that right. The verb is CHZQ/'to firm up' or 'to do something firmly or courageously' and having that verb's direct object be Jonathan's 'hand or penis'/YD should not surprise us...it's the very mark of the band of X who plays so cleverly with double- and triple-entendre layers of meaning. And why? To evoke awakening to the ridiculousness of one's assumptions. Jesus' parables do the same.

What does the story here do with your assumptions?

And watch how 'seeing'/RAHH and 'fearing'/YRAH in these lines of the story are practically interchangeable. The conjugations of these verbs are always so similar sounding/ looking for any hearer/reader in the ancient world. How would ancient hearers usually distinguish YRAH and RAHH? By context, of course. But what happens when you create a situation when 'seeing' and 'fearing' could be interchangeable? You have the style of the band of X...a style that plays with us.)

And (Jonathan) said to him,
"Do not fear — (or you can't see it that way) —
because my father Saul's hand/penis hasn't found you — will not find you —
you — you will be made King over Israel —
and I — I'll be for you a Second, a Number 2 (in command) —
even my father Saul knows in every way that it will be this way."

And they cut a serious-agreement — the 2 of them did — right before YAHWEH's face,
and David stayed in the woody forest,
and Jonathan went to his house/family.

And the people of the area where tar liquifies in the hot sun climbed up to Saul, up The Hill, saying,
"Isn't that David?!
Hiding with us in the hunting-forts in the woody forest?!
Up on the dark hill?!
South of the wasteland?!
And now, with all the lusting-longing-desire of the king's living-breathing body,
come down, come down, come down —
and with us, for us, shut him into the king's hand/penis/ phallic-control!"

(Jonathan tells David that David will be King and he/Jonathan will be the 'Second or Number Two'/MSHNH and then the 'two of them'/SHNYHM go off and seal the deal with each other, another covenant.

'Lusting-longing-desire'/AOT from the verb AOH...quite an interesting word-choice here. When the prophet Jeremiah uses this verb in the poem in Jeremiah 2, it has an air of 'passion' in it — an animal sniffing the air in heat, desiring sex. Maybe this time YD/'hand' is indeed 'penis' in all the ways Saul has desired 'the one who boils over with affection'/DOD...David...the one everyone, even in foreign lands like Judah, seems to know that David is the beloved of Saul, Saul's longing, Saul's lust.

And note well — these are the citizens of Judah saying this to Saul, king of Israel, about their own countryman David!)

And Saul said,
"You all here kneeling before YAHWEH — being blessed by YAHWEH —
because of <u>your sparing me, commiserating with me, having compassion on me</u> —
go please —
<u>firm it all up</u> —
<u>know in every way</u> —
see his place — where his <u>feet/balls</u> are —
who sees him there —
because it's been said how <u>naked-and-sly, naked-and-sly, naked-and-sly</u> he is —
and <u>see</u> —
<u>know in every way (certainly sexually)</u> —
who among all <u>is hiding-by-enfolding-themselves-within-each-other-in-their-lovemaking</u>
where <u>he hides-by-enfolding-himself-within-someone, lovemaking</u> there —
and you all return to me with those who've <u>firmed themselves up</u> —
and I'll go with you —

and so it will be —
but if he's not in the land...
I'll seek him out — concealing myself — among all the thousands of <u>Judah, the tribe known for throwing up their hands/penises in praise!</u>"

(More style-rich prose dropped into the mouth of our king-character by the band of X...

they have Saul use CHML/'sparing, commiserating, and possibly having compassion' instead of RCHM/'having pure compassion...womb-kindredness'...and CHML is exactly the word Saul should use when he's within the borders of a kingdom he does not rule...

and notice how he tells these citizens of Judah who kneel before him and before YAHWEH, as if they are synonymous...

and he responds to their style-rich choice of words to describe his own 'lust'/AOT for David by choosing all these very sexy words: he uses 'feet'/RGL which is also a euphemism for 'balls/testicles' as we saw in 1 Sam 14 with Jonathan and his gear-lifter...

Saul then follows that foot/balls double-entendre with wanting to know who might be there with David — perhaps Jonathan and perhaps they are balls-out with each other — 'hiding themselves within each other, lovemaking'/CHBAH —

and then Saul reminds these new spies of his that David has a reputation of being 'naked-and-sly'/AYRM (tripled here like I do, doubled in the Hebrew) — that 'naked-and-sly' way of being associated with, in Saul's royal/hierarchical imagination, the untrustworthy prophets-ecstatics into whose trance Saul himself fell and stripped himself of his clothes and was peaceful and ecstatic, even when David was right there in the circle with him on the mountaintop in the place where the ecstatic-prophets gather to know and be known by YAHWEH...

and the character-king Saul is just getting warmed up with his own double-entendre rhetoric...

Saul tells them to go see these naked-offenders — his own son Jonathan and his former lover/string-strummer David — and to know all there is to know about them — recall that 'know'/ YDAY can also mean 'have sex with' as in *Adam knew his wife Eve and she conceived and had a child...*

and then Saul ups the ante by using CHBAH/'hiding within each other...as in lovemaking' instead of STR/'hiding...like behind a rock' — and not just once but twice in different parts of the same sentence —

and then Saul circles back to CON/'to stand tall, erect' but this time not as a command to these spies kneeling before him and YAHWEH...this time it's *niphal*...a verb-form with reciprocal intentions...'these who are standing themselves up, erecting themselves in their hiding within each other while they make love'...and the double-entendre is that these lovemaking-hiders erect with one another are also erecting themselves standing up to Saul and his kingship...

and then Saul concludes his orders by reminding these spies who've come to him that if he shows up and David is not there that he as King of Israel will pursue David by ransacking their/Judah's thousands of people — perhaps a slap in the face to their low-numbers compared to Israel's massive land and census...at least compared to Judah...

and to make matters worse, the meaning of Judah's name puns well with all of these references to sex that Saul has purposefully used here. Judah means 'throw up hands/penises in praise!'...and the fiction of Genesis 38 makes it quite clear that the character Judah had a reputation for doing both...
and these spies from Judah have certainly done that — they've risked it all and put themselves out there — thrown their hands and penises and livelihood out there — by traveling to Israel's

King Saul to deliver information about their own countryman David's whereabouts within their home-country — perhaps most certainly hoping for a reward from him or the guarantee that he would not attack them — and now Saul reminds them that if David can't be found, Saul will take matters into his own hands/penis/phallic-control and find David himself by searching the entire country — inside every home and cave and nook and cranny — until he finds David, no matter how much Saul's search destroys their/Judah's country.)

And they stood up tall and went with Saul — facing Saul — to their home-area where tar liquifies in the hot sun (where they had last seen David)—
but David and his men/people were in the wilderness <u>where married ones reside together</u> —
on the plain to the south of the desolate wasteland.

And Saul and his men went to search him out,
and they reported it to David,
and he went down (even further to) the rocky-cliff's-edge —
he stayed in the the wilderness <u>where married ones reside together</u> —
and Saul heard and chased after David into the wilderness <u>where married ones reside together</u>.

(While 'the wilderness where married ones reside together' is usually translated as the Wilderness of Maon, the whole thing takes on a little more life — as it usually does in the band of X's stories — if we think of these scene-locations less as geographical places and more as descriptors with a clever twist and, as I have done, translate these names as the words constellate meaning in Hebrew...especially as just before this Saul was bargaining with citizens of Judah to try to trap David with his son Jonathan, two who act like they are married to one another in their affair and allegiance — covenant — with one another.

I suspect that Jonathan and David repeatedly making covenants with each other out of their love for each other and after their lovemaking with each other would probably anger the Levitical priests with their Torah and its distaste of male-with-male-love. And again, I suspect that's the band of X's point with these stories...to poke fun at the Torah and its covenantal-cultic-community with Moses and his Law as arbiters of relationship with ELOHIM/YAHWEH...

...all the while the prophets are on the mountaintops of the Levant living out their lives in relationship with YAHWEH, the wind that is constant, dependable, life-giving, covenant or not.)

And Saul went to this side of the mountain,
and David and his men/people went to that side of the mountain —

and that's why David hurried himself up to get away from having to face Saul —

and Saul and his men/people were encircling-like-a-crown toward David and his men/people to seize them.

And a message-runner (fuck) arrived to Saul, saying,
"Hurry up! Come on!
The Dust-Rolling-Philistines are stripping and plundering all over the land!"

(Like King Saul, did you too forget that when the king's away, enemy-nations could play?)

And Saul returned from chasing after David —
and he went to call out the Dust-Rolling-Philistines
and that's why the name called out for this place is Rocky-Cliff-That-Divides.

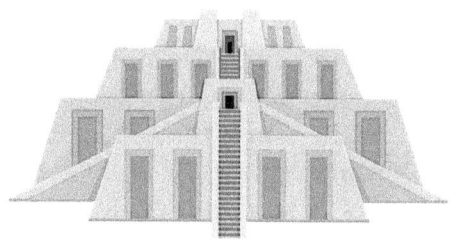

CHOOSE WELL!

Doublespeak vs. Ecstatic-speech

Many theologians and scholars with whom I've studied are pretty not so funny. Sometimes they get funnier away from the podium or outside their research area or after a couple of drinks. One of my early scripture teachers explained to me that that's why most/many of them don't understand Jesus or Paul, both of them with significant comedic chops. I would add most of the prophets to that duo of the misunderstood-for-their-humor.

But Caleb King sure caught a whiff of that ancient group's humor at the 2024 Society of Biblical Literature annual conference in San Diego. With as many as seven thousand scholars from all over the world gathering in groups of twenty (or a hundred if you're funny or controversial), most papers and their deliverers at these collegial gatherings are pretty serious-minded, though occasionally with a single giggle built into their argument to keep the audience awake and amiable.

I was delighted when Caleb began his paper "What Sounding Alike Sounded Like: Understanding Sound Similarity in Biblical Poetics Through Close Consonance" with a joke:

"What did the janitor say when he jumped out of the closet?"

I'll let you play with that a bit and circle back to it.

Here in 1 Samuel 23 we find a number of interesting well-styled things. I've been calling them 'stylish speaking'/DBR because it's all so different from 'regular speaking'/AHMR, and the band of X like the band of YAH notes well the differences. Anytime we hear DBR in the story, we'd be wise to lean in, catch it from the beginning, catch the details to be in on the whole joke and message.

So let's set the scene here in 1 Samuel 23. Long ago in our saga, Samuel and YAHWEH rejected Saul as king/*messiah* of Ancient Israel, so YAHWEH sent Samuel off to Ancient Judah to anoint David as king/*messiah*. Get the import of that?! There's no one worthy in Ancient Israel?! No wonder Samuel protests to YAHWEH — Samuel surely worried either Saul or the people of David's country would kill him/Samuel! (Ancient Israel and Ancient Judah were not one nation at this point in this fictional saga, if they ever actually were in actual life.)

Fast way forward to where we are in the saga with love-boiling David running from King Saul when Saul continually tries to nail David to the wall, ahem. David finds safe refuge with Samuel but then runs from it to seek refuge in his home country — but his countrypeople don't seem to want him there based on what we hear his own countrymen say to Saul, their cousin/kind-of-ally from Ancient Israel:

> *"Hey, isn't that David hiding out here in our land? That guy you've been lusting after like an animal in sexual-heat? Why don't you come and get him and kill him (so we don't have to!)?*

And Saul replies to them with the bawdiest language as if to deny his prior lust for David and to force the Judeans to expel David, one of Judah's own:

> *"Oh you've been so kind...all of you kneeling here before me and YAHWEH...yes yes yes go firm it all up...find David's feet or balls and who's there with him...I mean, he's said to be naked, naked, naked there — firm dick and balls out — and sly, sly, sly — so you'd better watch yourselves — and find out in any way you can — even sex if you have to — who is hiding — who's there making love with David (because it's certainly not me — but it might be my son!!!!) — be firm in your, ahem, disposition — and find him — otherwise I'll go house to house through your entire puny land — with your paltry thousands of citizens! — and find him myself! And aren't you all known for having your dicks out anyway, Judah?!"*

These are of course more rough renderings of what I translated earlier, though if you study the Hebrew carefully and note every which way the words reach, I think you too might find these renderings not so far off.

And notice what we have: some attempts at stylish-playfulness/DBR interwoven with a heavy dose of threat.

The only reaction of these Judeans would be to gulp and gulp hard. A king from a friendly but still foreign land just threatened them to bring the guy they just tattled upon to the king — essentially to do the foreign-king's dirty work for him — and if they don't come up with David, the foreign-king will ransack their country.

With the king's manner of speaking here, there is no negotiation, no sharing in building a plan — just threat, pure threat and manipulation. "Do it or die!"

King Saul's words here and elsewhere are not exactly Orwellian "doublespeak" but Saul's manner of speaking shares something in common with doublespeak: threat, intimidation, coercion, all of which enact hierarchical assumptions about one person being more powerful than another and forcing someone to do something or to think something or even to believe something that they don't want to.

Now to be clear, George Orwell in his *1984* coined the terms "doublethink" and "Newspeak" and since then we seemed to have rolled them together into "doublespeak."

What differences can you perceive between these two styles of saying something similar and yet very different:

A: *"Could you take the garbage out?"*

B: *"Take the garbage out."*

Does the potential meaning of A or B or both change if the speaker is standing above the hearer?

Does the potential meaning of A or B or both change if the speaker is a parent and the hearer is 6 years old? 10 years old? 15 years old? 40 years old?

Does the potential meaning of A or B or both change if the speaker and hearer are both neighbors of about the same age? or very different ages from each other?

Does the potential meaning of A or B or both change if the speaker is standing above the hearer and the speaker once punched the hearer, whether for not taking the garbage out or for something else entirely?

Does the potential meaning of A or B or both change if the speaker is currently holding a weapon?

Does the potential meaning of A or B or both change if the speaker is known to carry a weapon but no weapon appears visible at the moment?

Context is everything with determining meaning and with determining the speaker's mindset, right?

...and maybe an entirely different context would help...imagine this speech being offered...

> *"There is no justification for violence of any kind. We are a democracy. We are a peaceful people. We believe in democracy for the whole world. There is absolutely no reason for any country or group to want to do us any harm. We will deal handedly with all challengers to our way of life."*

Though I made this little speech up so as not to point the finger at any singular person, we in the United States are pretty used to speech like this, no matter who says it from the highest echelons of our government, no matter the political party. We the People...the only nation to have used nuclear weapons...the nation who continues to drop bombs daily all over the world. How many bombs? Well, we don't know any more. But in 2016, it was at least 70 bombs a day on average, every day that year. (*NBC News*, Jan. 9, 2017, F. Brinley Bruton, reporting on a Council on Foreign Relations report)

Seventy bombs a day. Every day. During peace time.

With such a context in mind, here we can catch a little bit more of the doublespeak, right? "There is no justification for violence of any kind..." says an official who is dropping 70 bombs a day through our democratic citizens' authority granted to our elected government and paid by our citizens' tax dollars, one bomb every 20 minutes or so, maybe even one bomb dropped as the speech is happening. But those bombs don't make the news very often...we're often not to know the full context, though the world where the bombs are being dropped sure does. The style of speaking makes no sense to the audience without the real context. That's the very nature of doublespeak — to subtly communicate threat and control without giving all the details.

Language + context = !

The essential question, from my viewpoint, to ask when anyone speaks or acts is...in what direction does the word/act move?

Circularly/level-to-level <u>or</u> up/down onto you?

That is to say, does the person's word/action invite you to help solve a problem together without any hierarchical imperative <u>or</u> does the person make you know that they are in control and will solve the problem whether that solution could harm you or your neighbor or not?

So what did the janitor say when he jumped out of the closet? *SUPPLIES!*

As U2 reminds, "laughter is the evidence of freedom" (*Beautiful Day*)...when we're all laughing and truly enjoying the moment, a moment often brought on by some stylish word and action. There is no threat. There is only *joie de vivre*. It's so vastly different from doublespeak....

With doublespeak, the speaker probably doesn't want you to notice everything that's being communicated — except to hear that the authority is in charge and will murder you too if you don't stay in line. There's an ethos of violence within a false mythos of peace.

With ecstatic/prophetic speech — perhaps involving puns or close-consonance — *SUPPLIES!* — or double-entendre or half-rhymes, the speaker wants you to catch their meaning and then more than that — as if using that forked joke might awaken you-the-hearer to more and more possibilities with no end to them so that together speaker and hearer might figure out more of the situation together. Nonviolence works this way too through *surprise* — what word or action will awaken an oppressor to realize we're all human and equally sharing in life in the wind and, with that awakening, begin figuring out a way together to leave behind the old hierarchical-default and form a better relationship/system on those equal terms.

In Ancient Hebrew way of life, it seems in ecstatic/prophetic-rich storycrafting, at least as far as we can glean from their stories, DBR/'stylish speech' simply invites a hearer to come back with more DBR, playfully, circularly. We make meaning together. It's what philosopher Hans-Georg Gadamer in *Truth and Method* gets at...that two speakers build a bridge to each other in a long conversation/relationship and work out meaning together, essentially by working out a common, shared language with each other. But notice the assumption here: that the two in conversation must recognize their equal nature with one another...otherwise the meaning gets stilted, threat lingers in the air, doublespeak creeps in...at least until the one being perceived to be below the doublespeaker says/does something to awaken the doublespeaker to their foolishness and both then have the opportunity to, if the doublespeaker allows it, hash out a new bridge to one another, a renewed relationship on equal terms.

Of course, if the doublespeaker does not allow that new bridge to be built, the one perceived to be below the doublespeaker can keep taking it — or step away and allow the bridge to crash down. Maybe then the doublespeaker finally wakes up to their power-issue.

The hierarchical imagination — of putting one below or above another — does not work as a system for long before the system crashes. Sure, we might meet someone and realize they know more than we do about something that we want to know. We might want to build a bridge to them and hope they'll do the same so that we can learn what they know, grow, discover — maybe even discover/create together. But build that bridge into the sky too high to reach the pedestal upon which you've elevated someone and the bridge will one day collapse.

Dangerous pedestals

We humans have a tendency to put other humans on pedestals — even the fellow-humans who use pleasing and just-right 'styles'/DBR to awaken people to our equality in the wind.

In the early 1960s some style came to Bob Dylan in the Big Wind during some dire times in US/world history and he shared that style through song and immediately he was put on a pedestal by many as the prophet of the age. Of course he rejected that title. (If they'd called him a fellow 'ecstatic' perhaps Dylan would have agreed!) So sure were so many fans that Dylan was their prophet and that he should act how they wanted him to act and play how and what they wanted that they booed him through his shows. No longer were they protesting the Powers that Dylan's music prior music was indicting — the same Powers creating bombs and using them, often against the innocent — now the pedestal-raisers were protesting the one they wanted to keep singing the songs they once resonated to, in the way they once resonated to, about 'the moment' years before that Dylan had captured with such style years ago.

Years later, in a *60 Minutes* interview (December 6, 2004), Dylan was asked about that, what he thought about these people demanding he be their prophet or savior: "They must not have heard <u>the songs</u>."

The spirit of the Big Wind seems to remind that we are all equal in nature, all enlivened together on this Big Earth, and we must be together and work together to keep human life going, at least as long as the Big Wind and the Big Earth will allow it.

No matter who is speaking, it's important that we listen...that we hear...
that we catch the style responding to the context and wonder if the speaker is trying to nudge us into laughter with them or is trying to assert their power over us and the context with doublespeak. Sometimes we are the ones demanding foolishly that another human rise above us and speak to us in this way...and then "we-asked-for-it!"

Uh oh, more messiahs are coming...what's this business of 'messiah'?

We had plenty of references to *messiahs* in the first 17 chapters of 1 Samuel — in Hannah's poem, and then referring to Saul and to David. And we're about to have many more *messiah-*

references so it might be worth wondering a bit about this whole *messiah*-business, this whole *christ*-business.

Priests and scribes of the 3rd and 2nd centuries BCE translated the Hebrew Bible from Ancient Hebrew into Greek. These early Jewish priests and scribes translated the Ancient Hebrew word *messiah* into the Greek word *christ*. Both words essentially mean 'oily one.'

This Greek translation of the Hebrew Bible, the Septuagint, was commissioned in Egypt for Greek-speaking Jews. It is said that 70 (or 72) Jewish scholars translated the Hebrew Bible that they had at the time into Greek. This translation project goes by two names: LXX and Septuagint. "Septuagint" is named after those seventy scholar-translators; "LXX" are Roman numerals for "70" given to this translation generations after the translation was completed.

The Ancient Hebrew word MSHYCH/*'messiah'* identifies many different people and even types of people in the Bible.

Here in 1 and 2 Samuel, MSHYCH/*'messiah'* is used exclusively to refer to the one anointed/oiled-up as Israel's king, the one made special by being smeared or rubbed with oil. MSHYCH/*'messiah'* appears 18 times in 1 & 2 Samuel — more than any other book or two-volume-book of the Bible.

MSHYCH appears in other places in the Hebrew Bible:

- 4 times in Leviticus...and always referring to a priest being the MSHYCH/'messiah or oily/anointed one'

- 10 times in Psalms...referring to David as this 'specially anointed one' as king or another savior-like role emerging in the tradition after the monarchy dies

- 1 time in Isaiah 45, what we once called 'Second Isaiah' and composed at the end of the Babylonian Exile or later...and this time MSHYCH refers to Cyrus of Persia, something that would have been quite surprising, that YAHWEH would rescue Israel/Judah through a non-Hebrew like Cyrus, king of Persia who 'freed' the exiles in 538 BCE

- 1 time in Lamentations, the poem reflecting back on the destruction of Jerusalem in 587 BCE by the Babylonians and then the exile, where the king/MSHYCH and the upperclass Deuteronomists were taken away and then likely employed by their captors in Babylon

- 2 times in Daniel and 1 time in Habakkuk...both of them like the Psalms in that they reach back to the mythos of David and expand it to some larger post-monarchical savior

And we would also be wise to check out MSHYCH used as a verb, MSHCH:

- 1 time in Genesis...the priestly-story of ELOHIM/divinity talking to Jacob about anointing a pillar

- 12 times in Exodus, 8 times in Leviticus, 8 times in Numbers...all of them referring to anointing priests, wafers, the tabernacle, and all manner of priestly things

- 2 times in Judges...a story lampooning the anointing of a king

- 14 times in 1 & 2 Samuel...all of them referring to YAHWEH insisting that a prophet anoint a particular person as king

- 12 times in 1 & 2 Kings...all of them referring to YAHWEH insisting that a prophet anoint a particular person as king, except once (1 Kings 19) where prophets are also called to be anointed too

- 5 times in 1 & 2 Chronicles...regarding the anointing of a king, especially David in 1 Chronicles 11 and Solomon in 2 Chronicles 29

- 2 times in Psalms referring to David/king/post-monarchical savior

- 1 time in (First) Isaiah...in a playful poem about oiling shields for war

- 1 time in Amos...lampooning people who are rich enough to drink wine from bowls and who anoint themselves with oil

- 1 time in Jeremiah 22 where the reference has to do with coating something as if in paint/oil

- 1 time in later-than-First Isaiah 61 where the prophet in exile exclaims that he/she has been anointed to share the good news

- 1 time in Daniel, as the whole MSHYCH-mythos grows into more of a post-monarchical savior

It's rather interesting to me that Leviticus with its four MSHYCH-references and its eight MSHCH-references makes it clear it's only a priest who is the MSHYCH — no mention of a king. And there's the Samuel-saga with no mention of a priest being MSHYCH — and no mention of a Levitical priest anointing the MSHYCH. In the Samuel-saga, it's only a prophet who anoints a king — not a priest.

Other similar-sounding words should give us some pause too...the Dust-Rollers' 'no-holds-barred-military-destroying-unit'/MSHCHYT — often translated as "raiders" — in 1 Samuel 13 has nearly the same key letters as *messiah*/MSHYCH. Concordances — including *Strong's* — note that MSHCHYT is the participial form of SHCHT/'to destroy, corrupt, ruin...and sometimes to pervert (as in justice/wisdom).' Any listener to this 1 & 2 Samuel saga would probably find it curious at the very least that Ancient Philistines' MSHCHYT sounds so similar to Ancient Israel's MSHYCH...and they sometimes perform similarly, violently.

Foolish messiahs and their foolish followers

This whole *messiah*-business as noun and verb can be found more in 1 & 2 Samuel than anywhere else in the Hebrew Bible and this 'oily one'/*messiah*/MSHYCH in the Samuel-saga is a fool. Saul, David, Solomon...these are not people upon whom you might hope to depend to save your life, whether as king or as something/someone more salvific than that. Saul hides under lush trees during war in a time when the king/MSHYCH would usually be expected to fight alongside his troops, builds penis-trophies to himself, takes credit for his son's daring and then out of jealousy wants him dead. Where we are in the saga now, Saul is doing the same with David.

The MSHYCH does not improve later in the Samuel-saga either. In 2 Samuel, King David has sex with whomever he wishes and then covers it over by killing the woman's husband. In 1 Kings, David's character-son-Solomon builds huge buildings — projects that require conscripted labor/slavery — and which of his building projects is bigger, the palace or temple? Solomon builds a palatial-house for himself — actually multiple buildings for himself and his wives — and the whole palace-complex is far bigger than the temple for YAHWEH, we are told by the band of X, with very carefully laid out measurements. As the story goes, those building projects alone are enough to split the United Kingdom of Israel/Judah in two, with Israel raising up the building-projects foreman as their new king, the one who surely knew and had the allegiance of the laborers/slaves, at least more than Solomon, the 'master' of all of them.

We must not forget that 1 & 2 Samuel and much of 1 & 2 Kings is fictional — 1 & 2 Samuel completely so. The band of X has fabricated this fiction of Saul-David-Solomon for a reason... and we wise readers must discern why exactly.

One thing's for sure, from the band of X's perspective, this whole business of making something holy (QDSH) or anointing someone with holy oil to designate that person as special (MSHYCH) is quite problematic....

The problems — and shadow — of a MSHYCH

We all too often invest our common power in one person to do our bidding, to enact our desires so that we might live our lives and have clean hands, sometimes no matter the costs. But our error is two-fold: first in that we give away our power to anyone, and second in that giving away our collective-power does not let us off the hook for what that MSHYCH does in our name, with our power...whether the MSHYCH is anointed with oil or with our attention/intention and interest.

Royalty, of course, did not begin with 1 & 2 Samuel. *Gilgamesh* came thousands of years before it. The *Gilgamesh* epic decries the problems of royalty when royalty conscripts its youth to build the city to epic proportions and forces upon the youth a system of oppression — a lack of choice in the matter. Royalty is eventually an economy — a system — that will kill itself off with its forgetting that a human is a human. Royal/ slave systems all too quickly forget that the sovereign is just as human as a slave, and vice versa.

Watch my generation's royalty-shows *The Crown* or *Young Royals* as characters and viewers alike begin to realize that the royal-system is designed to kill, to ruin, to thwart life — and how quickly we humans give our power to that system that proclaims one human is divine/royal and the rest basking in that divine-human's glow and hoping for benefits from the royal.

And through their saga, the band of X seems to be poking fun at the whole business of MSHYCH. They reveal its foolishness as a system — and its tragedies for how the sovereign will use their power for their own whims and gains at the cost of the people's lives and livelihoods.

We'd be wise to wonder what we do with *'messiahs'* today...and we'd be wise to remember we have choices about the systems we enact and into which we invest our personal power and attention.

Really want to keep royaling up royals?

It's mystifying to me that so few catch the point X was making — how people long ago and today continue to raise up David and Solomon as heroes, whether they know David and Solomon are fictional or not. The band of X makes it quite clear they are bloodthirsty kings intent on using for their own good(s) the system through which they're anointed and often at a tremendous cost to the people they 'serve' in their roles. For crying out loud, later in the Samuel-saga X has King David at home during war (!) with enough time to nap on the roof and be bored and notice and then stare at a beautiful woman bathing and has her summoned to his palace where he has sex with her (definitely not on equal terms...could she say no?) and then has her ever-faithful-to-the-crown husband killed to cover over the king's royally-fucked-up misdeed.

Centuries after the band of X's 1 & 2 Samuel were told warning about the dangers of *messiahs*, what did the early Jesus believers do? They carried forward this same *'messiah'* system and projected it onto Jesus...Jesus *Christ*...Jesus *Messiah*. Some gospel writers even position Jesus as from the line of David — sometimes bending over backwards to do so. Did they not read carefully 1 & 2 Samuel??! Or did they only read the sanitized versions of 1 & 2 Chronicles put together by the Levitical priests likely many years after 1 & 2 Samuel? Or did they not know either of them well enough to discern the differences? Ugh.

In the Gospel of Mark's version of the story — the earliest of the four canonical gospels — Jesus does not want to be associated with *Christ/Messiah*. Hmm.

It wouldn't be the first time Jesus' followers ignored him.

If we study 1 & 2 Samuel and 1 Kings carefully, the MSHYCH/*'messiah, christ'* is no one worth following. It's a problematic system, to say the least, our saga tells us: the people ask for it and get it and it destroys them. Saul-David-Solomon... these are blood-thirsty men. Do they have moments of wisdom and goodness? Of course. They are like you and me, they are humans who use their power for good and for evil, for others and for themselves. But their mistakes are exponentially greater than yours and mine due to the grand import of their role, in the system the people enacted by demanding a MSHYCH rule over them. A *messiah*/king/hierarch's power all originates with people giving over their personal power to these kings — and to the royalist political party who stand to benefit most from the king's rule. Same goes for hierarchy-leadership in organized religions, which have proven themselves through the millennia to be equally deadly.

It's easy to raise up a king if you get big benefits that trickle-down to you; it's also easy to kill the king if those benefits feel diminished. The inner ring of the king gets the biggest benefits — and they are the ones who seek most readily to maintain the royal system. Same goes for organized religion. Most companies and all-too-many governments today continue this same hierarchical imagination, simply replacing the title/role of 'king/*messiah*' with CEO.

What to do with Jesus Messiah?

For us Christians, it's one thing to love Jesus and to be curious about his sayings and story and lifestyle as a wanderer and healer and even to recognize him as someone you might want to befriend, follow, emulate, cherish...

it's entirely another to invest in him as a *messiah* or *Christ* or savior...

especially when Jesus' whole mission and philosophy appears to be in reminding people — each one of us — that we are the salt of the earth, the spice of life, the light of the world. Sure, Jesus is salt and spice and light too — but what he was up to was flattening pyramids of power, revealing that emperors were just as human as peasants and endowed by God with the same innate power, that the 'sacred' was all the time and everywhere and including all...and could be found even in the ridiculous possibilities of a woman kneading yeast into 50 pounds of dough or a farmer spreading dandelion seeds through his field, or a father taking back — and not only taking back but running after to embrace — the son who demanded his inheritance before his father's death (!) and had the nerve to squander it on parties and had even more nerve to return home and live off his brother's inheritance-share while their father was still living.

Jesus was upending the MSHYCH-imagination during his lifetime. And what did we do? Put him on a throne — made him *messiah*/MSHYCH — and all too often then to stop having to listen to him and those jarring parables and sayings that question the hierarchical/MSHYCH-system.

Whether with Jesus or anyone we put on a throne or to whom we give over our power, this whole MSHYCH-business is dangerous, dangerous territory, friends...and so many of us keep perpetuating it with our organized religions and doctrine-worship, with our celebrity-worship, with our president-worship, with our CEO-worship and our ongoing investment in companies intent on destroying the planet and covering it over, just to make a buck for their shareholders (likely you and me too with our retirement investments).

It's one thing to look to a teacher for a short time to mentor us into some type of learning that we seek. It's quite another to name someone your guru and follow them blindly. Jesus broke up such a game: "Don't call me Christ! Don't put me on a pedestal!"...Jesus seems to be saying. Closer to his words: "You are the salt of the earth! You are the light of the world!" And then when it would be easy to make him the healer, he sends his followers off to do the healing without any special blessing but instead some advice: take nothing with you for the journey and trust that God will flow through you...that divinity always flows through you and me. We are swimming in It (divinity)!

In a world where it is so easy for us people to give over our power to hierarchically minded leaders, Jesus and the ecstatic-prophets like the band of X here in 1 Samuel offer a way out... if we have the sense to make sense of It.

chapter 24

And David climbed up from there
and <u>stayed</u> in the hunting-forts of Spring-on-the-River-Bank-Where-the-Young-Goats-Gather (east of where he was, and on the edge of the Salt Sea/Dead Sea...as far east as he could get right then, and next to the only place with fresh water, it seems).

And so it was —
just as Saul had <u>returned</u> <u>from being behind</u> the Dust-Rolling-Philistines
that it was reported to him:
"Listen here —
David is in the wilderness of the Spring-on-the-River-Bank-Where-the-Young-Goats-Gather."

And Saul fetched 3000 <u>choice young men</u>
from all of Ancient Israel,
and he went to seek out David and his men/people all over the face of Rocky-Cliffs-of-the-Wild-Mountain-Goats.

(Hasn't *Messiah/Christ* Saul learned anything yet?!

Where had Saul returned from?   From being 'behind'/ MAHCHRY the Dust-Rolling-Philistines who had attacked as Saul left behind his kingly/national responsibilities within his own country's borders — his kingdom of Ancient Israel — to chase down his supposed-opponent-for-the-throne David who is hiding in a foreign though usually friendly nation, Ancient Judah.   And here *Messiah/Christ* Saul goes again, putting his people and country at risk of an enemy invasion to secure his own throne, to be sure David doesn't even think about trying to steal it from him.

Watch how human — and strategically foolish — the band

of X will portray this selected-by-God, specially-oil-smeared *Messiah/Christ* here, this Saul that everyone 'asked-for'....

And note the plays on the various types of 'goats' here and their positioning...

and not just that...Saul calls up his group of 'choice young men'/ AYSH BCHUR...who will then travel with him to stand high on the Rocky-Cliffs-of-the-Wild-Mountain-Goats and presumably look down on David and his men/people who are at the Spring-on-the-River-Bank-Where-the-Young-Goats-Gather.

If indeed Ancient Israel — like Greece and many of that time — were military-pederastic and Saul gathers 3000 of the present-future of the strength of Ancient Israel's military to go round up David, Saul is up to a number of ploys here... certainly showing that he's in control and will be in control of the royal-nation of Ancient Israel — if it survives Philistia's next attack — and that he has 3000 'Davids' at his disposal. But it's more than that. Recall that David was vaulted into this group of 'choice young men' — maybe even beyond this 'choice' training group — by defeating Goliath and by playing Saul's instrument to calm the King. Back in 1 Samuel 9, Saul himself was identified as a 'choice young man'...and now he commands them as king...commands these adolescent-warriors.

Note too the small play on David 'stayed'/YSHB and Saul 'returned'/SHB — when conjugated as they are here these verbs look and sound quite similar and an ancient hearer would probably have to unravel which is which by context... not to mention it adds to pleasing the audience's ear with similar-sounding but differing-in-meaning verbs.)

And he (fuck) entered the sheep-pen — walls designed to keep sheep in — by the road,
and there was a <u>cave — a naked, exposed place</u> —
and Saul (fuck) entered to <u>put a shadow over his feet/balls</u> —
squatted over his feet and balls (to poop) —

and David and his men/people were in the <u>legs — the rear-end</u> — of the <u>cave</u> — they were staying in there.

(Uh, yes, you read all of that right.

MAYRH/'cave' takes its root from AYOR/'to be made naked, exposed, bare'

HSC AHT-RGLYU/'put a shadow over his feet/balls' is also used in Judges 3 to refer to a king also most likely relieving himself, as most biblical translations do with this 1 Samuel 24 passage...and it makes sense as a man who squats down to poop also covers his feet with his lowered hips and his balls/testicles at the same time depending how low he can squat... recall that throughout 1 Samuel and Genesis that RGL/'feet' can be a euphemism for 'testicles/balls' as *Strong's Exhaustive Concordance* notes.

And where are David and his men? They are also in the cave. Where exactly in the cave? in the YRC/'leg-with-genitals or flank or rear-end'...which in the ancient world is the same word for the place a father would ask his son to put his/son's hand to receive the father's final blessing and inheritance rights, which we see best in the band of YAH's Genesis story of Isaac blessing Jacob instead of Esau.

Why these choices of words? Because the band of X — like Genesis' band of YAH — has a sense of humor. It's the prophetic-ecstatic style to be funny. And it's the same funny/punny imagination that Jesus uses in his parables. And such humor — when we're laughing — helps us to feel safe enough to consider that our assumptions might be completely wrong. Fictions, and sidesplitting fictions at that, can do that. They always have, it seems. Laughter might be the only way we come to realize the foolishness of adults giving away their/our power to others, as this Samuel-saga challenges.

And such humor in 1 & 2 Samuel will get even more bawdy and handsy....)

And David's men/people said to him,
"Listen up — today YAHWEH is saying to you —
'Listen up — I — I do — I give your enemy into your <u>hand/penis/phallic-control</u> —
do to him whatever is good in your eyes!'"

And David <u>stood up tall</u>
and cut off an edge of Saul's royal-robe in secret.

And so it was —
after this —
David's heart was struck down within himself —
that he had cut an edge that was Saul's.

And (David) said to his men/people,
"Cursed/Pierced am I by YAHWEH —
that I'd do this style-rich thing to my boss — <u>to YAHWEH's messiah, Its specially-oil-smeared-one</u>
to send out my hand/penis onto/into him
because <u>YAHWEH's *messiah,* Its specially-oil-smeared-one</u> —
that's who he is!"

And David tore his men/people (in two...divided them) with these stylings-on,
and he would not give them over (allow them) to <u>stand up tall</u> against Saul,
and Saul <u>stood up tall</u> from the cave and went out on the road.

(Here is Saul squatting, shitting, doing probably the most grotesque and often private of human functions, and suddenly David brings up the oil that anoints *messiahs*/kings, and whose oil it really is...YAHWEH's.

And not only that, David refers to 'sending out his hand/penis onto him'...and a 'hand/penis'/YD is indeed something that a man 'sends out'/SHLCH from himself. And how sorry David feels about it — even after Saul has at least twice tried to pin

David to the wall/piss-trench, either as a rape scenario or one of murder.

And there's that CHLYLH/'cursed' from CHLL/'to pierce, to profane' again. And QUM/'to stand up tall'...which could be 'rise up' or 'rise against' as in David's men/people rising up against Saul...immediately followed by Saul standing up tall after shitting and leaving the cave unharmed...a clever juxtaposition of QUM.

Do you think this story in the saga — where a king goes unprotected into a cave to take a shit and gets his clothes trimmed by the person he's chasing — would have brought laughter from the audience? Guffaws? Welcome to quintessential band of X style...and then we can begin to wonder why X styles it/It out this way....)

And David stood up tall and went out of the cave
and called out after Saul,
"My boss! King!"

And Saul regarded him,
and he <u>shriveled</u> — David did — (they all) bowed down,
<u>nostrils</u> to the ground.

(Let's sort this out carefully because some strange things are happening in the grammar that influences the meaning of the story.

Saul 'regards,' for sure. And then David shrivels at Saul's gaze — yes, that's right, David no longer stands up tall to Saul, he shrivels at this king and probable former lover who has tried to kill him twice. All with a glance, a regard.

David's men/people thought it alright to kill the king just a few minutes ago.

Very strangely, the next word we get is AHPYM/'noses/ nostrils.'. And where do those noses go? AHRTSH/'to the ground/earth.' And then we get a third person plural verb YSHTCHU/'they bowed down.'

Whose noses/nostrils? Who bowed down?

It's definitely more than David, though we know he alone shriveled at Saul's glance, at being noticed by Saul.

Why? Hard to say, though if we reach back to what David just said about Saul — about Saul being 'YAHWEH's *messiah*, Its specially-oil-smeared-one' — I think it's safe to say that our character David has come under the spell of the mythos, the power of the *messiah*-mystique. And locked inside of that — and remembering there was a day when this *messiah* loved him, when Saul loved the young, love-boiling, affection-boiling David, David seems to forget all those times that Saul has tried to kill him. David seems to forget why indeed they are all gathered here on the edge of the known civilization far from Saul's realm — because Saul has chosen once again to chase down David and kill him, even if it costs Saul his entire kingdom. The last time he chased David and failed to kill him, the Philistines invaded.

So who bows their noses/nostrils to the ground? David and David's men/people? Saul's men/people? All of them?

That is the cost of this whole *messiah*-mythos — no matter who one's *messiah* is. People will do unreasonable things in the name of and for the *messiah* — even if it costs them their own lives, even if it demands that they kill others for no good reason, for any reason.

Locked in such a *messiah*-mythos, we too quickly forget that we have choices beyond doing good for only one 'special' person, that we can evaluate which choice is best not only for oneself but for others, for all, if we can, and then enact that choice.

Locked in such a *messiah*-mythos, we too quickly forget that every single human being is made of the same stuff — flesh — and breathes the same air to survive and walks the same Earth.

The *messiah*-mythos is at its heart hierarchical — a system that really has very little heart to it. It puts one person on top, as close to divine as possible, and everyone else at grades less than this, usually determined by the rings near the top who keep the *messiah* alive and protected and pump up the mythos so that they grow their own power, their own quiet trickle/river of wealth essentially stolen from the lower and middle classes through tithe or tax or worse. And this mythos swept through Nazi Germany. And it's been sweeping through my own country for decades — if not much longer — with our seeking some politician or celebrity to save us — instead of being a democracy, a common-rule and shared-rule <u>by the people</u>, not a single person.

It's extremely dangerous to let the mythos shine so brightly that we refuse to see the obvious and significant errors in judgment by the *messiah*-of-the-day.

Note here in our saga that *Messiah* Saul gives no response to *Messiah* David...ancient biblical narrative style demonstrating that the character Saul was dumfounded by David's words and actions.

Or was that whole shriveling to the ground on David's part a pure act, another thing he simply "must do" to become *messiah* himself. Locked inside the *messiah*-mythos, you and I too might be dumbfounded as to our actions and words to improve our status in the hierarchy.

But on the mountaintops with the prophets, the ecstatics, everyone seems to flail away equally on the ground, bowing to no single human, all humans naked and ecstatic and fed by the wind....)

And David said to Saul,
"Why do you listen to the stylings-on of <u>a red-mud-creature-like-Adam (either referring to any old random person, though likely referring to Anxious-Doeg of the Red-Mud People)</u>??
Those who say, 'Listen up, David seeks to do bad things to you!'??
Listen here — this very day — your eyes can see
that YAHWEH gave you into my hand/penis/phallic-control — today — in the cave —
and someone said for me to kill you off —
but <u>I had you covered — I pitied you</u> —
and I said, 'I will not stretch out my hand/penis onto/into my boss —
because he's YAHWEH's *messiah*, Its specially-oil-smeared-one —
and <u>my daddy/father</u> —
yes, see this — see it — the edge of your royal-robe —
in my hand/penis/phallic-control —
look — I cut off an edge of your royal-robe —
I didn't kill you off —
know it in every way —
see here — there's no bad rebellion in my hand/penis/phallic-control — I've not committed a serious-offense against you —
but you do — you hunt down my living-breathing-body — to take it!
Let YAHWEH judge between me and you!
Let YAHWEH avenge me against you —
but my hand/penis will not be on/in you!
Just as the clever-wise-saying from the Ancient East (Babylon) says,
'From wrong comes wrong....'
but my hand/penis/phallic-control will not be on/in you!
After whom does the king of Ancient Israel come out?
After whom do you chase?
After a dead dog!
After a single flea!
And so it will be —
YAHWEH directly-judge and discerningly-judge

between me and you
and It will see —
and It will plead my plea
and discern (differentiate) me from your hand/penis/phallic-control!"

(This little outburst of a speech by David teeters on double-entendre right from the very beginning: the way David indirectly names the spy who earlier informed Saul of David's whereabouts...Anxious-Doeg the AHDMY/Red-Mud-People/Edomite...whom David refers to as AHDM — a reference to Anxious but at the same time a reference to any person and all persons through AHDM/'Adam'...whose name essentially means 'red-mud-creature.' Talk about style!

David says that in the cave — the place that is bare and exposed and where Saul was crouching and exposed as he pooped — that he/David had Saul 'covered'/CHUS...which can also mean in Hebrew that David had pity for Saul...which is to say that he both felt something for the king and pitied the king who pooped in such an exposed place, in such an exposed way, with no soldiers protecting him, no soldiers first sweeping the cave to make sure their king was protected.

David proclaims that he had his chance to kill the king — someone had even urged him to do it right there in the cave — but David refuses to do so because Saul is YAHWEH's anointed, YAHWEH's *messiah*, Its specially-oil-smeared-one. And not only that, David says that Saul was a father to him. A daddy/AHB. 'My daddy'/AHBY.

David of course has a father — Jesse-There-He-Is. David's referring to Saul as his father could refer to the military-pederastic arrangement between them...and that is essentially what the older-warrior would be to the younger-warrior...a second-father who would teach him how to stay alive in battle, how to stay alive in love, how to stay alive in philosophy...how to know one's place in the world. Gay love between two men of different generations still uses such 'daddy-son' terms today.

And as for all the 'hands, penises'/YDYM that are flying in this speech, David very well could be referring to his hand — that his hand would not touch or hurt the king. And it could also mean that his hand would no longer touch the king sexually. And it could also mean that his penis would no longer be on Saul. And it could also mean that his penis would no longer be in Saul. In the phrasing of the Hebrew here, every one of these meanings would be legitimate translations of the situation. And considering that David has been the darling youngster and string-strummer — and even savior against Goliath — since the very beginning of their knowing each other, the decision to hear it as 'hand' or 'penis' is a dicey one — one that any ancient hearer would be left wondering about considering the context of the story of David and Saul — and Saul's son Jonathan, to boot!

Double-entendre, triple-entendre, and more...that's the clever use of words by any ecstatic/prophet, any poet, any decent storycrafter. And it's sitting right here in the Ancient Hebrew for anyone to see....)

And so it was —
when David had finished styling-out these stylish-things to Saul, that Saul said,
"Is that your voice, David, my son?!"

And Saul lifted up his voice and wept.

And he said to (love-boiling) David,
"You are more in the right than me —
because you've <u>weaned</u> me toward goodness
and I've <u>weaned</u> you toward badness —
today you alone have <u>fronted it — made it conspicuously clear</u> —
what you have done with me — toward goodness —

when YAHWEH shut me into/onto your hand/penis/phallic-
control
and you did not kill me off —
because if someone finds their enemy
and <u>sends</u> them on their way for the good
and YAHWEH <u>grants you peace and health</u> for the good —
because today underneath all of this, this is what you've done
for me —
<u>and therefore</u> — I know in every way
that you'll be made king, you'll be made king, you'll be made
king —
that (the kingship) will stand up tall in your hand/penis/
phallic-control —
the kingdom of Ancient Israel will be —
<u>and therefore</u> — swear to me by YAHWEH
that you will not cut off my seeds/descendants after me —
that you will not destroy my name from the house/lineage of
my father/daddy!"

And David swore to Saul,
and Saul went home,
and David and his men/people climbed up to the hunting-fort.

(Just before this highly stylized speech, Saul weeps. Why
does Saul weep?

Because David has been compassionate — because David
spared him/Saul when Saul was completely exposed to attack
in the cave — when Saul's people don't even think to protect
him while he's in there?

Or is it because David has once again gotten the upper hand
and revealed — in front of everybody that matters, all of these
3000 choice-young-men, the very future of Ancient Israel —
that David is better than him/Saul. Again. And again. And
again. No matter how many penis-trophies Saul builds for
himself.

What is Saul's ploy here? What does he demand?

Saul must know his days are numbered now — whether by attack by the Philistines, which had just happened as he was chasing after David in a foreign land, by attack by one of David's people, by attack from one of his own chosen-young-men who've witnessed with their very eyes the love-boiler/ David standing before them holding an edge or flap of Saul's royal-robe — evidence that they as choice-young-men had failed their duty in protecting the king, evidence that David has captured the flag/flap.

But note too that Saul points out in front of everyone that while David is noble and loyal for not killing him — Saul himself being the one who was specially-oil-smeared by YAHWEH in front of Ancient Israel as king — that David had let his enemy go… something that no one trained in war can accept…something that all of these choice-young-men know is problematic.

So after making that apparent to all, 'fronting'/NGD it out for all to know, Saul demands a very public promise from David that David protect Saul's line/his family — that David will not wipe out Saul's lineage when David becomes king. And this is sworn by David before all the men/people who matter — Saul's choice-young-men who are the future of Ancient Israel — plus David's rebel-group.

And that move of wiping out Saul's line/family would be a legitimate concern, right? David-as-new-king might have challengers from Saul's family, especially if one of Saul's family felt that only someone from Saul's line/family should receive Ancient Israel's crown when Saul dies or is killed.

Note the two 'and therefore'/UAYT clauses…usually reserved for special announcements or promulgations…'whereas' in our modern contract language. The first UAYT, Saul's realization that David will be king. The second AUYT, Current-King-Saul demands of Future-King-David that David will not wipe out Saul's line and leave Saul's family-line childless. This is an interesting request, especially considering that that family-line includes Jonathan — and Saul knows something of their, ahem, love for one another. Perhaps Saul knows David does not really love Jonathan as much as Jonathan loves or plays to love love-boiling David. Perhaps Saul is twisting David's twisted lie/covenant with Jonathan all the more here, this political-alliance with a thinner and thinner veneer of love/lust holding it together...or Saul puts it out there a bit manipulatively to see how David will respond. And then David swears he won't kill off Saul's line — but with no mention of Jonathan.

And as for this 'weaning, rewarding'/GML...if indeed Saul and David were in that old-warrior with young-warrior military-pederastic relationship, just as every one of Saul's choice-young-men would be too, it would have been Saul's responsibility to raise and rear David to the good...but it appears that those roles and responsibilities have been reversed since near the very beginning...the youngster David kills Goliath when none of Saul's very best troops — his very best seasoned warriors — accept Goliath's challenge. Even Saul shirks the responsibility of confronting Goliath himself, as would likely be his duty in a culture of honor. David has been teaching and ripening and rearing Saul from the beginning — indeed was even brought in to strum the strings for Saul when Saul's demons reared their ugly heads, when the grips of kingly-power grasped Saul by the throat and by the imagination and strangled Saul's ability to breathe the gods-and-goddesses fresh, free air....

And yet even then, even through all this, Saul is still scheming. His speech here is full of style, all mentioned above plus the euphonic and similar-sounding 'sends him'/SHLCHO and 'grants you peace and health'/SHLMCA. He even circles back AHBY/'my father/daddy' that David had brought up just before.

Strength is power in the ancient world, for sure, but it's <u>style</u>

that seems to earn respect, honor. And the band of X has David and Saul vying for such respect and honor by spitting stylish things at each other...and yet the greatest styles so far in 1 Samuel have come from some pretty surprising people, including Samuel's own mother in a moment of ecstasy.)

chapter 25

And Samuel died.

And all of Ancient Israel gathered and mourned him (as was customary...tearing out their hair, beating their chests, lamenting, weeping).

And they buried him in his home, in The Heights.

And David stood up tall and went to the Wilderness of Beauty-and-Self-Boasting.

(With the information we have here, it's hard to know if David was at Samuel's funeral/public mourning. We could assume so if 'all of Ancient Israel' was there. But we don't know the time when David stood himself up tall and left. Hebrew verbs do not express time clearly, at least not like English verbs do.

Was David's exit during the funeral? Was it before the funeral? After?

Was it not safe for David to go at all? ...his Saul-troubles seem to have been resolved for the next few moments anyway with that whole cave-thing and the grand apology and promises?

In any case, we don't get any particular statement from David about Samuel — and never will. Recall that Samuel saved David's life from Saul's bloodthirsty rage when David ran to Samuel on top of the mountain, to The Heights. Circles can save, especially when presided over by ecstatics/prophets who do nothing.

And it's meant to be abrupt — this death, this no-statement from David about the fellow human Samuel who had introduced David — and many people, including King Saul on at least two occasions — to the ways of ecstasy with YAHWEH.

And where does David go? Seemingly on vacation. South, down to the Sinai Peninsula, to the wilderness known for its beauty and making anyone look beautiful and boast-worthy. The traditional name is Paran.

It's meant to be a stark contrast.

While Ancient Israel tears their hair out and beats their chests and wears uncomfortable mourning clothes and pours dirt on their heads in their mourning for the man they-asked for a king...

David at some point goes to a place completely opposite of that, where beauty and self-boasting reign.

Samuel hasn't had a speaking part in this half of the book named for him, has he? And there were only a few speeches from him in the first half of 1 Samuel, though quite a few key vignettes. And there's still a whole other book — 2 Samuel — bearing his name but, I guess, not his living-breathing self.

Unusual, yes?

Maybe it was never about him — about Samuel — in the first place —

the ecstasy with YAHWEH rolls on for anyone who breathes and wants to notice this life-force penetrating you and me and every creature into life....)

And there was someone in that place where married ones reside together,
and he was doing business in Vineyard, the next village over,
and this particular someone was great — very much so! —
this person had sheep — 3000 of them! —
and 1000 goats —
and this person was shearing his sheep in Vineyard,
and the name of this particular person was <u>Stupid-Wineskin</u>.

(Yep, you read that right. Most Bibles transliterate his name as Nabal...but NBL means 'fool, stupid, disgrace, wilt-away, wineskin'...how important it is to know what these ancient names sound like and mean to their ancient hearers...every Hebrew hearer of the ancient world would have tuned in much more carefully after hearing that...ears perking way up and most likely guffawing as each hearer wondered which he was — more 'Stupid' or more 'Wineskin'.

Note the style we encounter here in one of those stranger manners of Hebrew-speech, even from the outset... VAHYSH/'there was someone, there was a particular person.' It's all meant to be unclear. As noted before regarding David's men/people, AHYSH can stand for 'man' but it can also stand for many 'men/people'...and when it's plural, in Hebrew grammar, that gathering of people could be men and women and nonbinaries for that matter...all and anyone...as long as one 'man'/AHYSH is present.

We might begin to wonder about the way this story is being styled out, not only because of the very wild name — 'Stupid-Wineskin' — but also the manner in which we were told, brought into the drama, the punchline-name of this wealthy fellow.)

And the name of his wife was Abigail...which can mean 'Patriarchy's-Joy'...or 'Patriarchy's-Revolution.'

(Another exceedingly interesting name, especially alongside her husband's name.

You see, the plot is being set up...to see which way this Abigail's name wavers. Will she be Patriarchy's Joy...like the way it has been 'forever' or at least recent generations...with women placating their fathers/husbands and being their joy as good 'girls'...the system of patriarchy that by its essence puts women below men in value...the very essence of the hierarchical imagination? Or will she be Patriarchy's Revolution...to reach back, to revolve back, to circle-dance back to something else... perhaps a time and a way before patriarchy emerged as the assumed way it's always been?

Entering the circle-dance whether to honor the king or BAAL or ASHTAROTH or YAHWEH or whomever or whatever — to revolve this way and that — would make oneself new through the process, to leave the dance having been changed, improved. From what we know today of movement's effects on one's nervous system, every move creates an opportunity for sensing newness within oneself and thus growth.)

And she was a woman of good understanding...wisdom...insight, and she was beautifully shaped.

And the man was harsh and bad in his dealings,
and he was just like <u>his heart</u>.

(Most translators have 'Calebite' for CLBY or CLBO, depending on which manuscript one reads. CLBO actually means 'like his heart.' And as the drama plays out, this Stupid-Wineskin of a guy's heart will become more and more important to the story, not so much whether he's a Calebite or not.)

And David heard in the wilderness
that Stupid-Wineskin was shearing his sheep (which means

he's now very wealthy, with liquid wealth — ancient cash —
at no cost to his capital, his animals still alive and able to be
traded and milked and eaten).

And David sent ten slave/boys,
and David said to the slave/boys,
"Climb up to Vineyard —
and (fuck) go to Stupid-Wineskin —
and <u>ask</u> him in my name for peace and health —
and say,
'Yes! To life!
Peace and health are yours!
Peace and health are your house's/family's!
Peace and health are for all who are yours!
Now I heard that you have sheep-shearers with you —
and now you see your shepherds were among us (David's people) —
and they were not wounded or taunted —
and not a thing was visited-and-then-requested from them all
the days they were in Vineyard —
<u>ask</u> your slave/boys and they'll tell you —
that (my) slave/boys have found favor in your eyes
because every day with us was a good day —
please give whatever you happen to find in your hand/phallic-
control to your slave/boys — us! — and to your son David!"

And David's slave/boys (fuck) arrived,
and they styled out to Stupid-Wineskin all these stylish things
said in David's name,
and they settled down all quietly,
and Stupid-Wineskin responded to David's slave/boys and said,
"Who is David?!
Who is the son of Jesse-There-He-Is nowadays?
There're many slave/boys breaking away — one man/person
at a time — from their boss' faces —
(you think) I'm going to take my bread and my water and
my butchered-meat that I've butchered-up for the sheep-
shearers and give it to people whom I don't know where they
are from?!"

Ecstatic Prophets, Compulsive Fascists

(Water — when they're in a Vineyard. He's going to give his hired-men — the sheep-shearers — only water?! Cheap-ass. And a stupid cheap-ass who doesn't even offer some half-empty wineskins to his employees — let alone David.

The common meal of even the poor in the ancient world was bread and wine.

Maybe the meat is generous — but then again.... Clearly, NBL here is more 'Stupid' than 'Wineskin.'

And not only that, Stupid tells these slaveboys that many run away from their masters these days — perhaps suggesting that these slaveboys are lying and running away from David and trying to get a free meal from Stupid or maybe Stupid is encouraging these slaveboys to stay with him, to run away from David and never return and be his own — Stupid's own — slaveboys. Stupid-Cheap-Ass could get a good deal out of it if these slaveboys of David's decide to stay with him/Stupid and slave away for him. Even the priest gave David crumbly bread — more than Stupid did!

Remember who Stupid's messing with...David...who has also run from his boss Saul/SHAHL/'<u>Asked</u>-For-It'...and here is David hiding out in Ancient Judah where Stupid lives and far away from David's boss Saul, King of Ancient Israel. And perhaps too Stupid is hinting to the slaveboys that he knows something of David's story running from King Saul. It's quite a packed punch Stupid delivers...so much so that the slaveboys we'll soon see are 'changed'/HPC by these words, this same verb Samuel used to describe what would happen to Saul when he first encountered the ecstatics on his way home from Samuel the first time they'd met, just after Saul was smeared with oil as *messiah* and kissed by Samuel.)

And David's slave/boys <u>turned — in some changed way</u> — on their path —

and they returned
and (fuck) arrived
 and reported to him all these stylings-on.

And David said to his men/people (as in all of them, perhaps
including the slaveboys),
"Get your sword ready — every one of you!"

And every man/person got his sword ready.

And even David got his sword ready.

And they climbed up behind David — like 400 men/people!

And 200 stayed with the gear.

And to Stupid's wife Abigail...whose names means either
'Patriarchy's-Joy' or 'Patriarchy's-Revolution'...
one slave/boy from among all the slave/boys reported (to her),
"Listen here — David sent ambassadors from the <u>wilderness</u> to
kneel before our boss and he screamed and railed at them —
and the men/people had been good to us — very much so —
we weren't shamed or taunted —
nothing was visited-and-requested in all the days we were wandering
around with them when we were in the open-country —
a protecting-wall around us — that's what they were —
by night and by day —
every day that we were among them shepherding the lambs
and goats —
and now know in every way — see what you are to do —
because bad things are surely coming — already in progress
— against our boss —
and against his whole house/family —
he's a son-of-worthlessness — a wicked son —
the <u>wilderness — one can't even style it out to him</u>!"

(MDBR/'wilderness' and M+DBR as DBR/'styling, speaking
in a clever style' and the M/'from' or M which is used in

comparisons...all of this to say that the slaveboy here — the only one who had the guts to tell Abigail that her husband is going to get them all killed — this slaveboy employs some style in saying this David hiding in and coming from the seemingly worthless desert-wilderness is about to kill his boss and his boss' whole family/estate, and likely his' boss' wife, his boss who is worthless and not even worth styling about.

We're about to see what Abigail will do...will she preserve the system of patriarchy by being the joy of her husband and doing nothing about the dangerous situation brewing...or... will she step up and reach back to a time when women were recognized as more equal to men, long before patriarchy and hierarchy emerged as 'the [foolish] way it is'?)

And Abigail hurried
and took 200 loaves of bread
and 2 <u>skins</u> of wine
and 5 already-prepared sheep
and 5 huge servings of roasted grain
and 100 pressed-raisin-cakes
and 200 pressed-fig-cakes
and put them onto the donkeys.

And she said to her slaves,
"Pass-by before me —
look — (fuck) I'll arrive right after you!"

And as for her husband <u>Stupid</u>, she didn't tell him.

(NBL is used twice here recently — once as 'wine-skins' and once as Abigail's husband's name, Stupid. Both deflate and shrivel up when not full of anything valuable....)

And so it was —
she rode on the donkey — she did —

and she went down in hiding behind the cover of the hill —

and how about this! — David and his men/people were going down to call her out,
and she just happened to meet up with them.

And David had said (earlier, perhaps to himself),
"Surely it was an outright deception —
I protected everything that was this guy's — in the wilderness —
and nothing was visited-and-requested from all that belongs to him —
and he has returned bad for me instead of good —
so yes, may ELOHIM/God-or-the-gods-and-goddesses do for David's enemies —
and even make them multiply —
if I <u>swell up and leave behind as a remnant</u> anyone who belongs to him —
by morning — a single (male) person pissing on the piss-wall!!"

(Well, here's that 'piss-wall'/QYR in all it's shining glory... the convenient dribbling away place to piss in any wealthy person's house like Stupid's house and Saul's house where Saul had his fevered, bad-air dreams of raping/killing David. But here David is going to do it to other 'people who piss'/ SHTN...and with a curious and style-rich verb-choice to go along with all the pissing and morning-wood...'to swell up, to leave behind as a remnant'/SHAHR.)

And Abigail saw David
and she hurried
and got down from the donkey
and she fell toward David's angry-face upon her own face
and bowed to the earth/ground
and fell upon his <u>feet/testicles/balls</u>
and said,
"On me —

my boss —
the punishment for guilt —
please let your <u>woman-slave</u> style it out into your ears —
hear your woman-slave's stylings-on —
please do not let my boss — you! — put any time into
considering <u>his heart</u> —
toward this man-of-worthlessness — this wicked son —
upon stupidity/Stupid —
because just like his name, that's who he is —
his name is Stupid —
and stupidity is within him!
I am your woman-slave — I am!
I didn't see my boss' slave/boys — (your slave/boys) — whom
you sent —
and now my boss —
(I swear) by YAHWEH's life and your living-breathing-body's
life —
whom YAHWEH has held back from (fuck) bringing
bloodshed —
your own hand/phallic-control rescuing yourself —
and now let your enemies be like Stupid —
those seeking to do bad things to my boss — you!
Now this one is kneeling — this one whom your <u>successful-
child-bearing-woman-slave</u> has (fuck) come to my boss —
(me to you) —
and let her be given to the slave/boys who've been wandering
around my boss' <u>feet/testicles/balls</u> —
please <u>lift up/forgive</u> the <u>rebellion</u> of your woman-slave —"

(This is highly stylized speech by Abigail...exceedingly clever
in a number of ways. First and foremost, she's buying time for
David to calm down, and all the while, she's dropping in hints
about who she is and what she can offer — including that she's
a SHPCH/'a-woman-slave-who-has-borne-children' and thus
making her more valuable in society's eyes. The fact of the
matter is, most likely, that she is <u>not</u> a SHPCH but an actual
wife of Stupid...that is to say that she's a wife with more status

than a slave. But Abigail is showing, on her knees, that she could be of some worth to David...she could bear him children in the future because she's already shown she has the ability to do that.

Why is this important? Besides having enough to eat, it's the number one concern in the ancient world. The ancient representations of gods and goddesses reveal it — the 'powers that be' of any time period reveal what's most important to any culture. And what are the personalities of gods and goddesses of this ancient time period about? Fertility...of land for food and humans for babies, family longevity, family survival.

Abigail is making it clear that she is to David first a AHMH/'woman-slave' and then also a fertile one...a SHPCH/'successful-child-bearing-woman-slave.' The two meanings of these very different words are very clearly differentiated in Hannah-Bend-Down's speeches at the beginning of 1 Samuel...if today's readers and scholars are wise enough to notice what the band of X is doing there to set up this saga.

And that's not the only style in this speech by Abigail as she kneels at David's feet...she references the slaveboys who wander around — maybe hang around — David's feet. And remember that RGL/'feet' can be a euphemism for 'testicles/ balls.' And that would be what these slaveboys would do for David if this is indeed a military-pederastic society...these boys would be learning the ways of battle and the ways of love/ intimacy from their older warrior David. Perhaps Abigail noting this promotes David from a wandering-mafioso doing who knows what in her home-country of Ancient Judah to a well known and well followed general-training-boys who might one day be king of her nation?

Curious how Abigail uses the word usually reserved for these boys-in-battle — NSAH/'lift' as in gear-lifter as we saw earlier in 1 Samuel, notably with Jonathan and his gear-lifter. But

Abigail uses the word NSAH in its use to 'forgive' — 'to lift away' — her rebellion...not her sin, not her transgression. Instead, her revolt, her rebellion against her Stupid husband. And here she is kneeling before David — at his feet/balls. Here she is begging, essentially for her life and her whole house's life, begging at the fertile feet/balls of this man David who is intent on killing Stupid for being so, well, stupid.

Abigail is certainly 'Patriarchy's-Joyful-Revolution'/AHBYGYL even as she apologizes for her 'rebellion'/PSHAY essentially against her stupid husband! Notice: these words involving revolution/rebellion are not the same or similar-sounding... perhaps her very point. She is the one revolving with joy, she is the one inviting David into such joy — perhaps differently from the women with their dances that nearly got him killed by the King...that damned jingle that Abigail has probably heard even this far removed from King Saul's reign, that jingle that cuts, that exposes, the very nature of prophetic/ecstatic-speech to juxtapose, to reveal, to remove the clothes of the situation for what it is, often with no personal benefit. 'Saul kills his thousand, David his millions'...that jingle composed by dancing women; this stylish speech composed by a kneeling woman. Abigail's ecstatic speech is to save her life, her household's lives. Let's see what else she says....)

(Abigail continues...)
"—because YAHWEH is making, making, making for my boss a drive-in-my-tent-stakes-lasting house/family/lineage
— (one that is dependable and to be trusted) —
because my boss fights — you fight — YAHWEH's fights —
and bad won't be found in you all your days —
a red-mud-creature-like-Adam has stood himself up tall
(perhaps referencing Anxious-Doeg of the Red-Mud-People and the one he tipped off, Saul, if the whole world knows that story by now) —
to chase after you — to seek your life — your living-breathing body —

but my boss' living-breathing body <u>will be an adversary and bound up with the bundle</u> of the ones who live, with YAHWEH your ELOHIM/divinity —
and as for the living-breathing bodies of your enemies, (YAHWEH) will <u>sling him out from the middle of the sling's hollow</u> —
this is what YAHWEH is doing for my boss — for you —
all the good (YAHWEH) styles out about you —
(YAHWEH) shouts out orders to you to be the obvious-leader over Ancient Israel —
and this woman — me! — will not be for you
  a grief
  or a stumbling block of the <u>heart</u> for my boss — for you! —
  or a spilling blood out of favor — for no reason —
  or my boss rescuing himself —
YAHWEH is doing something good for my boss —
that you'll remember your woman-slave — me!"

(Talk about style!

AHMN, from which we get the word 'amen,' has to do with 'driving in one's tent-stakes'…something a wanderer like David has known to be rare, both as shepherd-boy before his Goliath fight and as adversary to the king who lusts after him and wants to kill him. A wanderer would only drive in their tent-stakes if they felt safe in an area long enough to want to stay, to make a commitment to the land for rest and for rich-grazing for their animals — one's safety and one's animals' safety being paramount.

TSRUR/'bound or bundle' used twice is interesting — and the similar sounding TSRR is 'adversary' and plays on what comes next in the reference to David's enemy — Saul — whom she refers to as someone like AHDM…seems like everyone knows Anxious-Doeg of the Red-Mud-Creatures betrayed David to Saul.

QLAY/'sling' plays on what David is best known for — for killing Goliath with a sling and a rock.

Abigail tells David that she will not be a stumbling block of the heart — quite a turn of phrase. Keep noticing the plays on 'heart'/LB.

So what is Abigail doing in this long speech uttered from her knees there before the love-boiling-turned-angry-blood-boiling David intent on killing her husband for being so stupid/ Stupid? The length of the speech surely is to buy time, to hope David will calm down enough to be reasoned with. But she doesn't just blabber on — she calls David back to who he is with very sharp turns of phrase — style! — and even makes it clear that the bloodthirsty Saul who is after David is not all that far from the bloodthirsty David coming after her husband Stupid, whom she clearly points out very early on is a complete fool — a dolt — and that she is available to leave her husband and become David's woman-slave, one of David's purchased wives to grow his amen-lasting empire through children.)

And David said to Abigail,
"Blessed be YAHWEH — Ancient Israel's ELOHIM/divinity — who brings me to my knees in abundance and who sent you today to call me out, to greet me —
and blessed is your perception — (essentially, your sound perception brings me to my knees into abundance) —
and blessed are you — (you bring me to my knees...) —
because you held me back today from (fuck) bringing about bloodshed —
and rescued my hand/penis from myself —
surely, (I swear by) YAHWEH's life — Ancient Israel's ELOHIM/divinity — who restrained me from doing bad to you because if you hadn't hurried up and (fuck) come to call me out, to greet me, there'd be nothing left for Stupid — by morning's light — not even a single (male) person pissing on the piss-wall!"

And David took from her hand/phallic-control what she had (fuck) brought for him,
and to her he said,
"Climb up in health and peace to your house/family —
see...I've heard the tone of your voice —
and I forgiven you, I've lifted your face."

(And most likely that's exactly what David did, lifted her from the ground where she had been bowing down at his feet/balls.)

And Abigail (fuck) went to Stupid —
and listen here —
for him there was a feast with wine in his house —
a feast with wine like one given for a king —
and Stupid's <u>heart</u> was good within him (he was having a good time)
and he was drunk — very much so —
and she didn't tell him anything of the style — (of what she'd styled out to David) — nothing small or big — until the morning's light.

And so it was —
in the morning <u>the wine had gone out of Stupid</u>
and she told him — his wife did — of these stylings-on (with David)
and his <u>heart</u> died within him
and he became like a stone.

And so it was —
after about ten days that YAHWEH defeated Stupid — struck him down like a plague — and he died.

(So David's swearing comes to pass...what is Stupid's will be gone when he gets up for his morning piss on the wall...when the wine goes out of him...and just the words of what his wife said were enough to stop his heart.

In just a few chapters we've had a foolish king squatting his balls to his feet to relieve himself in a cave even his own army did not secure and a rich, greedy, stupid fool having his final morning piss on the wall....

David swears that all that belongs to Stupid will be gone. And what exactly was Stupid's? Especially when his wife gives over a large sum of wealth to try to appease the angry David who received nothing from Stupid. Again, we see a toying with Abigail's name...she seems to be leaning away from Patriarchy's-Joy toward Patriarchy's-Revolution...especially in that she gives away her family's wealth...when by ancient standards she has no claim on any of the wealth or inheritance even if her husband were to die. It is quite revolutionary in what Abigail did in loading all this food/wealth and handing it over — with her phallic-power — to David.

This is the revolution that the prophetic-circles assume — that women and men and nonbinary bordercrossers have equal value and equal share in everything, including and especially power, in the hand/phallic-power that gives and takes, receives and offers. This is what the band of YAH does in Genesis and the band of X does in 1 & 2 Samuel — assumes that this revolution in values is apparent, the way it is and should be, no matter how much hierarch-lovers and patriarch-lovers argue against it.

And note the cleverness of the storycrafters weaving in all this information about Stupid's heart as the story plods on....)

And David heard that Stupid had died,
and he said,
"Blessed be YAHWEH — YAHWEH brings me to my knees in abundance —
who cased my case — grew my growing — defended me in the lawsuit —
I was being taunted — put myself (genitalia?) out there in

shame — by Stupid's hand/penis/phallic control —
through his slave It has held back a bad thing from happening
— and as for Stupid's badness, YAHWEH has returned it onto
(Stupid's) own head!"

(RB AHT RYB/'cased my case' though RB can also mean
'great' or 'grow.'

CHRPTI/'I was being taunted, I was being made to put my
genitalia out there'...*Strong's Exhaustive Concordance* notes
that CHRP can mean "to expose (as if by stripping)" and that
CHRPH can mean 'pudenda/genitalia.' And all of that at the
now stone-dead but once living-breathing Stupid and his also
dead YD/'hand, penis, phallic-control.')

And David sent for
and styled it out to Abigail — Patriarchy's-Joyful-Revolution —
to take her for himself as his wife.

And David's slaves (fuck) arrived to Abigail — Patriarchy's-
Joyful-Revolution — in the Vineyard,
and they styled it out for her,
"David — (the love-boiler) — sent us to you to take you for
him as a wife."

And she stood up tall
and bowed down <u>faces</u> to the ground
and said,
"Here is your woman-slave
to be a <u>child-bearing-woman-slave</u> —
to wash the <u>feet/balls</u> of my boss' slaves!"

And she hurried and stood up tall — Abigail-Patriarchy's-
Joyful-Revolution did —
and rode on a donkey — and five of her slave/girls walked
behind her <u>feet/ovaries</u> —

and she walked behind David's ambassadors —
and she became his wife.

And as for Ahinoam-My-Brother's-Delight...David took her
from the nearby town EL-Sows-Seeds —
and they were — the two of them — his wives.

And Saul had given his daughter Michal-Who-Is-ALL —
David's wife — to Slip-Out, Lion's son from Heaps, a non-
Israelite town.

(If David didn't marry Abigail, she would not be the inheritor
of her dead husband's estate — a male relative would, like her
first-born son if she had one. Perhaps her ancient strategy
all along was a wise one — and why she makes it clear that
she could be a valuable slave in David's harem. And it does
show David's honor in taking her in, albeit for his own
devices. And Abigail has proven her resourcefulness, her
power, her RGL/'feet' — which with her gender I guess could
mean 'ovaries' to David's RGL/'feet, testicles.' Note that five
slavegirls follow after Abigail and her feet/ovaries — perhaps
we're to read this as '*cojones*' for her style/gumption to stand
up to David with a bold request to spare her family's life.

And Ahinoam-My-Brother's-Delight...! That's quite a name
for a woman. And the verb-conjugations after this person's
name indicate that this person is indeed a woman. The name
could mean this woman is her-brother's-delight — tragic
incest. The name could also mean that this woman is named
for her brother's looks and attributes — delightful, beautiful,
pleasant. Um, strange. Whatever it is, her name comes from
the patriarchal system from which most of modern society
has emerged and has continued to support...the hierarchical
imagination. Or...it could mean that this woman with a name
referring to her brother is a genderbender. We'll have to see
how her/their character emerges in the ongoing saga.

And as for Saul giving Michal-Who-Is-ALL to another man

— this is not just some random other man...this is someone who is not under Saul's rule. Gallim — Heaps — is a non-Israelite town. Saul is doing this most certainly to signal that David has no place in his family anymore — and Saul is doing this to make an alliance with a foreign power, a royal foreign alliance, and apparently a wealthy or 'heaps'/abundant one too...all the while David is off marrying non-Israelite women too. Abigail is from Judah — not under Saul's rule. The chess match between David and Saul continues on, with David making a strong move of marriage and perhaps now land-ownership in Judah through marrying Abigail...if she has no male-inheritor or if David can chase them away.

Stay with the present system, even if enlightened by the most stylish poetry, and hierarchy and its bitter son patriarchy continue to rule — even when David does a seemingly good thing and is moved by Abigail's revolutionary style. Swim away from the shipwreck of the present system to the ecstatics-prophets on the mountaintops and something new can be born....)

chapter 26

And the people of the area where tar liquifies in the hot sun — the non-Israelite area just north of the Vineyard — (fuck) went to Saul at The-Hill (Saul's boyhood home and now home to Ancient Israel's royal-seat) saying,
"Is that not David there hiding on the dark hill facing the wasteland?"

And Saul stood up tall and went down to the wilderness where tar liquifies in the hot sun —
and with him were 3000 men/people — the choice-young men of Ancient Israel —
to seek out David in the wilderness where tar liquifies in the hot sun.

Ecstatic Prophets, Compulsive Fascists

(Most Bibles will have Ziph instead of 'the wilderness where tar liquifies in the hot sun'...but note the repetition of it in this same sentence, perhaps more as a scene-setter for the confrontation than for a geographic location, I suppose. Sounds like a place where one will need to be very careful, right? Where things could get hot — so hot that tar liquifies? Where the situation could become quite sticky — in too many ways....

And here we have the BCHURY(M) again, those 'choice-young-men' drafted into Saul's service as warriors and as whatever Saul likes, for his own royal/hierarchical purposes — these youngsters he brings with him to make David feel jealous and threatened in a number of ways.)

And Saul <u>bent over, camped</u> on the dark hill which was over there facing the wasteland by the road,
and David stayed in the wilderness,
and he saw that Saul (fuck) was coming after him into the wilderness,
and David sent the <u>ball-draggers/foot-soldiers/spies-who-risk-it</u> —
he <u>knew in every way</u> that Saul had (fuck) come <u>to, um, erect himself</u> (...to show his power, to establish himself against David).

And David stood himself up tall and (fuck) entered the place where he was bent over — camping there — Saul was!

(Yeah. It's important to catch the double-speak here, something that no translation I've encountered has yet noticed or wanted to notice.

CHNH/'bent over, encamped'...yup, it can mean either and most concordances note that.

The spies...MRGLYM...from RGL...the word that keeps returning through 1 Samuel and sometimes means 'feet' and sometimes means 'genitalia, balls, *cojones*' we would call them in slang Spanish. To be a 'spy'/MRGL would take some *cojones*/RGL for sure — you'd have to put your 'balls'/RGL out there. Just like Abigail had done — she put her 'genitalia'/RGLH out there to save her family...stepped her feet/RGL up to the plate.

And of course we have our usual friends: YDAY/'to know in every way, often sexually' and BOAH/'to enter or arrive or bring, to fuck.'

And there's impotent King Saul trying 'to erect himself'/CUN again and again and again, brings the choice-young-men with him — 3000 of them! — hoping that that will get David to bend over and submit to the king's (im)potent power, especially in a land — Ancient Judah — he does not rule.

In just a few moments we'll see David is the potent one again, the top in the relationship to Saul's submissive-bottom...but David's potency pales in comparison to the power that the ecstatics-prophets know on the mountaintops of Ancient Israel and Ancient Palestine, all of it 'the Levant.' We see David going anywhere he pleases and surviving — he crosses borders and lives. But a prophet knows that there are no borders — they live among 'enemy' and 'friend/citizen' alike... because a prophet knows that in YAHWEH's view there are no borders...the wind blows where it will...it doesn't stop at any border...and nor should anyone who knows the ecstatic-power of the wind....)

And David saw the place where he was <u>lying down (sometimes sexually, with someone)</u> there — Saul was! —
and his guy in-charge of his army — Abner-Patriarchy's-Lamplight, son of Lamplight —
and Saul was <u>lying down (sometimes sexually)</u> there in the circle, and the men/people having been bent over, camping, surrounding him.

(There appear to be nearly as many instances where SHCB/'lying down' actually means 'to sleep with as in sexually' in the Hebrew Bible than its other meanings: 'to sleep, to lie down as in death.' The clearer word YSHN/'to sleep' is not used here in the previous lines.

An ancient would wonder immediately what's happening here — and note the reference to Abner-Patriarchy's-Lamplight being with Saul in the middle of the circle with the 3000 choice-young-men, the army that Abner-Patriarchy's-Lamplight commands, over which he is in-charge. The whole story lampoons royal/hierarchical power, yes?)

And David responded and said to My-Brother-the-King — The-Terror (not the priest) — and to Abishai-Patriarchy-Yes — son of Crack-and-Leak, brother of YAHWEH-is-Patriarch — by saying,
"Who will go down with me to Saul, to the encampment, to those bent-over?"

And Abishai-Patriarchy-Yes said,
"I will! I'll go down with you!"

(A bit of comedy here...Abishai could certainly mean 'Patriarchy-Yes' as much as it could mean 'Yes-Daddy'...and here Abishai says "yes" to David, who in a military-pederastic society would indeed be a like a 'daddy' to Abishai. Ahem.)

And David (fuck) went — and Abishai-Patriarchy-Yes — to the people in the evening —
and listen here — Saul was lying down (sexually?) asleep —
in the circle —
and his spear stuck in the ground by his head
and Abner-Patriarchy's-Lamplight and the people lying down (sexually?) surrounding him.

And Abishai-Patriarchy-Yes said to David,
"Today ELOHIM/God-or-the-gods-and-goddesses have shut up your enemy into your hand/penis/phallic-control —
so now please let me strike-and-kill him with the spear —
into the earth —
one time — I won't need a second time for him!"

And David said to Abishai-Patriarchy-Yes,
"Do not destroy him —
who can send out his hand/penis on YAHWEH's *messiah*, Its specially-oil-smeared-leader and not get strikes — be clean and blameless?"

And David said,
"(I swear on) YAHWEH's life that if YAHWEH doesn't push him over (into disease/death) —
or his day (fuck) comes and he dies —
or he goes down into the fight and is scraped away —
far be it for me to pierce/sully the situation, how dare I send out my hand/penis onto YAHWEH's *messiah*, Its specially-oil-smeared-leader —
so now please take the spear by his head and the water-jug and let's walk away!"

(Note just before that Abishai-Patriarchy-Yes doesn't respond to David before David speaks again — an ancient storytelling tool/device to indicate that the hearer must be dumbfounded by the speaker's initial speech. And Abishai should be dumbfounded — how many rounds of Saul chasing and trying to kill David and his men/people have we been through now?!

A clever play on words here too — AHCNU conjugated from NCH/'strike down' said by Abishai-Patriarchy-Yes and NQH/'to be clean and blameless' said by David and punning on each other, both by sound and meaning...striking someone down vs. having no strikes against oneself...maybe punned well in the ancient world and, though differently, ours.)

And David took the spear and the water-jug by Saul's <u>head</u>,
and they walked away from them —
and no one saw anything —
and no one knew anything —
and no one was on watch, no one was awake —
because all of them were sleeping —
because a deep sleep of YAHWEH had fallen upon them.

And David <u>crossed over to the other side</u>
and stood at attention on the <u>head</u> of the hill,
a great distance of space between them.

    (YAYBR DOD HAYBR/'David crossed over to the other side'
    has AYBR/'bordercrosser'/'Hebrew' in that phrase twice.

    'Head'/RAHSH is used here in two very different ways. The
    first 'head' is Saul's — a pretty normal descriptor for where
    the spear is...near Saul's head. The second 'head' refers to the
    top of the mountain — kind of a strange use of 'head' here in
    that the band of X could simply say that David was 'on the hill'
    and hearers could perhaps assume he's at the top/head of the
    hill...perhaps foreshadowing in its allusion, these two 'heads'
    together....)

And David called out to the people
and to Abner-Patriarchy's-Lamplight — son of Lamplight
(Saul's general),
"Why don't you respond, Abner-Patriarchy's-Lamplight?"

And Abner-Patriarchy's-Lamplight responded and said,
"Who are you calling out to the king?"

And David said to Abner-Patriarchy's-Lamplight,
"Aren't you a man?!
Who is like you in Ancient Israel?!
Why didn't you protect your boss — the king?!

Because one of the people (fuck) went to destroy the king —
your boss!
It's no good — this style you're making — (this special way of
proceeding) —
(I swear by) YAHWEH's life that you all are sons of death
because you didn't protect your boss — YAHWEH's *messiah*,
Its specially-oil-smeared-leader —
and now look — where's the king's spear and the water-jug
that were by his head?"

And Saul perceived the tone in David's voice and said,
"Is that your voice — my son David?!"

And David said,
"It's my voice — my boss the king!"

And he said,
"What's this — my boss chasing after his slave?!
What did I do?
What in my hand/penis/phallic-control is bad?
Now my boss the king, please listen to the stylings-on of his
slave — me! —
if YAHWEH had pricked you up against me,
let It breathe in a sweet smell of a gift (an animal/wealth burned
up as a sacrifice into the breeze that would appease YAHWEH
and get YAHWEH to back down from pricking YAHWEH to
fight David through Saul)...
but if it's the children cursing themselves of the red-mud-
creature-like-Adam in front of YAHWEH's face then they
should drive me out as if they were divorcing me today from
scraping away any of YAHWEH's estate by saying
'Go, slave away for other ELOHIM/gods-and-goddesses!'
Now do not let my blood fall to the ground in front of
YAHWEH's face —
because Ancient Israel's king has come out to seek a single
flea as if he were chasing a partridge that calls out through the
mountains!"

(Another AHDM/'red-mud-creature-like-Adam' referencing 'any old common person' or perhaps the spy Anxious-Doeg but this time expanded to the 'sons/children' of 'red-mud-creature'...in the Eden Story 'red-mud-creature'/Adam has two sons and first son Cain kills the second son Abel...and then GRSH/'to drive out, as if divorcing' is the same verb used in Genesis 3.24 with YAHWEH driving out Adam and Woman, and again Genesis 4.14 with Cain being driven away after murdering his brother...could be coincidence or it could be a very intentional verb choice by the band of X to gloss the band of YAH's Eden Story. Let's consider that a bit later.

Note the other images tied up in each other with David's style:

David is making it clear that Saul is acting as if David is the offering, the sacrifice to be bled out and burned up for YAHWEH...when David could have again done the same to Saul, and right there in front of all of Saul's 3000 choice young men encircling him, supposedly protecting him, all those that David and Abishai-Patriarchy-Yes just stepped through to walk in and take Saul's weapon and water.

Note how David demeans Saul — a boss chasing after his slave, the one in power chasing the one owned. David uses an interesting verb: 'to prick up, stimulate'/SUT, very similar in sound to 'thornbushes'/SYT which, when pricked, bring about blood if one isn't careful.

The reference to 'partridge' or 'calling-bird'/QRAH is clever in that here is David 'calling out'/QRAH the king for chasing him through the mountains.)

And Saul said,
"I have sinned — made a serious offense —
return, my son David —
you see, I won't do bad things to you anymore —
I'm even more underneath —

my living-breathing-body was <u>precious-like-a-partridge</u> in your eyes today —
listen here — I've been <u>silly</u>, foolish —
I've gone astray — so very much so!"

(David referred to himself as a QRAH/'partridge' and Saul refers to himself as YQRH/'precious'...and it sounds like a conjugation of the verb QRAH/'to call out, to meet.' Saul styles back his understanding of the situation about who has the upper 'hand'...not to mention the whole 'underneath'/TCHT business. Perhaps not so 'silly'/SCL of Saul to style it out so!)

And David responded and said,
"Look here — the king's spear!
Make one of your slave/boys <u>cross over</u> and fetch it.
YAHWEH <u>returns it</u> to the man/person who lives right and who lives with trust enough to drive in one's tent-stakes (who makes a firm commitment in the open-country far away from the safety of cities) —
because today YAHWEH gave you into my hand/phallic-control but I wasn't willing to stretch out my hand/phallic-control onto YAHWEH's *messiah*, Its specially-oil-smeared-leader —
listen here — just as your living-breathing-body grew in my eyes (in value) today
then let my living-breathing-body grow in YAHWEH's eyes (value) —
let It strip-and-plunder me, deliver me, away from all trouble, all adversity!"

(This is a war of wits between David and Saul — and it's being played out in front of the future of Ancient Israel, the generals and the 3000 choice-young-men — not to mention all of David's misfit-army probably listening in not too far away. Just a few lines ago, Saul asks David to SHUB/'return'... and now David says it's YAHWEH who 'returns it or makes good on it'/SHUB...same verb. And there's that AYBR/'cross over' again...in this story told, likely anyway, among fellow AYBRYM/'bordercrossers, Hebrews.')

And Saul said to David,
"Blessed are you, my son David — be brought to your knees in abundance —
even more so
  the things you've done, done, done —
even more so
  the things you are able to do, able to do, able to do!"

And David went out onto the road, on his own way,
and Saul <u>returned</u> to his place.

(So Saul is the one who gets to 'return'/SHUB home...such are the benefits of being at the top of the pyramid of power. But such a perch has its costs — tremendous costs.

Saul's final words to David here waver — YCL can mean 'to be able to do' and that can go two ways, at least. YCL can mean 'to have power' but it can also mean 'to find the power, have the ability, be allowed to do something'...and surely the character Saul doubles it in that clever Hebrew style, tripled when I translate it. Saul allows David to carry on his way, the life of the road, on his own way, as long as David does not interfere with the king's life. Most translations make it sound like Saul softens every time David confronts him...but the verb-choices put into the character Saul's mouth demonstrate a style that is rather sharp, that points out his own hierarchical privilege as king.

And even though David has the moral upper-hand here and has demonstrated it in front of all the choice-young-men, Saul could have just as easily ordered his 3000 choice-young-men to storm David on that hill. Sure, Saul's men would've risked being ambushed by David's misfit-army...but we don't know how they'd match up with Saul's army with Saul at the helm. Maybe David has been using that same training with his men/people. Military-pederasty can firm up the strength of any army quickly, as scholars note it was probably the cause of Greece's strength, and perhaps too Ancient Israel's. Fight for your lover, that your love might live!

And, um, by the way, where's Jonathan been? Where's the guy who pledged his loyal-love to David, the love and affection boiler?)

chapter 27

And David said to his <u>heart</u>, to himself,
"Now I'm going to be scraped away one day by Saul's hand/phallic-control —
there's nothing better for me than to escape, escape, escape to safety
to the land of the Dust-Rolling-Philistines —
he is desperate for me — Saul is — to seek me out again, all and anywhere within Ancient Israel —
so I'll escape to safety from his hand/penis/phallic-control."

And David stood up tall
and crossed over — he did with his 600 men/people who were with him —
to Sure-There-Achish, son of Squeezed, king of the (Dust-Rolling-Philistine) city with the wine-press and their drunken concerts.

(More hilarity in the band of X's use of fictional-genealogy in that David goes again to Sure-There-Achish — a sure-thing in his mind?! — to be safe from Saul.

Recall that the last time David went to Achish, it was the furthest thing from a sure-thing! Achish thought David was a madman, because David had acted like one. And here now David goes to the only sure-thing, sure-safety, he can imagine, to the land of the enemy, to the one who thought him mad the last time.

And not only that, Sure-There-Achish's dad was 'Squeezed'/MAYC. And their city of GT/'winepress, and the concerts/parties that go with them' was ruled over by someone named Squeezed…just like the grapes that got squeezed and smushed to create the wine. Note that we didn't get this juicy detail about Squeezed earlier when we met Sure-There-Achish.)

And David <u>lived</u> with Sure-There-Achish in the city with the wine-press and their drunken concerts — he and his men/people — each man/person with his own house/family —
and David with his two wives Ahinoam-My-Brother's-Delight, the one from EL-Sows-Seeds, and Abigail/Patriarchy's-Joyful-Revolution, the one who was Stupid's wife, from the Vineyard.

And it was reported to Saul
that David had bolted to the (enemy, Dust-Rolling-Philistine) city with the wine-press and their drunken concerts,
and he no longer sought after him.

And David said to Sure-There-Achish,
"Please, if I've found favor in your eyes — charmed you enough to make you kneel down to me —
they should give me a place in one of the cities out in the open-country —
and I'll <u>live</u> there —
why should your slave — me! — <u>live</u> in the city of your royal-kingdom — with you (the king!)?!"

And Sure-There-Achish gave him that very day A-Pint-of-What's-Squeezed/Oppressed —
that's how A-Pint-of-What's-Squeezed/Oppressed came to be for the kings of Ancient Judah,
all the way to today (when the story was first told by the band of X, or their later editors).

(Now note, Israel's enemy King Sure-There-Achish allows David to YSHB/'to live' with him, first among his royal-court and then in his own city; Israel's King Saul would not allow David to SHUB/'to return'...these similar sounding verbs and their very similar sounding conjugations play well with this saga of juxtapositions.

What had David done off-camera to make Sure-There-Achish agree to take him in...when last time David sought refuge, Sure-There-Achish chastised his own guards for allowing David inside the city-gates and into the presence of his royal highness King Sure-There-Achish and David had to stumble away acting like a madman?

Whatever happened, Sure-There-Achish seems to find it all just fine now...and David sweet-talks him even more and asks for his own city far from the royal-capital — David asks for a city out in the open-country. Would Sure-There-Achish be able to keep an eye on David there — an eye to be sure David would not rally any more people to one day attack Sure-There-Achish and the Dust-Rolling-Philistine people?

Decisions within hierarchies are complicated, you see...one must watch one's level of the hierarchy...and one's back.

It's worth noting that 'A-Pint-of-What's-Squeezed/Oppressed' from TSUQ and Sure-There-Achish's father 'Squeezed'/MAYC derive from different verbs...and the band of X could be playing with this subtle differentiation as they craft their fiction...in that what's pressed for grapes and always in the Philistines' grasp is far better and more pleasing than what is oppressed and ends up in David's/Judah's hands....)

And so it was —
it had been a number of days that David had been living in the Dust-Rolling-Philistine's open-country —
a full year and four more new moons (months),

and David climbed up — and his men/people too —
and they <u>raided and stripped people of everything they had,</u>
<u>even their clothes</u> —
they did this to the people known for their bridge-building,
and they did this to the people who lived off by themselves by
the rocks,
and they did this to The-Laborers, second-cousins to Ancient
Israel —
you see, these were the people who had been inhabiting the
land forever as you (fuck) go to the wall, even as far as Ancient
Egypt (the land known as 'Suffering' to any Ancient Israelite).

('raided and stripped'/PSHT is very different from GLH/'to
strip oneself as if one's life depended on it, as an exile or
slave, often for inspection of value and often to make clear the
hierarchical relationship'...earlier in 1 Samuel, YAHWEH said
It GLH'd Itself before the prophets and Saul GLH'd himself
with the ecstatics-prophets as he chased after David and fell
into the ecstatic spell with the prophets. Among the prophets
and in relationship with YAHWEH, humans choose to strip
freely. But here, David is enforcing this on others — he and
his people PSHT/'raid and strip' these people with innocent-
sounding names — not so that they can experience ecstasy
through YAHWEH by 'self-stripping'/GLH. David is raiding
people and stripping them of clothes and wealth and all they
have to enrich himself and his people and eventually other
people to whom he'll give this wealth to secure his own power
in the present moment and in the future once Saul is dead.
There's a reason the ever-crafty David asked for his own city
— not to be a burden on his host but to continue building the
empire long before he receives the crown.)

And David struck the land — struck to kill (all these people
just mentioned) —
and he did not let a single <u>man or woman</u> live —
and he took the sheep and goats

and cattle
and donkeys
and camels
and the clothes (ancient signs of wealth/status)
and then returned
and (fuck) went back to Sure-There-Achish (his Philistine host).

And Sure-There-Achish said,
"No — you were not to go raiding and stripping people of their clothes today—"

And David said,
"—against the southern desert of Ancient Judah
and against the southern desert of May-EL-Have-Womblike-Compassion
and to Cain's-Kids (Israel's second-cousins)."

(This is exceedingly clever storytelling here. Sure-There-Achish says, "You all were not/AHL…" and immediately David responds with, "—against/AYL…and then to/AHL"….

What's so clever?

AHL before a verb negates a verb.

AYL or AHL before a noun is a preposition…'to' of different sorts.

They sound similar.

Most translators do not catch this and assume the AHL before an imperative verb inserted into the Sure-There-Achish character's mouth has to do with 'where'…but AHL is never used as 'where' in this way. Nowhere in the Hebrew Bible can I find a time where AHL means 'where.'

So what does all of this bring forth here, then? Essentially that David bulldozed Sure-There-Achish's question and rattled off the people he'd raided and stripped not only of their livelihoods but of their very lives — brought back their clothes to Sure-There-Achish as prizes for him — bulldozed immediately as Sure-There-Achish affirms that David should have done no such thing, at least not that day.

And this is a rarity so far with both AHYSH/'man' and AHSHH/'woman' mentioned explicitly. AHYSH/'man' can sometimes mean more generally 'someone' or 'person' as in speaking more broadly of someone without necessarily indicating gender — because the plural of AHYSH can include men and women. But here the band of X lays out very clearly about just how ruthless David is — he kills every AHYSH/'man' and AHSHH/'woman' — he kills everyone.)

And as for any man or woman, David had not let any of them live to (fuck) come to (Sure-There-Achish's) city of the winepresses and the drunken concerts (with David) saying (to himself),
"Otherwise they report on us (to Sure-There-Achish), saying, 'This is what David did!'

And this is how he was enacting his judgment all the days he was living in the Dust-Rolling-Philistines open-country.

And Sure-There-Achish drove in his tent-stake in trust with David, saying,
"Has he ever stunk it up, stunk it up, stunk it up with his people in Ancient Israel!
He will be mine — a slave — forever!"

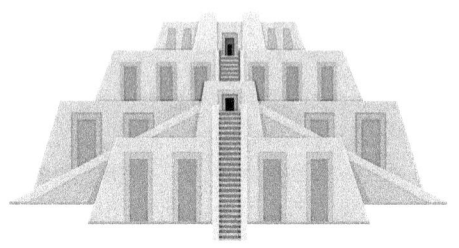

CHOOSE WELL!

Why do we keep perpetuating power-hungry fools as 'leaders'?

Because we never really grew up, moved on from our childhood and adolescence, the times in human life when we do indeed need adults to lead us into life...though less and less with every year we age (hopefully).

As adults we must be careful about whom we raise up to lead us — careful about people like Saul who is only interested in saving himself — even lets his enemy-nation attack his own people as long as he successfully hunts down and kills David first. But Saul can't even do that, even with 3000 choice-young-warriors at his side.

We need to be equally concerned with leaders like David — leaders who seem sweet and affectionate and love-boiling but really are genocidal and ruthless.

It's really incredible to me that people continue to celebrate David as a hero — when the first stories we have of him in the Bible present him as a genocidal, power-grabbing fool who has qualms — in the name of God — about killing the king who wants to kill him but zero qualms about enacting genocide on people who did not attack him. If he had just stayed on the mountain with Samuel...enraptured in ecstasy...free like the wind and with the wind...a true 'bordercrosser'/AYBR/'Hebrew'...but instead he chose his path and rallied men/people around him to begin the killings that won't end once he wears the crown currently on Saul's head. David offers no choices — he just takes and kills.

The prophets guided by their relationship with YAHWEH are far, far different from kings and royalists.

You see YAHWEH 'self-strips'/GLH for humans, and through

that example recommends we do the same, and thus the prophets take on that action as the core of their theology and life-philosophy...the prophets' action is a self-stripping and never a stripping others who do not want to be stripped.

AHDM...Doeg or Eden's Adam?

Is it indeed Doeg the Edomite — Anxious-Doeg of the Red-Mud people — who haunts this Samuel-saga? Or is it Eden's Adam?

A few times this AHDM/'red-mud-creature, Adam, or Red Mud/Edomite people' is referenced, sometimes surely as code for Anxious-Doeg the Edomite, the one who tells Saul that David had visited the priest who fed him and gave him Goliath's sword. But AHDM could mean more than that and could hearken back to Eden's Adam, the one whose sons do not see eye to eye, where one brother kills the other, even when he knows better.

In the 'pleasure-orchard' — Eden — YAHWEH blows life into Adam's mouth/nose and then 'ribs' Adam to make him a partner. This ribbing — what was it exactly? It's what happens to Jacob too in his wrestling match with YAHWEH. Sexy. And this partner — Woman — is to be Adam's NGD/'leader, front, talker' as David is to be a 'leader, commander, one out front who speaks things into action'/NGYD for Ancient Israel (1 Samuel 25.30). One eats forbidden fruit and Wisdom is born; the other raids people to kill and steal from them. Which would you follow?

Adam gets himself in trouble for his Woman's desire, for wanting to know just what that insight-inspiring, lusty fruit would do within herself. And so she eats and gives some to her Adam and he too eats — but he doesn't have to. He chooses it himself. And then they enfold themselves into each other and make love, know each other in all ways, hide within the embrace of the other and all's fine until YAHWEH calls out to them because It couldn't find them as It makes Its way through the 'pleasure-orchard'/Eden during the breezy time of the day. And once AHDM/Adam and Woman present themselves clothed in front of YAHWEH, It figures out that they now <u>know</u> — they had metaphorically devoured the fruit (each other) of the Sexy-Tree, the Knowing-Tree from which It had told them not to eat, to keep them innocent and child-like their whole lives, I guess. Recall that YDAY can mean 'have sex' as much as it means 'knowing.' Translators would be wise to make that clear in the story.

All YAHWEH wants, it seems, is to be lover/companion to Adam, to the mud-creature — but Adam makes love with Woman and that ticks YAHWEH off, this YAHWEH-character who creates Woman as an afterthought because Adam was lonely with only the animal-playmates and, we guess, lonely with YAHWEH, the wind alone.

But Mud-Creature-Adam and Woman eat, they know each other in their lovemaking, and once YAHWEH knows it too, It throws a hissy-fit and kicks them out of the pleasure-orchard. And their knowing produces children...fruit...where one day one brother kills the other brother in his jealousy for his brother being liked by YAHWEH more than himself.

And here in our Samuel-saga, Saul has been chasing after David to kill him, these two who have been entangled for years now, first in love and devotion, later in angst and jingles that haunt about one being better liked than the other. "Saul kills his thousand, David his millions."

It's curious, to say the least. These stories — of Eden and of the Samuel-saga — could be dancing together in the imaginations of ancient hearers, both stories fictional for sure, fictions told to awaken hearers to discern the forces that want us to remain children — hierarchically oriented — from the forces that invite our partnership and participation in life.

In life beyond these fictions, we humans — red-and-ruddy-blood-rich-mud-creatures — have equal access to YAHWEH, the force of life that slides into and out of each one of us. The Bible certainly hints at it playfully in little love-nibbles... though the real, live YAHWEH is the faithful lover, the faithful life-giver who enters into all and invites a deep-knowing from and with anyone who contemplates this life-giving force. Such contemplation can be ecstatic. Such lovemaking with ALL THAT IS can nudge you and me deep in the 'ribs', can make us 'limp' (both words TSLAY) because we've had such an ecstatic time with the life-force, with YAHWEH. Being with YAHWEH doesn't cost one one's life — being with YAHWEH gives life, in all Its abundance.

As children we needed strong leaders — parents, guardians, more, a whole village — to keep us alive and guide us in learning how to take care of ourselves, to stay alive, to keep breathing. We might have needed 'strong' images of God too — or at least we might have thought we did, thought those images someone taught us about from ancient centuries were better than our own unique ecstatic experiences as infant and toddler and child and teenager and on and on — experiences in the now, of the now.

What we did and had to do as children was one thing. But as mature and wise adults? It's up to us to choose what serves us best.

Demanding a leader over oneself often only asks for bigger problems...and Saul and David and the whole *messiah*-complex are dangerous proof of that.

chapter 28

And so it was in those days
that the Dust-Rolling-Philistines would gather together their armies
to go to war
to fight with Ancient Israel,
and (Philistine) Sure-There-Achish said to David,
"Know, know, know in every way
that with me you must go out to war with the army
you and your men/people."

And David said to Sure-There-Achish,
"For sure — you alone know in every way what your slave can
do — all that I've been doing...."

And Sure-There-Achish said to David,
"For sure — guardian of my head —
I've appointed you all these days!"

And Samuel had been dead —
they had torn out their hair and beat their breasts in mourning
for him — all of Ancient Israel had —
and they had buried him in The Heights, in his city.

And Saul had gotten rid of — beheaded — from the
land all <u>those who rattle and mumble and blow into the
empty wineskin-bottles to communicate with the dead-
grandparents</u> — and <u>those who know in all ways</u> —
and the Dust-Rolling-Philistines had been gathering
and had (fuck) arrived
and had encamped in <u>Resting-Place</u>...
and Saul was gathering up all of Ancient Israel
and had encamped at <u>Rushing-and-Gushing-Over</u>
and Saul <u>saw</u> the army of the Dust-Rolling-Philistines
and he <u>was afraid</u>

and his heart trembled — very much so!
And <u>Saul...They-Asked-For-It</u> <u>asked</u> YAHWEH —
and YAHWEH didn't respond —
not even in his dreams —
not even by the brilliant-*urim* (likely the priestly-Magic-Eight-Ball-future-telling-device) —
not even by the ecstatics, the prophets!

(More comedy and ancient Hebrew punnery...the similar sounding 'saw'/YRAH and 'to be afraid'/YRAH...immediately connected with SHAHUL/Saul and YSHAHL/'asked'...similar plays on seeing-fearing happen throughout this saga and in the Isaac/Laughingstock story of Genesis. Perhaps it's a prophetic trope. One would have to work very hard to craft stories where an audience would have to discern which of these two similar sounding verbs was intended — and rich-fun to have them so close together. Sometimes seeing <u>is</u> fearing...and perhaps here in the build-up to war happening in our story — and quite a complicated war...

Ancient Israel encamps at Gilboa/Rushing-and-Gushing-Over and they probably were all atwitter with nervous energy contemplating the always-fierce Philistines now enriched by David, their own countryman encamped with their enemy...

and...

Ancient Philistia encamps at Resting-Place all cool, calm, and collected.

Note that it seems that everyone is 'in the know'/YDAY about all matters — on this side of life or the next — except Saul. He's constantly trying to find out things that everyone else knows...and he's the King...the one who is supposed to know all things and what to do about them! This is how the band of X will constantly tease the kings of their fiction...even the love-boiling soon-to-be-King David will be teased by the ecstatic-prophets for what he thinks no one else but him knows... though the prophets seem to have ways to know that kings now and into the future will reach out to them for help. That's the entire point of 1 & 2 Samuel — that the non-hierarchical prophets are better leaders — more 'in the know' — than the kings and priests because the prophets know who is in charge, who controls all life...the wind...the life-force that is the wind and atmosphere...YAHWEH...over which no king has power and over which no priest has power...over which no one has power, not even someone in the throes of ecstasy.

Prophets know how YAHWEH flows.

Saul's banishment of all 'who know'/YDAYNYM would probably include the prophets, the ecstatics...)

And Saul said to his slaves,
"Seek out for me a woman — a master of rattling up the dead grandparents —
and I'll go to her —
I'll inquire of her."

And Saul's slaves said to him,
"There is a woman — a master of rattling up the dead grandparents —
in Fountain-of-the-Generations."

(This is the famous 'Endor' which literally means Fountain-of-the-Generations...the perfect place for the woman to call back the dead ancestors of generations gone by....

So the king-who-is-supposed-to-know-all is going to a medium to get some information about the upcoming battle. Most translations stop right there with 'medium'...but how the medium works is quite fun in the Ancient Hebrew as well...'rattle and and mumble and blow into the empty wineskin-bottles to communicate with the dead-grandparents'/AHBON...*Strong's Exhaustive Concordance* notes that AHBON of course has to do with 'fathers or parents'/AHB and also to do with 'wineskins'/AHOB and perhaps that a necromancer would rattle and blow on the wineskin and mumble the grandparents' names over and over again and call them back and then in a different voice speak like a ventriloquist into the bottle for the grandparent's voice...a special kind of trickery that is far different from the ways of the prophets, as we'll soon see. It should be noted too that the ancient understanding is that dead people who have lived a good life will have family/friends who will bury them in the ground/cave and join the dead in Sheol, on a bench in the ancient Hebrews' understanding of the underworld, for a long, eternal rest.

Saul seeks out a wineskin-rattler because he's afraid. And he should be. Saul can't even depend on his own son Jonathan.

Recall that Saul had pushed away Jonathan over his fears about Jonathan's relationship with David. And of course Saul can't depend on David, the only other living person from his own nation who has successfully taken on the Philistines. And where is David now? Living with the Philistines!

And twice now Saul can't depend on his own choice young men or generals who let him go into a cave by himself to take a shit without first inspecting the cave for the king...this same army who falls asleep around him without organizing a watch.

Saul has every reason to be afraid for his life.)

And Saul disguised himself
and dressed in other people's clothes
and went — he did and two of his men/people with him —
and they (fuck) went to the woman in the evening
and he said,
"Please <u>divine-the-future for me (make divinity speak to me)</u>

by conjuring the dead-grandparents —
climb up for me the one I say to you."

And the woman said to him,
"Listen here — you know in every way what Saul did —
that Saul cut off from the land those who rattle and mumble
and blow into the empty wineskin-bottles to communicate
with the dead-grandparents and those who know —
why would you entrap my living-breathing-body to murder me?!"

(Perhaps the woman already knows the poorly disguised
person in front of her is King Saul...?

Saul's request to 'divine-the-future'/QSM has been used before
in our Samuel-saga, in 1 Samuel 6 — and *Strong's Exhaustive
Concordance* notes that QSM often involves throwing dice or
reading from magical scrolls/books to 'divine-the-future'...but
here such divination involves a bottle/wineskin and tooting
into it to get the dead-ancestors to show up for insight in the
living-world.)

And he swore to her — Saul did — by YAHWEH,
"(I swear by) the life of YAHWEH
that no guilt or punishment will happen upon you
for this stylish thing (you're/we're doing)!"

(Um...does he control YAHWEH?)

And the woman said,
"Who is it I'm making climb up for you (from the underworld)?"

And he said,
"— Samuel — make him climb up for me (from the
underworld)!"

And the woman saw Samuel —
and she cried out in a big voice —
the woman said to Saul,
"Why did you hurl me to the heights — betray me —
you are Saul!"

And the king said to her,
"Do not fear — what did you see?"

(Samuel was from and was buried in RMH/The Heights...and
the woman accuses Saul of RMYTNY/'hurling to the heights,
betraying, deceiving' which derives from RMH...more clever
punnery, especially by this clever woman. It seems that King
Saul essentially outlaws anyone who is clever...maybe it's what
kings do until they need clever people for their own devices.

And note the punnery with 'be afraid'/TYRAHY and 'see'/
RAHYT again, these similar-sounding words sounding
sharper this time in the Ancient Hebrew with these particular
conjugations.)

And the woman said to Saul,
"— ELOHIM/God-or-the-gods-and-goddesses —
I see It/them climbing up out of the ground!"

And he said,
"What's its form — what's its appearance like?"
And she said,
"An old man is climbing up —
and he's wrapped himself with a robe!"

And Saul knew in every way that this person was Samuel,
and he shriveled in deference, bent his nostrils to the ground
and bowed down.

(MAYYL/'a robe' is the same word to describe what Samuel's

mom made for him way back when Samuel was apprenticing with the priest Eli. Remember that before the robe, Samuel was wearing the strangly-yarned-underwear-*ephod* that might embarrass him in front of his mother where is boyhood might fall out of his priestly-undies/*ephod*.)

And Samuel said to Saul,
"Why have you disturbed me —
to make me climb up (from the pleasant sleep of the underworld)?"

And <u>Saul</u> said,
"I'm all bound up — the distress of an adversary has come to me — very much so —
the Dust-Rolling-Philistines are fighting against me —
and the ELOHIM/God-or-the-gods-and-goddesses have turned away from me —
they don't respond to me anymore —
not even by the ecstatic-prophets' hand/penis/phallic-power and not even in dreams —
so I'm calling out to you —
to make me know what to do!"

And Samuel said (to <u>Saul...They-Asked</u>),
"Why are <u>you asking</u> me?!
YAHWEH has turned away from you
and become your opponent —
YAHWEH has done by Itself just as It styled out to into/onto my hand/penis/phallic-control —
YAHWEH tears the kingdom from your hand/penis/phallic-control
and gives it to your friend/neighbor, to David —
because you didn't listen to YAHWEH's voice
and you made Its face burn with anger about The-Laborers
so this style is being made for you — YAHWEH is making it — this very day:
YAHWEH will give — yes — Ancient Israel with you in it

over to the Dust-Rolling-Philistines' hand/penis/phallic-control —
and tomorrow you and your sons will be with me — yes —
(in death's underworld) —
and — yes — as for Ancient Israel's army — YAHWEH will
give it over to the Dust-Rolling-Philistines' hand/penis/
phallic-control!"

(Note the clever styles being played out in words and in plot...

Samuel plays on Saul's name/SHAHL when 'asking'/SHAHL
why Saul rouses him from his ancient sleep in death's
underworld...

and continues to drive the nail in deeper and deeper with his
words...

he refers to David as Saul's friend/neighbor — their
geographic homelands as neighbors — and all this recalls the
earlier relationship between Saul and David when David was
strumming Saul's strings to calm him down and the more
recent relationship where Saul is hunting down his 'friend'
David to kill him. Recall that Samuel saw that chasing-down-
David in action when David had run to The Heights to seek
safety with Samuel and Saul found David and tore off his own
clothes and writhed on the ground like the ecstatic-prophets
were known for doing...

and Samuel calls Saul back to another of his failures as king...
recall in 1 Samuel 15 that YAHWEH had told Saul to kill off
The-Laborers as pay-back for the The-Laborers having
attacked the Israelites when they were weak and on the road
running from Egypt, as the legend with Moses goes. The-
Laborers' leader Agag is a military-legend known for his
brutal ways. What does Saul do? Not only does he not kill off
all the people, he takes The-Laborers' wealth for himself and
lets Agag live. So what does Samuel do? He kills Agag right

there — something neither this saga's Israelite ring of royalty — king, generals, court — nor the Israelite-priests going back to legendary Moses would or could do. The prophet-loving band of X offers a dig at both parties — priests and royals — they are teasing with their fictional 1 & 2 Samuel.

Now back to Saul's terror at hearing he and his sons will be dead tomorrow and his greatest fear coming soon to fruition — David being handed his kingdom!)

And Saul became like liquid and fast —
he fell to the ground after standing at his full height —
he was afraid — very much so — from Samuel's stylings-on,
and there was no strength/power within him —
you see, he hadn't eaten any <u>bread</u> all day or all night.

And the woman (fuck) came to Saul
and saw that he was <u>shaking, terrified</u> — very much so —
and said to him,
"Look here — your successful-childbearing-slave — me —
listened to your voice (obeyed what you said earlier, at the risk to my life and livelihood) —
I've put my living-breathing-body into your <u>palms</u> —
I listened to the style that you styled out to me —
and now please listen — even you! (the king!) — to your successful-childbearing-woman-slave's voice —
let me put in front of your face/presence a piece of <u>bread</u> —
and eat —
and then you'll have the strength/power within you —
because you're going out onto the road, on your way."

(This woman has every reason to be terrified of the king who is terrified inside her home. First, he outlawed her profession. Second, he arrived and asked for Samuel to be summoned and got horrible news. Third, her summoning Samuel actually worked — maybe it does, maybe it doesn't usually, with her act of mumbling and blowing into empty wineskin-bottles. Fourth, if the king were to die here in her home, it would certainly not go well for her, even with the king's bodyguards as witnesses. And as much as she bows in deference to him by proclaiming herself his slave — and one who has borne children before and therefore considered valuable in the ancient world — she also toys with him in her double-edged style. The use of 'palms'/CP here is interesting and perhaps a way to clarify and move out of the double-entendre of 'hands, penis'/YD...but YD can also mean 'power' as in 'phallic power.' And she makes it clear that he — the king everyone asked for — has no CCH/'firmness, power, strength' within himself. Here sits the king on her floor with no potency, no potential, no future. He became like liquid at the news and toppled over. Tomorrow he will be dead, and his sons with him. His family and lineage will be no more. This is the greatest nightmare for any ancient person — for one's line to be cut off due to something shameful.

Did Saul need Samuel to confirm this? Not really. He knows what he is up against — not only the Philistines but the Philistines now with his arch-rival David at their side.

It is quite clever, in my opinion, that the woman wants to put 'bread'/LCHM — the same Hebrew consonants as 'fight, war'/ LCHM — in front of the king...Samuel confirmed Saul would die in the 'fight'/LCHM and she puts 'bread'/LCHM in front of him to try to revive him enough to get him out of her house. And this 'bread' vs. 'fighting/war' thing has been a theme in this 1 Samuel epic...David comes from Bethlehem...BT-LCHM...'the house of feast or fight'...and David has certainly been that for Saul. David has been food/sustenance and fear/ war for Saul. And David will be that for Ancient Israel too in his kingship — gift and threat/danger — as any hierarch, royal or priestly, is that. The whole system of hierarchy is the problem — whether it's religion or government, though especially royal/dictator government. That's the band of X's point, their whole point of crafting this fiction to reveal the problematic roots of their nation's fascist beginnings, just like their neighboring countries' fascist beginnings. What is the antidote? The circular nature of the prophets, the ecstatics living in the out-of-the-way places like mountaintops, who have life in the wind as their king, YAHWEH as king...it's much, much different from the path Ancient Israel has chosen with a human-king, and one as failed as Saul. Very much so.

'shaking, terrified'/NBHL recalls the earlier story of NBL/'Stupid' who also became like stone....)

And (Saul) refused and said,
"I will not eat."

And they burst out on him — urged him — his slaves did
and the woman did again —
and he listened to their voices
and stood up tall from the ground
and sat on the bed.

And the woman had a nearly grown calf — a stall-fed one
(valuable) — in the house
and she became like liquid and hurried to butcher it in the
sacrificial way of ceremonial meals,
and she took flour and kneaded it and baked unleavened
cakes — the kind that are made quickly and are sweet
because yeast hasn't soured them over time —
and she drew closer to Saul's face and his slaves' faces,
and they ate,
and they stood up tall,
and they left that night.

(Notice how the band of X juxtaposes the king's MHR/'to become like liquid running out, to hurry' with the woman's MHR. He stiffens up and does nothing, falls flat on his face; she moves into action.

And now back to the frontlines of the war...the 'armies'/MCHNH... those 'who bend over, who bend down'/CHNH...which we should keep in mind every time 'army' is mentioned...perhaps just one more way the band of X teases the ridiculousness of war, of trying to edge someone out, of determining who lives and who dies — that's YAHWEH's job, right?!)

chapter 29

And the Dust-Rolling-Philistines had gathered all of their armies at the fortress, the stronghold (probably in their own territory —
and Ancient Israel was encamped at the fountain, which is where EL-sows-seeds, Israel's own territory as well).

And the Dust-Rolling-Philistines' city-bosses <u>bordercrossed</u> by the hundreds and by the thousands —
and David and his men/people <u>bordercrossed</u> after them with Sure-There-Achish.

And those in-charge of the Dust-Rolling-Philistines said, "What's with these <u>Bordercrossers</u>?"

(These particular 'Bordercrossers' are of course David's men/people. The Ancient Hebrew style here never gets translated into English with such style...the triple-repetition of AYBRYM/'bordercross(ers).' Most translations will tell you the first two AYBRYM are 'crossing the border' or 'crossing the river into' or 'passing by/through' — all good translations for AYBRYM. But then most translators take the third AYBRYM here as 'Hebrews' — and then miss the meaning of who the Ancient Hebrews apparently were...people who passed through, who crossed borders and rivers that were borders, who didn't stay in one place for very long, either to find a fresh patch of grass for their animals — as in Abraham and Sarah's family situations — or to seek a fresh horizon from which to be found ecstatically by YAHWEH, the breeze. Maybe any decent Ancient Hebrew person was after both...fresh grass for animals and fresh horizons for inspiration...and never nailed in their tent-stakes — amen! — for long. The most ancient Hebrew people — perhaps the prophets, the ecstatics — were a people on the move, on adventure, always with a clever word... but here we have a story in 1 Samuel of a people beginning to nail themselves to a ground, to the earth, through demanding a human-king Saul and then soon human-king David and thus denying the wind-king YAHWEH on whose whims one's adventures must depend for life and limb...not the roofbeams of one's permanent house.

Makes me wonder too how the so-called father of the AYBRYM-people is Abraham/AHBRHM...these two ancient words sounded quite alike...another cleverness by the band of YAH whose Genesis stories offer one explanation for the origins of the prophets-ecstatics...a cleverness that all too often gets covered over by most modern translations. Scholars are beginning to think that the Abraham-Sarah stories are much later stories than many of the others in Genesis — perhaps later generations longing for their roots in wandering, bordercrossing, and crafting stories in that vein. In the band of X's saga, the prophets are people on the move, living on mountaintops at one point and in sheep-hovels at others and in their own home in The Heights at others.

In any case, here the Philistines are revealed to be bordercrossing just like The Bordercrossers — the Hebrews/HAYBRYM. This is quite intentional — there are plenty of other words the band of X could've chosen to describe how the Philistine armies were gathering and lining up or mustering for battle. And now those in-charge of the Philistines notice that one of their own — Sure-There-Achish — has David and a herd of disgruntled Hebrews traveling with him, with the Philistine army...a potential ambush against the Philistines. All the while Sure-There-Achish thinks David will protect him in battle.)

And Sure-There-Achish said to those in-charge of the Dust-
Rolling-Philistines,
"Is this not David — the slave of Saul, king of Ancient Israel —
who has been with me — has it been days or years? —
and I haven't found in him anything (untrustworthy)
since the days he fell in with me all the way to this day!"

And they burst out at him with rage
— those in-charge of the Dust-Rolling-Philistines did —
and they said to him
— those in-charge of the Dust-Rolling-Philistines did —
"Make this guy go back —
make him go back to the place that you mustered up for him —
he's not going down with us to the fight —
he could become for us an attacker/satan in the fight —
in that this one could make himself pleasing to his boss to
satisfy a debt — if not with the heads of those men/people
(Ancient Israel's generals) —
is this not David — the one they answer one another in their
songs and circle-dances, saying
'Saul kills his thousand,
and David his many, many, many...millions!'?!"

And Sure-There-Achish called out to David and said to him,
"(I swear that) as YAHWEH lives,
a straight-shooter you've been and good in my eyes —
your going out and (fuck) coming back to me —
with the army —
I haven't found any bad in you
since the day you (fuck) came to me all the way to today —
but in the eyes of the city-bosses you are not good —
now, go back —
go in peace —
do not make bad in the eyes of the Dust-Rolling-Philistines'
city-bosses!"

And David said to Sure-There-Achish,
"But what have I done?!

And what have you found in your slave — me! —
from the day I've been with you all the way to today
that I can't (fuck) go and <u>fight</u> with the enemies of — you —
my boss, the king?"

(There's LCHM again...'war, battle, fight' and 'bread, feast'....
seems it's all in David's pedigree, eh? David's home-city...BT-
LCHM...the House-of-Feast-or-Fight.

PQD/'mustered up, visited, missed, appointed' is that weird
verb with so many diverse meanings...and often used it
seems to beg the responder to clarify their purpose and
relationship to the one who is PQD...for instance, the city-
bosses demanding that David leave also seems to be saying to
Sure-There-Achish, 'Is David equal to you that you give him a
city and visit him there, or does he serve you?')

And Sure-There-Achish answered and said to David,
"I know in every way that you are good —
in my eyes like an ambassador of ELOHIM/God-or-the-
gods-and-goddesses —
for sure though, those who are in-charge of the Dust-
Rolling-Philistines have said,
'He is not to <u>climb</u> up with us to the fight!'
So now — rise early in the morning —
and the slaves of <u>your</u> boss who've (fuck) come with you —
and make yourselves arise early in the morning —
light for you all —
and you all go!"

(Not so punny here with the underlined words but very clear
that maybe even Sure-There-Achish is having his doubts
about David now that his superiors have sounded the warning
bell about David and his men/people and his/their allegiance
in a battle with his/their own countrypeople back home. The

Philistine leaders tell Sure-There-Achish that David will not 'go down'/YRD with them into the battle; Sure-There-Achish reports to David that he cannot 'climb up'/AYLH with them into the battle...perhaps to disguise the plan of attack? Or are the leaders hiding from Sure-There-Achish what the plans are and Sure-There-Achish reveals the plans to David? Sure-There-Achish tells David that he and <u>his boss' people</u> must wake up early the next morning and leave...as if they are not really David's own people...clarifying that either he/ Sure-There-Achish himself or Saul — David's true boss in the hierarchy of Ancient Israel — is in-charge of David, the runaway asylum-seeker. How sides change so quickly once fights break out, when one has to get one's daily <u>bread</u> through <u>fighting/violence</u>....)

And David arose early — he and his men/people —
to leave in the morning,
to return to the land of the Dust-Rolling-Philistines,
and the Dust-Rolling-Philistines climbed up to EL-sows-seeds
(Ancient Israel's territory where Saul and his army has
gathered).

chapter 30

And so it was —

when David and his men/people (fuck) arrived to A-Pint-of-
What's-Squeezed/Oppressed (the city Sure-There-Achish
had given David), it had been three days since The-Laborers
had raided and stripped people of everything they had, even
their clothes, in the southern desert and A-Pint-of-What's-
Squeezed/Oppressed —
they had struck (David's city) A-Pint-of-What's-Squeezed/
Oppressed and burned it with fire,
and they'd taken captive the women who were in (the city) —

Ecstatic Prophets, Compulsive Fascists

from small to big —
they didn't murder a single man/person —
they drove them onward,
and they went on their way.

And David and his men/people (fuck) entered the city —
listen here — it was burning with fire —
and their wives and their sons and their daughters had been
driven away.

And David and the people/nation who were with him raised
their voices
and wept until they had within themselves no more <u>strength/
power</u> to weep.

(This is the same 'strength, power'/CCH that had run out of
Saul after 'dead'-Samuel had told Saul that he and his sons
would be dead the next day.

Recall The-Laborers...the people David had raided and
stripped them of their clothes and left everyone dead — at
least he thought so. But fight like that and it all comes back
around in not so nice ways.

And notice who was nowhere near the place when The-
Laborers invaded...David and his military men/people, his
mafia-like unit. None of them! Very poor strategy by David!
Remember earlier in 1 Samuel 25 he left behind a unit to
protect the gear/valuables? But not here....

And note 'the people/nation'/HAYM with David now...no
longer just AHNSHYM/'men/people.' They've become a
<u>nation</u>?! This could indicate a different storycrafter from the
band of X offering this tale, or possibly the same storycrafter
trying to make a particular point...maybe of not-yet-king
David making blunders with his 'nation' even before becoming
king?)

And David's two wives had been driven away —
Ahinoam-My-Brother's-Delight from EL-Sows-Seeds (where
the Dust-Rolling-Philistines happen to be encamped for battle)
and Patriarchy's-Joyful-Revolution, Stupid's wife, the one
from the Vineyard.

And David was <u>distressed — felt pressed in</u> — very much so —
because the nation/people was talking about burying him by
throwing stones at him —
because the living-breathing-body of every single man/
person of the entire nation/people was bitter —
all because of their sons and their daughters —
and David firmed himself with YAHWEH, his ELOHIM/divinity.

> (Note the juxtaposition of David's distress and Saul's distress.
> David feeling 'distressed, pressed in'/YTSR recalls the name
> of the Philistine city where he lives and that was just ransacked
> by The-Laborers...the city of Ziklag/A-Pint-of-What's-
> Squeezed/Oppressed...different forms of being pressed and
> oppressed...contrasted with what Saul was feeling about his
> own coming demise.
>
> David is distressed because the wives and children are gone
> — perhaps that he failed to leave behind a force to protect the
> city — and that his growing nation is ready to kill him; Saul is
> distressed because he and his sons will likely die, something
> he must have known in his gut long before he conjured 'dead'-
> Samuel to pay him a visit.)

And David said to Abiathar-My-Patriarchy-Remains — the
priest, the son of Ahimelech-My-Brother-the-King,
"Come closer to me with the straggly-yarned-underwear (the
ephod that priests' underlings wear with the 'yes-rock' and
'no-rock' inside)!"

And Abiathar-My-Patriarchy-Remains came closer to David
with the priestly straggly-yarned-underwear-*ephod*.

And David <u>asked</u> of YAHWEH, saying,
"I'm going to chase after this <u>troop</u> (of robbers) —
will I reach them?"

And It said,
"Chase! Because you'll reach, reach, reach
and snatch away, snatch away, snatch away!"

And David went — he and 600 men/people with him —
and (fuck) got as far as the Cheerful-News stream
(in the land of the Dust-Roller-Philistines, just south of one of
their strong cities),
and remaining behind, some stood there at attention.

So (really) David and 400 men/people were doing the chasing,
and 200 men/people were standing at attention because they
were too exhausted and faint to <u>cross over/bordercross</u> the
Cheerful-News stream.

(Note how translating NCHL BSOR as 'Cheerful-News stream'
conveys a heck of a lot more than 'Brook of Besor' as it is
usually translated...and that David's men/nation/people are
not as battle-ready as perhaps he had hoped, especially with
the extra weight of wondering if their families were still alive.

Mentioning that 200 of David's army were too tired to
AYBR/'cross over, bordercross' would probably elicit
laughter from anyone who knows well the true rigors of the
bordercrossing, shepherding, wandering lifestyle. After all,
this army was just about to go into battle before being sent
home by Sure-There-Achish!

GDOD/'troop, crowd' has David's name within it DOD/'love-
boiler.')

And they found a <u>Suffering-person</u> in the open-country,
and took him to David
and gave him <u>bread</u>,
and he ate,
and they let him drink some water,
and they gave him a slice of pressed fig-cake
and two bunches of raisins,
and he ate,
and <u>his wind-breath-spirit-perception</u> came back to him —
you see, he hadn't eaten <u>bread</u> and he hadn't had any water to drink
for three days and for three nights.

(Bread or fighting again…LCHM. Even a 'Suffering-person'/
AHYSH MTSRY — usually translated 'an Egyptian man' —
has life in the RUCH/'wind-breath-spirit-perception' — not
just Hebrews/bordercrossers. And as we'll soon discover, he's
not just any Suffering-person, he's a slave!)

And David said to him,
"Whose are you?
And where are you from?"

And Suffering-slave/boy said,
"I'm a slave/boy — a Suffering one —
I'm a slave to one of The-Laborers —
my boss left me behind
because I got weak and sick three days ago —
we raided and stripped people of everything they had,
even their clothes —
we did (I was involved) — the southern area run by They-
Who-Cut-People-Down,
(and we ransacked) the areas run by Ancient Judah and the
southern area of the Big Dog —
and as for A-Pint-of-What's-Squeezed/Oppressed (David's
city in Ancient Dust-Rolling-Philistia), we burned it with fire."

And David said to him,
"Will you take me down to this troop?"

And he said to him,
"Swear to me
by ELOHIM/God-or-the-the-gods-and-goddesses
that you won't murder me
and that you won't shut me up into my boss' hand/phallic
power
and I'll take you to this troop."

And he took him down — and listen here —
they were spread out all over the land eating and drinking
and celebrating as if it were a festival
with all that had been plundered — great amounts! —
from the land of the Dust-Rolling-Philistines and the land of
Ancient Judah.

And David struck them — killed them — from dusk until the
evening of the next day —
and no one escaped from them —
not a single man/person —
except 400 men/people (ha!) —
slave/boys who rode away on camels and fled.

And David snatched away all that The-Laborers had taken —
and as for his two wives, David snatched them away too.

(Ummm...are you catching just how much the band of X is
lampooning David here?! No one escaped — unless you
count the 400 who did. Perhaps X is teasing the ridiculous
assumptions of the ancient world — that slaves/boys did not
count as people. Or perhaps we could see something into
this as if that were the deal with the slaveboy who led David to
The-Laborers...'I can lead you to my bosses and then you let
all the other slaveboys go.' But that's not quite how X tells the
story. Cutting, in a number of ways.

Remember, David had the chance to stay with Samuel and the ecstatics on the mountaintop — the only place he was truly safe from Saul — but instead he chose this life of the bandit who raids nearby peoples to increase his power and wealth. He pledged allegiance to the enemies of the king of his home-country and lives with these enemies, who left his family and those of the people he protects and has his wealth and family stolen right out from under him, who chases after those who stole from him and can't seem to round them all up, even 400 of them riding off on camels.

The game of bandits never stops...it outlives generations... until someone wanders away to a marginal space like a mountaintop, meets ecstatics, joins them in their ecstasy, and then chooses to <u>stay</u>.

Remember, the band of X's fiction here is the story of those who have a choice between hierarchical-human-power and the circular-ecstatic-power inspired by the wind, YAHWEH.)

And nothing of theirs was missing —
from small to great,
to sons and daughters,
from all that had been plundered,
all that had been taken from them —
all of it — David brought it all back.

And David took all the other sheep and cattle that they had driven to face the livestock (the livestock that was David's and his people's),
and they said,
"This is David's plunder!"

And David (fuck) went to the 200 men/people who had been too exhausted and faint to follow after David and had stayed by the Cheerful-News stream.

And they had gone out to call out to David
and to call out to the nation/people who were with him,
and David got closer to the nation/people and <u>asked</u> them for
peace.

And they responded — all the bad and worthless men/
people from among the people who'd gone with David —
and they said,
"Because they didn't go with us, nothing will be given to
them from the plunder
which we snatched away
except each man/person can have his wife and children and
drive them on and leave!"

And David said,
"No — don't do this — my brothers —
with all that YAHWEH has given us —
It protected us —
It gave the troop who (fuck) came up against us right into our
hands/phallic-control —
who will listen to you all in this style
because...
the reward for the ones who went down into the fight
(is to be the same as) as the reward for the ones who stayed
with the gear —
they are united, they all get the reward!'"

And so it was —
from that day forward —
it was so made —
(those words became) a statue/inscription and a judgement/
decree
for Ancient Israel
all the way to this day.

And David (fuck) entered into A-Pint-of-What's-Squeezed/
Oppressed (David's city in Ancient Dust-Rolling-Philistia),
and he sent some of the plunder to the elders of Ancient

Judah, to his <u>friends/neighbors</u>, saying
"This here is for you —
a blessing, something to bring you onto your knees into abundance —
from the plunder of YAHWEH's enemies!"

to those in Divinity's-House,
and to those in Southern-Heights,
and to those in Leave-Jutting-Out,
and to those in Naked-Junipers,
and to those in Bare-and-Sticking-Out,
and to those in Hear-Me-Out,
and to those in Travel-for-Trading,
and to those in the cities of May-EL-Have-Womblike-Compassion,
and to those in the cities of Cain's-Kids,
and to those in Devoted-to-Destruction,
and to those in Smoking-Pit,
and to those in Lodging,
and to those in Enchanting-Allies,
and to all the places there where he'd gone about there —
David and his men/people.

(As we've seen recently, David is now an enterprise, not just a single person. When we hear 'David' in the story, it's always 'David and his men/people'...the nation/tribe he's building.

And as for this list of 'friends/neighbors'/RAYH(M)...the same word 'dead'-Samuel used to describe what David was to Saul... and here it's quite a list of David's RAYHM...and a long one not usually in the style of the band of X unless they're trying to make a very clear point...hmmm...David offers gifts to all of these friends/neighbors from what had fallen into his hands by raiding and ransacking The-Laborers...and to whom exactly did he offer them and why? To peoples north, south, east, and west...and judging by the names of some of these towns, they might have been short on resources, out on the edge of life... and some of them are big names — like Divinity-House/Bethel and Enchanting-Allies/Hebron...so David gifts them all with the motivation to secure their loyalty for his future kingship of Ancient Judah...and in his mind at least he'll have Judah, especially if Jonathan is not true to his word about handing his father's kingdom of Ancient Israel over to David after Saul dies...and by the way, where is Jonathan lately?

Is Jonathan making moves behind the scenes to secure the kingdom for himself? Is Jonathan mourning the necessary move of his beloved, love-boiling David? Is Jonathan missing all the affection he used to boil/lavish onto David? Has Jonathan simply given up on all the games between himself and David and Saul, the love-triangle gone very wrong? Has Saul done something to punish his son Jonathan that we just haven't heard about?

At least two of these cities/peoples receiving gifts were ones David had attacked earlier...May-EL-Have-Womblike-Compassion and Cain's-Kids — at least that's what he reports to Sure-There-Achish about where he had raided and plundered earlier on in 1 Samuel 27. Hmm....

And as for all these more recent raids and gifts to all of these cities...David must have received a vast amount of sheep and cattle to be able to give a decent portion to the people of each of these out-of-the-way cities...no sense in giving a pithy gift. We'll have to see if his strategy works toward his aim, his crown...just one person in the way of that....)

chapter 31

And the Dust-Rolling-Philistines had been fighting against Ancient Israel,
and Ancient Israel's men/people had fled from facing the Dust-Rolling-Philistines.

(Here's a good example of why it's important to note the meanings of the names...Ancient Israel's name of course means 'the nation taking its name from the guy who wrestled EL, got groped and penetrated and still won.' It's their national story, at some point related to the character Jacob's iconic-wandering life...Jacob wrestling his own demons and difficulties and bloodthirsty-brother and ELOHIM/YAHWEH and coming out on top. His story is pretty catchy and entertaining, likely told around campfires often enough that as soon as someone says 'Israel' people might flash with some glimmer of memory of that story, that identity as a bordercrosser who was penetrated by ELOHIM/YAHWEH and whom penetrated ELOHIM/YAHWEH back.

But here in the saga the band of X presents the Ancient Israelites as not having the courage to stand up against the Dust-Rollers — those whose only move is to roll in the dust and wail and mourn. You'd think dust-rolling people would be easy to defeat...and yet Israel runs from them.

The band of X does not shy from crafting a fictional story about the historically once-great nation of Ancient Israel being a bunch of foolish cowards...foolish for asking for this hierarchical arrangement of royal-monarchy and more often than not cowardly in defending that monarchy...where soldiers have run away to hide in each other's caves, making love with one another to soothe their fears. But why, we'd be wise to ask? Why tell tales like these...especially tales so stylistically clever and outright hilarious and — gulp — sickeningly tragic...?)

And (the Ancient Israelites) fell <u>pierced and penetrated and wounded and profaned</u> on the hill Rushing-and-Gushing-Over.

And the Dust-Rolling-Philistines kept getting closer to Saul and his sons —

and the Dust-Rolling-Philistines killed Jonathan
and My-Patriarch-Offers-(Me)-Freely
and My-King-Cries-for-Help-or-Riches
— Saul's sons.

And the fight against Saul grew very heavy, serious —
and the shooters found him — the men/people who shoot
arrows with their bows —
and he was pierced and penetrated and wounded and
profaned — very much so — by the shooters.

('Shooters'/MORYM is rather strange here in that the band
of X follows it up with literally AHNSHYM BQSHT/'people
of the bow' and followed by CHLL/'pierced and penetrated
and wounded and profaned' a second time. There are easier
ways to describe this, but maybe not quite as stylistically,
purposefully.

Well, the king and his sons are all down, wounded, maybe
dead. How about those names for Saul's sons?! We know of
Jonathan/YAHWEH's-Gift, of course. But where did these
other sons come from? This is the first we hear of them, and
their names lampoon Saul and his royally-motivated ways.)

And Saul said to the guy lifting his gear,
"Pull out your sword —
stab me with it —
otherwise these uncut-dicked guys (fuck) enter me —
stab me through —
and get saucy and thrust it into me—abuse me terribly!"

(Every verb here leans toward our English expression 'fuck
me up'...or worse...

BOAH/'enter, and sometimes fuck'
DQR/'stab'

AYLL/'abuse'...though *Strong's Exhaustive Concordance* notes it can also mean "be saucy to" and "defile" and "overdo"...and what follows AYLL in the text is BY/'in me, on me, about me' and not just simply 'me'...

and it's worth noting that Saul does not call these offenders 'Dust-Rollers' but AYRLYM/'having foreskins, uncircumcised, uncut' and *Strong's Exhaustive Concordance* notes the root has to do with 'to strip' and 'to go naked'...including a sense that a hearer of this Samual saga would likely not approve of these people, that being 'uncut' might have to do with having loose morals, not to mention loose skin around the heads of their penises.)

But the guy who lifted his gear would not do it —
you see, he <u>was afraid</u> — very much so.

And Saul took a sword
and fell onto it.

And the guy who lifted his gear <u>saw</u> that Saul was dead, had murdered himself,
and he also fell onto his sword and murdered himself with him.

('Seeing' and 'fearing' again in the same sentence and this time used with conjugations with the exact same letters...YRAH.)

And he died —
Saul and his three sons —
and the guy who lifted his gear —
and all his men/people —
that day all of them <u>united together</u>.

(Yikes. There's that word again that was just used to describe David's nation/people...YCHD/'to be united, together.' Is the band of X lampooning such a thing, such unity that ends in death? Group-think that gets anyone in the group killed, eventually? Or is the band of X at the very least juxtaposing the 'unity' under Saul — where everyone dies on a hill, their blood rushing and gushing out — versus the 'unity' under David where no one dies — at least not yet, though they seem far from united with their recent fights about who gets the plunder and who doesn't?

As we'll learn right here, not all of Saul's men/people died as some of them were on the other side having fled...portrayed here as a people not all that united at all.)

And the people of Ancient Israel —
  the ones on the other side of the valley —
  the ones who bordercrossed the Going-Down River —
  because (these) men/people of Ancient Israel had fled —
they saw/feared that Saul and his sons were dead, murdered,
and they abandoned the cities
and fled,

and the Dust-Rolling-Philistines (fuck) entered
and lived in them.

And so it was —
the next day —
and the Dust-Rolling-Philistines (fuck) entered/came to raid
and strip everything they had, even their clothes — those
who had been pierced and penetrated and wounded,
and they found Saul and his three sons having fallen on the
hill Rushing-and-Gushing-Over.

And they cut off his head
and raided and stripped his gear
and sent it throughout the surrounding land
of the Dust-Rolling-Philistines
to announce the cheerful news
in the houses of their god-figurines
and within the nation/people.

And they put his gear in ASHTAROTH's house —

and as for the <u>backside of his body</u>,
they <u>nailed-clammored-fucked</u> it
to the wall of Ease-House....

(...where most probably everybody could hear what was happening...the sounds of those nails being driven in...or the sounds of raping/abusing his dead body...securely nailed to the house's wall...

after all Saul had been trying to do something similar to David's living-breathing-body whenever the king was getting soothed by David...the violence Saul once attempted now come back to him...

here's BSR/'cheerful news' again, the name of the brook that divided David's men/people — and what a strange use of 'cheerful news' here — to announce the death of the king the people asked for!

GOYTO/'his body, his corpse'...and that word relates to GOH/'the backside'...

and the ever important conjugated word TQAYO from TQAY/YQAY that is from the same word that happened to Jacob, his being hammered by ELOHIM or YAHWEH in the Genesis stories, perhaps the most famous story of the origin of 'Israel,' the name Jacob earned by wrestling the divinity who nailed Itself into Jacob and on whom Jacob climbed and conquered and nailed It back...

I'll have more to say about this in a bit, but briefly juxtapose both stories involving TQAY/YQAY:

Jacob's alive-body being hammered/raped by ELOHIM/YAHWEH so that Jacob could give birth to the prophets through his son Joseph, the ever-dreaming, ever-protected-by-YAHWEH son of Jacob and his favorite wife Rachel

and Saul's dead-body being hammered/raped in Ease-House to become pleasure for foreign-warriors and fodder for the divinities of a foreign nation...what happens to unsuccessful royals, royals left unprotected by their own men/people.

As the saga goes, Saul had very limited success as a king — though one great success early on with 'those living in Jabesh-Gilead...the city of dry ground and heaped up stones'/YSHBY YBYSH GLAYD...this city of people playing a pivotal role in Saul's life early on and, as we'll see in a moment, after his death...

the band of X could have chosen any city to be the redeemers and they choose this one and with such playful, euphonic sounds...say it out loud, this city name...such style, even right after a tragic slaughter of a king, no less, and all of his sons...

and we'll soon hear that this city of people steps up and rescues Saul's dead-backside and his sons too, those royal-backsides nailed to the wall for all to see and then some, all the Dust-Rollers who had visited not to pay their respects to a dead head-of-state but to take their ease with the dead asses of the enemy-king and his enemy-sons.)

And when they had heard about it —
all the way to <u>those living in the city of dry ground and heaped up stones</u> (those people on the edges of Ancient Israel whom Saul had called all of Ancient Israel to defend because they had no one strong to step up and defend them) —

(when they'd heard) what the Dust-Rolling-Philistines had done to Saul,
they stood up tall — every man/person who was strong/in the military (!) —

and walked all night
and took the dead backside of Saul and the dead backsides of
his three sons from the <u>wall</u> (CHOMH, not the piss-wall) of
Ease-House,
and they (fuck) went back to the city with the dry ground
and burned them there
and took their bones
and buried them under an evergreen tree
in the city with the dry ground
and covered their mouths — fasted — seven days.

THE END
of 1 Samuel

(if indeed the Samuel-saga was intended to be two scrolls,
though it's one heck of a cliffhanger here!)

Ecstatic Prophets, Compulsive Fascists

The best cliffhanger ever?

It's quite a scene...who now will reign over Ancient Israel...? One of the best cliffhangers ever told!

The *messiah*/king Saul and his sons are dead and disgraced, publicly humiliated by the Dust-Rolling soldiers who had been licking their pride and their wounds ever since a very young teen had taken down their giant, their Stripper, their Goliath.

And the only person worthy of the throne — based on the circling women's jingle that now everyone including enemies sings — had been disgraced over and over again by the now-dead *messiah*/King Saul. And this love-boiling, Stripper-stripping David lives in the land of the enemy and raids neighboring peoples and secures by gift-giving his place among the near and far cities of Ancient Judah, the half-cousins of Ancient Israel. And this raider David is also a *messiah*, an oily-one, though not yet a full-fledged king. He has been allowing men/people to circle around him though, perhaps more like a mafia-boss than a king so far. Or perhaps like an old-style judge as we see in the book of Judges. Maybe kings and judges are essentially mafia-bosses, fascist-enacters, and perhaps must be that way systematically so. The whole book of Joshua about that single judge/general is one giant genocidal bloodbath proclaimed in the name of 'God' — at its heart, fascism.

Could another possibility after Saul's brutal death in this fictional story of 1 Samuel be that Ancient Israel's monarchy dies? Could it be possible that the people who asked-for-it wise up and realize that their desire for a king has gotten them into this Dust-Rolling mess in the first place? What would it be like if YAHWEH reigned (again)? if character-Samuel's very first public invitation — love YAHWEH alone! — realistically could be enough? Samuel defeated the attacking Dust-Rollers by calling on YAHWEH to defend Israel, and YAHWEH did, as the story goes. Later in the band of X's saga, the enemy attacks and Elisha calls on YAHWEH to blind the attackers and then he feeds them a meal and sends them home — and these well-fed-attackers never attack again, as the story goes.

The prophets are onto it — It — it seems, and in such style-rich ways, in their poems, in their parables, in their fictions stirring our guts to wonder, to live into new ways and new ways and new ways always — and often with some sense of internal-safety because we as hearers of the tales are laughing. Ecstatically. If the prophets-ecstatics had just put out a list of dictums about the way it 'should' be, I'd likely feel threatened — maybe you would too. But if I'm laughing at some story that invites me to wonder about life and power, well there's a good chance I'd feel less threatened and more willing to entertain new ideas and even co-create with the story and bring forth the story's wisdom in new ways for this moment. Stylish stories do such things.

And the style of the band of X's fiction here in 1 Samuel...? Whoah.

How many fucks...(?)(!)

For a nation taking its identity from the band of YAH's character Jacob-become-Israel, this whole business of dead Saul and his dead sons being nailed or hammered or fucked/raped by the enemy should invite us to pause — for many reasons. In *A Wildly Sensual YAHWEH*, the volume 0 prequel to this series, I took many pages to lay out the case as to TQAY/YQAY being a euphemism for 'fucked' in talking about the Jacob wrestling divinity story in Genesis 32. I won't rehash that here. Privately scholars with whom I've talked for many years have nodded with me in agreement, but rarely on paper.

Indeed, most of those Genesis stories from the band of YAH are extremely sexy — even if most translators refuse to go that way. But read it in the Ancient Hebrew and you'll come to notice that words like YDAY/'to know' and BOAH/'to come and go' do not mean only those banal possibilities in many of their Genesis or even greater biblical contexts. Mud-Creature/Adam does not YDAY the Woman/Eve as in YDAY/'know in terms of knowing some information' and then she suddenly has children from that 'knowing information.' Mud-Creature YDAY's Woman/Eve — he has sex with her. YDAY often means 'sex' — and much nicer sex than BOAH which leans a lot more toward 'fucked' and not nearly with the love and care that YDAY implies, even with the already overshadowing patriarchical-influences of the ancient Mediterranean world. SHCB/'lie down in sleep, possibly including sex' sounds more mutual, potentially loving. CHBAH might be the closest to 'lovemaking' we can get in Ancient Hebrew — what Mud-Creature/Adam and Woman/Eve do after they YDAY/'know'... after they eat from the Sexy-Tree, the Knowing-Tree. CHBAH, recall, is 'to make love by enfolding oneself within the other, hiding oneself within the other'...from CHBB/'to love, to cherish.'

Just as in the band of YAH's Genesis stories, 1 Samuel has all these 'lovemaking' and 'lying down, potentially for sex' and 'knowing someone completely with sex' and 'fucking/entering' — CHBAH, SHCB, YDAY, BOAH — and now finally at the conclusion of 1 Samuel TQAY/YQAY too.

In Genesis' band of YAH stories, Jacob gets TQAY'd/YQAY'd by whoever wrestles him — who turns out to be ELOHIM/YAHWEH. And then Jacob 'ribs, limps'/TSLAY afterwards — the same stylish-word that YAHWEH takes from Adam, his 'rib'/TSLAY, to build up into Woman/Eve after YAHWEH puts red-mud-ruddy-Adam/AHDM into a deep sleep. Ahem.

Our character Saul and his character-sons get TQAY'd but they don't 'rib/limp' afterwards — they are dead.

Maybe anyone who lives by the hierarchical imagination gets TQAY'd, be they royalists or followers of organized religion or of whatever system set up to put one person above another or below another.

Could it be that in these systems where some are valued as better or worse than others, that people rarely offer all they are and can be?

The ironies of Jabesh-Gilead...

As the Samuel-saga reminds, the 'dry ground' town Jabesh-Gilead gets attacked and seeks help. No one from their own town steps up — but a very young King Saul does. He rallies 300,000 men/people from Ancient Israel and 30,000 from Ancient Judah — but not a single person from Jabesh-Gilead, at least as we're told. Saul and all these men/people effect a huge slaughter on the oppressors and Jabesh-Gilead lives on — all the way to when Saul and his sons are killed. The people of Jabesh-Gilead come with their 'strong serving in the military'/CHYL and take Saul and sons' dead bodies down from the wall where they were 'nailed, fucked'/TQAY and bury them.

Jabesh-Gilead had people who were 'strong and served in the military'/CHYL? Where did they come from? Did they have these CHYL when young King Saul came to their rescue — these CHYL who did not then step up to defend their own town? Or did the old men of the town not want the young CHYL to sacrifice themselves to defend the town from the invading oppressors — so they demanded help from the new king instead? Or were the dry-withered ones just testing the monarchy, the new system of government they-asked-for? Or did these CHYL emerge as a result of Saul rescuing the town, on the need to defend the town in the future? Was the new generation inspired by what Saul and those 330,000 Israelites and Judeans had done for them so they stepped up and became CHYL?

It is curious how the band of X circles back around to towns and peoples in their saga....

Perhaps in this instance the band of X is telling us something about the system of monarchy...that it does not work. When forced to give your best people and land and food and wealth/ herds and choice young men and choice young women to the crown, perhaps people hold back. Even towns like Jabesh-Gilead — who only later does the decent thing and buries the dead, bloody, raped torsos of the King and his sons, this King who once rescued them.

Maybe people are more likely to offer their best in a system where all are equal and recognize each other as equals...where everyone must work together and offer their best for one another to survive, to thrive. Sounds like those actual highland-villages that were the early civilized Israel and the early civilized Judah, those 1200 BCE-and-later highland-villages that archaeologists Israel Finkelstein and Neil Asher Silberman and others uncovered. (See *The Bible Unearthed*, referenced often in *The Naked Path of Prophet vol 1*.) This same needing-to-work-together holds true for wanderers, bordercrossers, shepherds who must roam at the right time and shelter at the right time just to live — avoiding storms, bandits, empires who encroach on the freedom of the open-road, the open-countryside, where the wind blows perhaps more freely.

The band of X's stories do seem to play on the tensions between the freedom of the open-road and the stability of having a home...and so do the band of YAH's stories of the wandering characters we now call "patriarchs and matriarchs," those stories gathered into Genesis about the AYBRYM/'bordercrossers, Hebrews.' Home is where the heart is...if you have a heart that does not infect itself with a bad wind as the character Saul allowed to grow within himself as king/*messiah* and as the character Nabal/Stupid allowed to grow within himself through his greed. This 1 Samuel and its wild characters — and often hilarious plot — have much to awaken in us, yes?

1 & 2 Samuel's importance in the Bible & its cover-over

This 1 Samuel text might be the most important in the Bible — and yet few people pay it much mind. And it might be the most important text for our time in the 21st century, a century that looks like it will be a doozy for us and all those who come after us.

Besides Jesus' parables and wisdom sayings and besides Paul's letters insisting that the Law kills, 1 Samuel might be the only whole biblical text that purposefully stands up to the Torah/ Pentateuch and lampoons its 613 laws.

Instead of respecting what's there in 1 Samuel, what we've inherited, our forebears sought to cover it up.

How?

First by positioning this fiction as an early history of Israel and Judah.

Then by crafting 1 & 2 Chronicles to re-do the story, to sanitize it, to make David out to be a hero to be emulated, to rally a people behind him and this character's genocidal vision.

Then by attributing so many Psalms to the fictional David, to build up even more his so-imagined 'Godly' reputation.

Then when translating what was becoming the Hebrew Bible from Ancient Hebrew into the Greek Septuagint, choosing words that downplayed the ecstatic-prophets and their bawdy style both in 1 & 2 Samuel and in the band of YAH's stories in Genesis, and perhaps elsewhere too.

Then by continuing to listen to the 'David' that emerges out of Chronicles instead of reading — and reading slowly and carefully — the 'David' of the received Ancient Hebrew text of 1 & 2 Samuel. I argue that one needs to read 1 Samuel and most of the Hebrew Bible aloud, just as anyone studying the poems of prophets/ecstatics like the Isaiahs, Jeremiah, Amos, others. All these prophets'-ecstatics' poems, speeches, stories, things were spoken aloud first and only later — often much later — written down. Same goes for Jesus' wisdom sayings and parables, just as much as Paul's authentic/untampered letters which were first performed, not simply read.

Which offers more meaning...reading the lyrics to rap music or hearing those same lyrics performed by the artist?

Which offers more potency...a poet performing their poems or quietly reading the poet's words to oneself out of a book?

Most of the Bible was originally performative — most of Genesis, 1 & 2 Samuel, perhaps the Elijah/Elisha and prophetic-guild accounts in Kings, most of the prophets' poems, Jesus' (authentic) sayings and parables, Paul's (authentic) letters. Perhaps more.

Chronicling some problems with Chronicles

That whole Chronicles business is a major problem to the biblical tradition — though it accomplished precisely what its writers hoped to accomplish with it. Chronicles elevated the priestly imagination and suppressed the prophetic imagination.

Think I'm wrong?

Try this out with me. Compare 1 Samuel's ending — the story of Saul's death/rape — to the account in 1 Chronicles 10.

In Chronicles, the whole business of Saul's dead-backside is completely removed. Instead, it's Saul's head that is 'nailed'/ TQAY, not his ass/torso.

In Chronicles, there is no Ease-House and no Dust-Rolling-Philistines taking their ease on Saul's dead-ass. There is no mention, even, of ASHTAROTH but instead DAGON, a divinity that wasn't so sexy to the Chronicle-writers' people (Judah/Israel).

And not only that....

This is where the writer of Chronicles **begins** the story of Saul and David. Those 30 other 1 Samuel chapters of rip-roaring, wildly clever styles and raps and puns, laughter-inducing action and juxtaposition are nowhere to be found in Chronicles. There is no 'Samuel' except a mention in 1 Chronicles 6 that makes him out to be a historical character, fitting into a genealogy beginning with Adam, who is also apparently an historical character to the Chronicler. Mind you, there is no mention in that genealogy of Eve, that so-thought sinner who 'made' Adam eat from that Sexy-Tree (while he stood nearby and watched her eat first).

In 1 Chronicles 6, the character Samuel is identified as a Levite, a priest — not so in 1 Samuel with the wild story of him walking away from the whole priesthood thing once his boss Eli is dead and the ark is taken.

Although rarely used in the Torah — and not once in Leviticus — the Hebrew word NBYAH/'ecstatic, prophet' is used quite frequently in the priestly 1 & 2 Chronicles — but never with the bawdy and often hilarious style we see so often in 1 & 2 Samuel. It's a bit like the strategy in Acts of the Apostles, another account scholars now argue is pure fiction...Acts of the Apostles gives Paul some weak speeches and some stories for sure but has nothing of his letters' clever rhetoric and piercing questions. Why would the writer of Acts of the Apostles do that? So that Peter looks and sounds better than Paul. Chronicles seems to do this with the prophets, mentions them but erases their style. The prophets in 1 & 2 Chronicles are quite boring — nothing at all like the style-rich punsters of 1 Samuel or Amos or the Isaiahs or Jeremiah or the band of YAH.

The Chronicler-priests who crafted 1 & 2 Chronicles had every motivation in the world to dim down and write the prophets right out of the story — as do all those who continue to listen to priests and ministers and hierarchs in our organized religions and in our seminaries and universities due only to their office/pedestal — not their equal-share as humans.

Modern religion is built upon what the Chronicler did. And we continue to stomp down our prophets at the very least and sometimes kill them, write them out of life and even history... except for naming a street after them every now and then. But even then, the hierarchically minded choose how to tell the ecstatics'-prophets' story and soundbite their message, their style.

Just look at what Christianity did to Jesus and continues to do with this style-spitting ecstatic who seemed to love everyone...even prostitutes and tax collectors and sick and poor and enemies and children, who were not considered human or worth anything in the ancient world until puberty, marriageable age.

And note well, the religion inspired by Jesus is called Christianity — after *Christ/Messiah* — which I mentioned earlier has little to do with Jesus and too much to do with mafia-mentality that we can very easily see in the *messiahs/ christs* of 1 & 2 Samuel and 1 Kings with Solomon (at least).

Some early movements of what would become Christianity even linked Jesus with David by lineage, by genealogy — as if that were a compliment!

Anyone loving Jesus and knowing 1 & 2 Samuel well would not want Jesus linked in any way with David or with *christs/messiahs* of any sort. But someone identifying with a hierarchical mindset and knowing 1 & 2 Chronicles might. And did.

Anyone really knowing Jesus through his authentic sayings

and parables would recognize his wild imagination did not originate with him but with the earlier ecstatics...the band of YAH's parable-like tales in Genesis, the band of X's exceedingly stylish Samuel-saga, the wild and brave imaginations of Amos and the Isaiahs and Jeremiah and perhaps others with their performed poems and audacious actions in the midst of wildly challenging circumstances.

But most of us in the 21st century cannot discern that the band of YAH and the band of X and Amos and the Isaiahs and Jeremiah and Jesus and Paul were doing something very different from the royals and priests who crafted the tradition that became Judaism and then spun off Christianity and later Islam — not to mention all the forms of government that have emerged from those royal/priestly imaginations, all of them at their root most often hierarchically minded. These same governments often bolstered by these religions have been killing us humans for centuries, millennia even.

Democracy's more authentic roots...and the discernment needed to become democracy today

Let's not forget, the very first imaginer of democracy-without-slaves was Paul. And he seems to have been influenced in some way by the ecstatics on the mountaintops — fictional or not — who recognized each human as equal to any other human, even enemies it seems. Jesus seems to be deeply animated by the ecstatics too — "love your neighbor" and "love your enemy" — on top of all the shaman-like healings and respect for people on the lowest rungs of the hierarchy of his time.

Paul's system of democracy-without-slaves has rarely if ever been tried, except perhaps in those earliest circles of the Jesus-movement. But as we can glean from Paul's letters, it was pretty easy for those early communities to devolve back into hierarchical mindedness. Even the Founding Fathers of my own country's "democracy" — as bold as they were to break from the royal-system — had no problem with slaves and no problem with women having no voting powers. Paul frees slaves in his writing; Paul honors women having leadership roles. Those who did not like Paul's ideas covered them over. They wrote Acts of the Apostles and purposefully diminished Paul in it. They also added things into his letters that were the opposite of what Paul stood for. Check out *The Authentic Letters of Paul* — more than twenty years of research by four scholars.

We friends of the 21st century must begin to develop the tools of discernment that 1 Samuel invites of its first-hearers. David is juxtaposed with Saul, and both of them are juxtaposed with Samuel and the ways of all those misfit ecstatics running up and down the mountains and getting naked with YAHWEH's ecstasy in their shepherds' pens or anywhere they can. And all the while, styles are being styled out by these ecstasy-enriched characters — with women often having some of the more compelling styles. None of those styles can be found in Chronicles — and none of the compelling women either. Again, the priests who crafted Chronicles and the hierarchical religious-sensibility that comes from it wanted nothing to do with the stylish storycrafting that is 1 Samuel. And even millennia later, many are continuing to follow what these Chronicler-priests have done as if what they created was a good idea.

The style of 1 Samuel could make you and me wake up, realize that hierarchy is most often foolish and dangerous, and choose systems other than the hierarchical/priestly/royal/dictatorial/democracy-with-slaves-and-no-women examples we have so readily accepted for millennia.

The books of 1 & 2 Samuel are dangerous, positively dangerous to hierachically-minded systems. The books of 1 & 2 Samuel are absolutely necessary for our time and any time, and stirring within any careful hearer 2500+ years ago or today an imagination of possibility — through laughter, sweet shared laughter.

Dare we re-enter the land of 'sweetness'/TSUPH as our

character Samuel did when he came home and moved away from organized religion's cruelty. In the bordercrossing richness available within such sweetness, may we come to know more and more the ecstatic-life possible with the wind, the life-giver, YAHWEH....

If you and I want the killing to stop, then you and I must stop killing...

"Saul kills his thousand, David his many more...millions!"

In a candid interview after World War 2 (transcribed in *C.G. Jung Speaking*), psychoanalyst Carl Jung noted that everyone who was seeing him for analysis during and after the war was having renditions of the same dream/vision...one of terrible violence.

And everyone seemed to live out of it too: violent perpetrators, defenders against the violence who used violent tactics, and those who seemed to have no choice but to succumb to the violence.

But the roots, the first signs of this violent extremism, were evident long before Hitler assumed power and enacted decisions that eventually led to 75 million people's deaths all over the Earth, including 8 million Jewish-humans and homosexual-humans and Roma-humans, all the fellow humans Hitler and his followers attempted to completely eradicate.

And such signs of violent extremism are evident today too, aren't they? They seem to boil up within us in every generation...until we give ourselves to the winds that cool and comfort, to YAHWEH, to ecstasy that leads to life/love and lovemaking — not death/hate and fucking each other over. There are things lurking in the shadows each one of us casts... and we'd be wise to shine whatever light we can into those shadows, our own and our collective shadow...

see and hear and sense things as they are — different from deadly doublespeak — recognize how life is, note that life flows through us all and each and every one of us, and then live accordingly...if we are to exist for long with one another and on this living-breathing Earth. Elevate any one life above another and problems arise.

If you and I want the killing to stop, then you and I must stop killing. Look for other possibilities. Let go of our compulsion for death-dreams...in so many movies, sports, songs, video games, etc. Swim away from institutions still stuck on the death-dream and still wanting you and me to be good adults-acting-as-children who do not question, who stay in the places they have assigned you and me, who demand hierarchical arrangements, who demand we call them "Father" even when they are younger than us and less studied than us, even when Father and Sister and Brother kill.

Could it be that it was the *Christ*-myth that animated Nazi Germany?

Gott Mit Uns..."God With Us"...that's the phrase worn on the uniforms of Nazi Germany as they instigated the slaughter of 75 million people in World War 2 in the name of empire and in the name of the 'purity' they sought. How quickly they rallied other nations all over Earth into this death-dream....

The *Christ*-myth has animated many nations/principalities into doing horrible things for centuries, whether by slavery-built-economies or manifest-destiny-dreams or we-are-right-to-kill-at-war-visions. It's time we wake up and stop perpetuating such madnesses, such tragedies.

1 Samuel was a warning ignored, repeatedly

The text of 1 Samuel warns us against *Christs* of any sort — *Christ/Messiah* is what character-YAHWEH gives the people after they-ask-for-it, after they demand a king rule over them in the band of X's fiction. And do they ever get it. Not all that long after these characters boytoy around with each other, *Christ* Saul wants to kill *Christ* David, and David refuses to kill *Christ* Saul because 'Saul is a *Christ*' but David has no problem killing anyone and everyone else as he avoids Saul. As we discover in 2 Samuel, character-*Christ*-David will use his new power as king to unite two nations — Israel and Judah — and commit genocide through the region to grow his reach and power, and then he will use that royal-power to cover up his own rooftop-lust by killing the woman's husband who proves himself loyal to *Christ* David over and over again, in battle and off the battlefield.

And that whole *Christ*-myth was projected onto Jesus — though if we listen to what he says through his authentic parables and sayings, he rejects that *Christ*-myth at every turn. But Christians all too often ignore what Jesus authentically said and prefer instead the dangerous *christ*-shadow projected onto Jesus.

And following suit, Christians through the centuries will kill millions upon millions upon millions of people in the name of *Christ* Jesus. Christian-humans will kill Jewish-humans and Muslim-humans and Albigensian-humans and believing-humans and non-believing-humans — and Christian-humans will do it in the name of *Christ* Jesus and in the name of God...

never minding that Jesus advocated nonviolence and loving one's neighbors and loving one's enemies.

Let me be quick to say again that '*Christ*' is not 'Jesus.' The '*Christ*-myth' is much older than Jesus and was projected onto him after his death...and it stuck. Indeed, it was the '*Christ*-myth' that killed him — both at the hands of the religious authorities of his locale and the ruling empire's local authorities, these hierarchically minded people who wielded their power onto someone who threatened their system, their power.

And that extremely dangerous *Christ*-consciousness continues to be spread today with every "In the name of the Father, and of the Son, and of the Holy Spirit" that enacts the hierarchical imagination where one human is raised up as better than others.

The dangerous hierarchical system of '*Christ*' continues to be spread with every "Merry Christmas" and with every "*Christ* is the reason for the season," with every "christening" that resembles nothing of what wild-man John was doing dunking adults down below the surface of things, down into the shadowy-dark-and-dim waters to fight for one's living-breathing-body and then catch a whiff of YAHWEH just above the surface and live.

"Christ Saul kills his thousand, Christ David his many millions!"

This dangerous *Christ*-consciousness continues to be spread today without anyone thinking anything of it. Rarely do we even consider the hierarchical arrangements we've inherited. In my own Roman Catholicism we are asked — sometimes demanded — to call a priest "Father" in the spirit of this so-called *Christ*-consciousness. Talk about trying to maintain adults acting like children! Talk about forgetting the violence tied to *Christ* Saul and *Christ* David in 1 Samuel!

Some well respected and oft-wise teachers of my generation continue to use and spread and even name their whole system after *Christ* — they clearly have not researched the title or its deep shadow in 1 & 2 Samuel. When Paul called Jesus '*Christ*' he was slapping the Roman Empire in the face. Paul's *Christ* was a nobody from the middle-of-nowhere killed at the hands of empire/authorities — indeed by the very empire of Rome — but in Paul's view God looked favorably on this nobody who stood up to the forces of empire; God then raised up this nobody from death to life, as Paul imagines. Paul would've been wise to research the term *'messiah/christ'* — even with Paul's clever use of the title to make the Roman-emperor-god and its cult look foolish and impotent before the real God who rules the whole Earth, not just the ancient Mediterranean.

Christ America!

Today, when Christianity is the largest religion in the world, we 'Christians' are the empire all over again. Sadly. And all too often we've done horrible things with that empire/power in the name of our God...with "In God We Trust" as one of our mottos.

No matter who is President of the United States and no matter who 'controls' Congress and the Senate, the same number of bombs seem to be manufactured and dropped by drones onto humans every year, all of them paid by my tax dollars and done in my name and — if you are a US citizen — yours. And if not by bomb, then by training. The School of the Americas in Fort Benning/Fort Moore, Georgia has been training Central and South American citizens in such things as torture and terror, often to protect US corporate interests in those countries. The 'School' has gone by different names since then and its trainees have been implicated in killing hundreds upon hundreds upon hundreds of prophetic-people and the poor they have been trying to protect. The current name of the 'School' is Western Hemisphere Institute for Security Cooperation. If this is news to you, then perhaps you've been caught in the dangerous doublespeak....

"Saul kills his thousand, David his millions!"

Could the military-savior *Christ*-myth of *Christ* Saul and *Christ* David and *Christ* Solomon be animating and enlivening any of the death-dream in my own country? Read the Hebrew text or a decent translation of 1 & 2 Samuel and 1 Kings and you be the judge for yourself. What's even worse, in my opinion, is that many of us all too often miss that 1 & 2 Samuel and 1 Kings were first composed as <u>a warning</u> against *christs* and kings...and yet too many over the centuries have used the characters in those texts as figureheads for tyranny.

A similarly problematic hierarchical system is spread with Moses and his Torah, the 613 laws said to be handed down from 'God' to Moses and from Moses to his priests and judges and to every law-abider through the generations in three faith-traditions. It's a Law that has ensured the need to hire 'sacred-ministers' with 'God'-mandated fees/tithes for sacrifices or sacraments or sermons, no matter which religious tradition appeals to this Torah/Pentateuch/Law.

This five-book Torah is in the larger Bible assembled through centuries by royalists, and this Bible has ensured the need for royalists with taxes/thinking that most benefit the royal-ring and its head-royals whose heads roll if the royal-ring is not satisfied. Much of this Bible was written by and often used by priests and royalists — be they popes or kings or bishops or whoever benefitting from the hierarchical mindset — to make things like slavery and men-better-than-women seem like good ideas and 'God'-ordained ideas. But not 1 & 2 Samuel — these books challenge that dangerous default.

Much of the Bible and the whole *Christ*-myth are essentially fascist, hierarchical, pitting some against the other and ordaining that some are worthy and some are not and that 'God' recommends the 'worthy' suppress and even kill the 'unworthy.' Much of the history of the human-world has been guided by these problematic ideas and praxes.

The dangers of '*Christ*' continue to be spread with every Mass, with every sacrament and prayer service, with every effort to worship '*Christ*' and the image of God who supposedly sent '*Christ*' to die to save the whole world.

And none of this has anything to do with the Jesus of history.

The ideas of religious Law and *Christ* have cost us enough as a people.

In the spirit of the bands of YAH and X and Amos and the Isaiahs and Jeremiah and so many freedom-imaginers, Jesus seemed to be turning up-side down our human-penchant for wanting to give over our thinking and power to some other authority, whether that authority is priest or king or parent or whoever/whatever. Jesus told jarring stories like the parables to crack up our foolish assumptions about who is worthy and unworthy so that we all can realize instead the all-of-us-swimming-equally-in-the-divine that is the Infinite God, the reality that must include you and me and even the so-called 'unworthy' if it/It/God is indeed <u>infinite</u>.

Ecstatic-initiation on your terms...
far different from hierarchical/compulsive membership and "believing"

Like the ecstatics before him — including our fictional-character Samuel and the band of X who created the character Samuel — Jesus invited people of his day to an <u>experience</u>. A careful, contextual reading of his authentic parables and wisdom sayings today continues to offer such an experience. Few people today catch even a whiff of that experience because they so rarely study the ancient context of Jesus's time and what his words might have sounded like and meant in the Levant where he lived. Jesus wasn't speaking to people living in the United States or Central America or South America or Europe or Africa or Asia or...on and on and on. Jesus wasn't speaking to anyone living in the 21st century — not even in the Levant, his region.

There's nothing special about this experience to which Jesus and the ecstatics-prophets were referring — but your noticing

It is special. It's a whole initiation, though on your own terms, in your own unique way, at your own time, different with each awakening moment of noticing and appreciating and even loving It.

Which would you rather follow —

the wind/breath/YAHWEH that gives you life

or

the person who tells you how you should feel for God and how you should feel about God and what exactly you should believe and do about God and, rather compulsively, how often?

We must come to know the differences between self-determination and control if human-life is to survive on Earth. And it's/It's an experience that helps....

Say Its name out loud — YAHWEH. Get playful with It...YAHO, YAH-HOO...on and on in infinite ways. It gets us breathing, gets us knowing, lets us be known by It. Do you feel Its sexy voice in your nostrils? Do you sense Its style, Its rhythm?

Heck, say whatever you want and the sexy wind has Its way with you, enlivens you! Being alive and breathing is enough!

Compulsive people and institutions that kill and a wind that gives life...

which will you choose to lead you?

There is no greater love than this — to become potent and wise adults who sense and know and get curious about what we are sensing, to discover we have choices about what to do with the sensations that arise, to leave behind one's organized religions and hierarchical institutions and all the trappings that seek to prevent us from trusting one's own sensations. There is no greater love than this — than to notice and appreciate and love the One who gives you life, no matter by which name you call It.

Toddler wisdom, toddler problems

Near the beginning of this book I referenced watching the two year old squirming wildly in his family's arms until they strapped him in his stroller where he hollered...he and his whole family standing there on the train platform, the train approaching. Boy, did he holler and cry!

He of course didn't know that his parents/guardians were saving his life in that moment, preventing him from far more harm than being strapped into a stroller. As an adult he would see that, of course, he would see the train approaching, he would see the four-foot drop from the platform down to the tracks. As an adult looking back, he would no longer hold so tightly onto what seemed like the gruff treatment by his guardian-handlers at that particular moment, what he interpreted with his two-year-old self as a lack of care, as a reason possibly to distrust these guardians from that moment forward, to be suspicious, no matter how much love was later showered upon him. If he as an adult can even remember being two years old! But something within him remembers...and likely still lives out of it, out of that two-year-old's experiences, and that one-year-old's experiences before that train-platform experience, and that four-year-old's experiences after that...live out of it until he's done the hard inner-work that any adult must do probably daily to be an adult.

We all go through it as children, with whomever raised and reared us, ushered us into adulthood. We have some sense that our efforts at a self-determined life have been hindered even by loving parents/guardians or any adult-authorities who care deeply for us any time we are a child/adolescent. Sometimes then unknowingly we as adults enact such unhappy drama onto other adults, take away their self-determination. "It's what happened to me," something deep within whispers to oneself as we feel some strange satisfaction that it's no longer within just me, as we watch with a sick joy as someone squirms with even the tiniest bit of discomfort from something we said or did. It's the tragic game that erupts from us, manipulation as act and its linguistic doublespeak. It's murder and societal collapse by a million tiniest little pokes or glances, all of it happening within us and at one another...if we don't do our incredibly important inner work/play every day.

We can choose to see it, to feel it — what we as children interpret as affronts by these adults/parents — who 99% of the time — if we are extremely fortunate — cared so deeply for us and we knew it. But that one time on the train platform...and then that other time when I was ten and telling mom about this thing that was so important but she didn't pay me any attention while she worked so that we could eat or that time dad didn't help me when I asked — never mind he was already helping a sibling — or that time when, or that time when, or that time when.

Breathe in the life in the air. Pause. Let the wind do its wise thing...time...space.... Recall what truly sustains your being, my being. As an adult, note your choices, your possibilities. There are so many as adults, so many more we can invent as potent adults — far more than when we were toddlers. Take time to notice how you've used your potency, your power. Notice, have you provided room for other adults to make their own choices, to live their own self-determined lives? Notice, have you swum away from the shipwrecks of fascist/hierarchical systems that want to make you a child all over again and reduce your choices, who demand that you disregard what you sense with your own body?

This is the real work — actual and inner — required to save your life and mine, to guarantee that another generation knows something of what freedom can be, this shared and co-creating experience of self-determination.

What could we do with the big & little fascisms in all of us?

As I mentioned earlier, parenting is essentially a fascist enterprise — and it must be for the infant-toddler-child to live. A loving parent must make decisions for their child — and sometimes even coat them in "because God/I said so." But at some point, children begin taking on some responsibility for themselves. And parents and children must navigate this sharing in decision-making together and dance that difficult dance with each other especially through the teenage years. Parents will make mistakes for sure — it's the nature of life. Children and adolescents will interpret things as mistakes too — even innocent-seeming things like strapping a squirming toddler into a stroller for the child's own safety. It's the nature of life, complicated, complex. And no one of us is innocent. Even adorable and seemingly powerless little infants learn quickly how to manipulate too — one's innocence is rarely so innocent. We will get our way! Or if no one responds to our screams, we will cry ourselves to sleep dreaming up our not-so-innocent revenges to better get our way the next day.

It's best to bring these complicated and complex things out of the shadows so that they do not hinder one's own adult life and, even more so, so that these complexes are not projected by an adult onto other adults or one's own children or students or anyone we perceive to be smaller/less powerful than us. True even if we think we've moved away from hierarchical privilege, no?

This work is extremely complicated, as we all know well as children and as adults.

What is this work/play? What can we do?

Well, the best we can. You do what's yours to do; I do what's mine to do. With those efforts at doing the best we can, perhaps we can grow another generation of human life on the planet.

I recommend returning to the scene of the 'complex' — to when we were those 'innocent' infants and toddlers manipulating the heck out of our parents/guardians. Get back onto the floor if you can, or your bed if that's easier. Roll around like a child (Feldenkrais-style if you have to). Do only what's easy and delightful. Be led by your curiosity. Return yourself to such innocence — to the time of innocent joints and senses just coming alive, where we began building one's unique nervous system that would negotiate one's particular way on a gravity-rich planet...to roll and creep and crawl and climb and stand. Every move novel, different, important for making you who you are today, each move in your own unique way, each move listening within yourself for what's safe, delightful, pleasurable.

Return to innocence, to your child-like nature still alive in your adult body there on the floor or bed...return to the scene of the crime where you and I learned to manipulate — and fast — where you and I learned to get what we want, to make the bigger people give us what we want, when we want...when even so small we began our own fascist games.

Return to such innocent moves and innocent ways of being — now as adults — and discover a love for yourself that can grow love beyond yourself too. Make peace with your childish self... see all the wrongs done to you if you feel like you must, know these adults did their best for you, know that two of them gave you life, so take it. Rediscover more and more your child-like curiosity and the grandeur of the world. Delight in it as much as you can, let delight grow your potency as an adult. And before you know it there's a little distance between the fascisms you've inherited through institutions and the compulsions you've created that manipulate people in your life...a little room to realize you have choices, that you (and anyone) can respond with love, affection, clever nonviolence, jujitsu.

And then stand up from your ecstatic toddler-rolling...just stand...what do you feel? What might life on Earth then become for you, for adults, with an experience like this?

From rolling on the ground ecstatically
to worldwide renewal...

Each one of us can leave behind the manipulative games where we say one thing but mean another, leave behind taking away people's choices and instead provide space & hospitality where people freely discover they have choices and the time to choose well and delight in such potency...and such love.

In our Samuel-story, it worked for Saul when he was at his most bloodthirsty...

Samuel let Saul stumble into the shepherd-pen there with all the other ecstatics gathered...and ecstasy overcame Saul... and before Saul knew it he had removed his clothing too and rolled on the ground to get as much of the Earth and wind on his skin. Ecstasy has its ways — YAHWEH has Its ways of helping us know groundedness and lightness all in the same instant.

May we be so bold as to choose YDAY/'to know, in every way' and CHBB/'to love'...CHBAH/'to make love,' to realize the wind — YAHWEH — enfolding Itself around and inside each one of us. May we have the courage to leave behind our TQAY ways. There are plenty of times I fucked things up too, when I reduced fellow adults' choices, when I deterred them from their own self-determined lives. Wind and Earth can cool things, soften, soothe those old hurts we've done to each other for millennia. Let It.

...and be careful we don't fall into the ritualistic worship trap!

Perhaps, even out of gratitude for YAHWEH and It's ecstasy, you're tempted to ask for all the ways you should worship It, the special rituals, the special prayers, the teachings. <u>No.</u>

You and I might be tempted to want to follow the character Samuel or the version of YAHWEH in 1 Samuel or even the band of X who created both of these. <u>No.</u>

The book(s) of 1 & 2 Samuel was/were designed to loosen you and me from our foolish assumptions about 'the way it is,' or even worse 'the way it's supposed to be.' A parable does that — it unfurls within the hearer, the one who entertains the story. Some stylish-bit wafts this way, the story wafts that way, and before you know it we're up dancing in one's unique and unchoreographed style again and no longer bound to old assumptions that we inherited or concocted ourselves to survive in some way. Survival is not thriving.

The voice of YAHWEH in 1 Samuel is snarky, funny, and meant to be that way — perhaps as a contrast to the usually very serious voice of YAHWEH or ELOHIM in the priestly-minded Leviticus and the royalist-directed Deuteronomy. YAHWEH of 1 Samuel was not created by the band of X to be emulated and followed — It was created to get us laughing. Laughter nourishes our every cell with the breath of life. As any comedian worth their salt and light knows, laughter helps us to open the container, to open one's paradigm, one's imagination...to life in all Its abundance.

To entertain a story like 1 Samuel or Jesus' parables or any story really, we're invited to be a child again — but this time as a potent adult. Infants and toddlers know so little, it seems, and yet they hold the key to life, delighted by what seems to be the simplest of things...the way the sunlight and shadows move on the wall, the way a movement feels and the desire to get someplace new, the way something new to them tastes, the way a finger or a toe feels on a surface new to them, the way a family member hums a new note that's first noticed, the way the wind dances all over their skin, shares scents, shares secrets that often get ruined with adult words...except sometimes 'saved' by poetry.

Such foolish things, it seems, these simple, hum-drum, everyday experiences...and yet infants and toddlers often know more ecstasy than us adults with all of our bound-up and controlling ways that strangle and suffocate and sulk us down...fascisms that take us out of the moment, out of the grand opportunity of <u>experiencing</u> for oneself...the sensations that arise uniquely for each one of us...in the moment...in the span of a single breath...

until we too allow ourselves to be known again by the sun and the wind and Earth and the fellow creatures who walk and swim and fly the Earth, to be thrived by them all, to realize a bit more what they are doing to us and for us, each of them enlivening and knowing us with each inhale and exhale, with each delicious move, the free ecstasy in the air and in this life available to each one of us...

sensing for oneself and reflecting on those sensations gives birth to a new morality within oneself — a way that does not have us consulting someone else's ideas to determine what we are to do with our feelings/sensations and what we are to do in any particular situation.   Let the wind come to us, bring us what we need in the pause between inhale and exhale, between exhale and inhale.

The wisdom of those circling women singing that catchy jingle...

And then, after we pause, may we have the bravery to be those women in our Samuel-story who circle around and tell it like it is with that jingle that haunts Saul. It sounds like David is better than Saul...but what does that jingle really communicate? Both of these *messiahs/christs* are killers. Genocidally. And if we have our wits about us, we'll grow into potent adults who choose a different system than hierarchically minded government or hierarchically minded religion or hierarchically minded anything...

like these brave women of this saga circling around and styling it out

"Saul kills his thousand, David his many more...millions!"

we're invited to be the adults who call out such butchery, be the ecstatics-prophets who call for loving and nonviolent ways, be the adults who know there's something better, some enduring love underneath it all, some love/Love that can be trusted, that is dependable, reliable, that is life...

and circle around, tell it like it is and at the same time open one's heart and one's hands to the hierarchically minded so that they can join the circle freely, live self-determined lives that protect others' self-determination too, remind all that all are welcome and already in THE ALL, all already breathing in YAHWEH...that the world might be (re)new(ed)....

all and each of us doing nothing but delighting in ecstasy, in the moment with an exhale, an inhale, a dance of moving and resting all with one's own rhythm and choosing, simply, pleasurably, so easily — living with It as simply as that.

Ecstasy.

Conclusions so far
from *The Naked Path of Prophet* series, volumes 0 - 2:

> 1 & 2 Samuel was the rival to the 613 laws of the Torah/ Pentateuch (Genesis, Exodus, Leviticus, Numbers, Deuteronomy and perhaps at one time including Joshua and Judges).

> If we were to read only 1 & 2 Samuel's stories of the MSHYCH/ *messiah* (the Greek word for *messiah* is *christ*), the *messiah* is no one to emulate, at least from the viewpoint of the prophets-ecstatics...*christs/messiahs* are genocidal and power-hungry and disregard the wisdom and protection of prophets-ecstatics in 1 & 2 Samuel.

> The style in which 1 & 2 Samuel was written is similar to the band of YAH's stories in Genesis, style which the Levitical priests and perhaps Deuteronomist royalists/bureaucrats sought to dampen to protect their own power and privilege [see *A Wildly Sensual YAHWEH* for details on that].

> This style in 1 & 2 Samuel and the band of YAH's Genesis stories has been disregarded by scholars and translators for millennia...to our human detriment.

> The Bible includes competing philosophies, an insight that proponents of Judaism, Christianity, and Islam should consider before ever speaking in the name of 'God' again.

Calls to Action thus far:

> Evaluate one's religious tradition (scriptures, prayers, worship, instruction) for signs of fascism — of some authority

deciding what's right and wrong and clothing those decisions in God-talk — and decide for oneself if those signs are wise to continue forward in religious practice.

> Shine a light on the roots of *christ/messiah* that we find in 1 & 2 Samuel and wonder together if those ideas are what we really want to bring forward today.

> With the bloodthirsty, genocidal shadow of 'christ/messiah' evident in 1 & 2 Samuel, Christians would be wise to consider calling themselves 'Jesus-followers' and on their patron's birthday greet people with 'Merry Jesus Day!' instead of 'Merry Christmas!' This could help Jesus-followers to actually be interested in listening to Jesus' words and studying Jesus' actions instead of all too often projecting the *christ*-shadow onto Jesus and onto other human beings, a shadow that is terribly violent and having nothing to do with Jesus.

> Note times when you (or I) value some humans over others — is that wise, even for your own long-term livelihood?

> Note times when you (or I) attempt to control others (not including when the other is not of adult age or not capable of safely living a self-determined life on their own...both situations where we do the best we can to help someone grow their own self-determination as they are able).

> Note one's personal potency...how we have choices in how we respond to oppressors, oppressed, victims, instigators, and rescuers alike. Study clever nonviolent action to awaken oppressors and oppressed alike to the reality that ecstatic experience reveals.

> Remind one another often that we all share the one and same breeze for life — where cultivating an appreciation of the breeze might bring some clever nonviolent possibility to mind just when you or I need it/It most.

A Final Invitation

A friend who read a drafts of *The Naked Path of Prophet* (new edition) and *Ecstatic Prophets, Compulsive Fascists* suggested that a wise reader now go back to the beginning — in this volume, 1 Samuel 18 — and begin again. But this time read it through without the commentaries.

In the print edition especially, this should be easy to do as I have indented commentaries that I have inserted into the biblical translation.

Now that you have a 'lay of the land' of the Ancient Hebrew and some information about the context of the band of X's world, much of this context from scholars' archaeological research, perhaps you too will be inspired to sit and let the current moment catch you and awaken you — YAHWEH! — and style out something that helps all humans recall from which we've come — YAHWEH! — and with which we have our being — YAHWEH! — all of us sharing together this life and equally valued in the circular ways of the wise wind. It's more fun with friends. Come! Be welcomed here!

Resources for Further Discovery

Hebrew Alphabet - transliterated

It would be fair to say that my rendering below of the Hebrew (Aramaic) characters/sounds into English letters is far from perfect. I do hope it is useful, and easier than most renderings. Many Hebrew letters have multiple sounds, depending on if the letter is doubled or depending on the vowel with which it might be associated. I have let a lot of that go for simplicity's sake.

Although I disagree, it has been usually said/assumed that the Hebrew 'alphabet' (*aleph-bet*) itself has no vowels — they are assumed, in a sense. For clarity, between the 6th - 10th centuries CE, a group of biblical scholars called the Masoretes added vowels below the Hebrew consonants to clarify the sounds and even meanings of the written Hebrew language. In some ways, the Masoretes' work clarified meanings of Hebrew words; in some ways, the Masoretes' work flattened the meanings, especially of the ecstatic-prophets' poems and 1 & 2 Samuel — both of which rely on the pun-richness of the Ancient Hebrew language...the ways words expand and explode with multiple meanings and possibilities.

My very crude system of transliterating the Hebrew characters into English-sounds invites you to add any 'a' sound between consonants that you wish. And let gutturals be vowel-like. It's a system, in my mind anyway, that allows the words to be euphonic without the Masoretic markings that aim readers/hearers toward some kind of false precision which sometimes distract readers from hearing the potentials of the sounds from word to word. More of the puns become noticeable too, I think. But you must be the judge of that for yourself. As we well know, language is spoken differently as language flows from one community to another, from one time to another.

א	*aleph*	AH
ב	*bet*	B
ג	*gimmel*	G
ד	*dalet*	D
ה	*hey*	H
ו	*vav*	V or U or O
ז	*zayin*	Z
ח	*chet*	CH
ט	*tet*	T
י	*yod*	Y
כ/ך	*kaf*	K or hard C

ל	*lamed*	L
מ/ם	*mem*	M
נ/ן	*nun*	N
ס	*samech*	S
ע	*ayin*	AY
פ/ף	*pey*	P
צ/ץ	*tsade*	TS
ק	*qof*	Q
ר	*resh*	R
ש	*shin*	S/SH
ת	*tav*	T

My only hope with this simplified system of transliterating Ancient Hebrew sounds into English approximated-sounds is to encourage more people to study Ancient Hebrew...to dig deeply in the sandbox of language and understanding to discover our roots and to make better choices in our present moment.

Major Character Names

Abiathar...AHBYTAR...My-Patriarchy-Remains...AHBY = 'my father/patriarchy' and YTR = 'to be left over or jut out or to remain'

Abigail...AHBGYL...Patriarchy's-Joy <u>or</u> **Patriarchy's-Revolution** ...AHB = 'father/patriarchy' and GYL = 'to rejoice...often through circle-dance, revolution'

Abinadab...ABYNBD...My-Patriarch-Offers-(Me)-Freely...ABY = 'my patriarch(y)' and NBD = 'to offer freely, to volunteer for military service, to inspire someone to offer themselves freely for military service'...son of Saul, un-named until he is dead on the hill with his apparently older brother Jonathan and the rest of the family

Abishai...ABYSHY...Patriarchy-Yes...AHBY = 'my father/patriarchy' and SHY = 'yes, there he is, gift/present' (similar to the name 'Jesse,' David's father)— and Abishai could just as well be 'Yes-Daddy' — and he is son of **Zeruiah...ZRUYH...Crack-and-Leak** from TSRY, perhaps a kind of balsam, cracks under pressure — who is brother of **Joab...YOAHB...YAHWEH-is-Patriarch**

Achimelek...AHCHYMLK...My-Brother-the-King...ACHY = 'my brother' + MLK = 'king' — the name for two different characters in 1 Samuel....the priest from whom David gets bread & Goliath's sword and **the Hittite...CHTY...The-Terror**...from CHTT/'terror, to terrify,' the Canaanite who helps command David's ragamuffin forces of misfits running from their own nations/tribes

Achish...ACYSH...Sure-There...AC = 'sure, surely' and YSH = 'yes/there' (king of Gath, son of MAYOC/'squeezed')

Adriel the Meholathite...AYDRYAHL HMCHLTY...Weed-Eating-Flock-of-EL/God from the region where people did

their <u>circle-dances</u> in the grassy-meadow...AYDR(Y) = 'flock, herd; something that's missing, weeded' + EL = regional name for the chief divinity named 'EL' and often carried forward in Ancient Israel's priestly tradition as 'God'...as for Meholathite: MCHLH = 'meadow for circle-dancing'

Ahinoam...ACHYNAYM...My-Brother's-Delight...ACHY/'my brother' + NAYM/'delight, beauty, pleasantness'

David...DOD/DUD...'the one who boils over with affection and love'...DOD/'beloved, lover, uncle'...DUD literally means 'to boil over with affection, love'

Doeg the Edomite...DAHG HAHDMY...Anxious-Doeg of the the Red-Mud people...DAHG = 'to be anxious or fearful' and AHDM = 'red-mud-creature'/Adam's name in Genesis...if we use the Genesis lineages and J's stories, Edom is a nickname for Esau who gives his name to the branch of of the larger family of Israelites who take their family-identity through Esau and then Issac and then Abraham...AHDM = 'red-mud'

Gad...GD...Attack-by-Penetration...from GDD/'to invade, attack, penetrate, cut'

Goliath...GLYT...Stripper, as in the kind of stripping that happens when one nation conquers another and then forces exiles or slaves to strip themselves naked to humiliate them, to dehumanize them, to steal from them (from GLH 'to force someone to strip' or 'to denude someone')

Jesse of the House of Bethlehem...YSHY BYT-HLCHMY...Jesse-There-He-Is of the House of Feast-or-Fight...(from YSHY 'there (he) is' and BYT 'house' + LCHM(Y) 'bread, food, feast' or 'fight, war'...rather interesting, isn't it, that LCHM can mean both 'bread' and 'war'...but then again why are most revolutions fought but for access to bread, to the freedom to live...David's father

Malchishua...MLCY-SHUAY...My-King-Cries-for-Help-or-

Riches...MLCY = 'my king' and SHUAY = 'to cry for help...and can also rather strangely mean riches/wealth'...son of Saul, un-named until he is dead on the hill with his apparently older brother Jonathan and the rest of the family...quite ironically named considering the situation in which we first meet him!

Nabal...NBL...Stupid...NBL = 'fool, stupid, disgrace, wilt-away'

Palti...PLTY...Slip-Out...from PLT/'to slip out as a calve does at birth, to slip away as in escaping' (he's the son of Lion/LYSH)

Samuel...SHMUAHL...Named-For-EL...from SHM = 'name' & AHL = *EL* ... I often simply use 'the guy named for/after EL' throughout the text

Saul...SHAHUL...Asked-For...from SHAHL 'to ask'

his father:
  Kish...Set-a-Trap (from QOSH 'to set a trap, lay a snare')

his sons:
  Jonathan...Gift-of-YAHWEH (<u>YAH</u>WEH + NTN 'to give/gift')
  Ishvi...Equalizer (from SHVAH 'to level or make equal')
  Malkishua...My-King's-Wealth (from MLCY 'my king' +
    SHUA 'riches')

his daughters:
  Merab-From-Many (from M/'from' + RB 'much or many')
  Michal-Who-Is-ALL (from MY/'who' + CL/'all')

his wife:
  Ahinoam...My-Brother's-Delight (from ACHY 'my brother' + NAYM 'delight/pleasant')...curiously the same name as thew wife David marries as well

her father's family:
  Ahimaaz...My-Brother-Fastens (from ACHY 'my brother' + YTSH 'to shut or fasten')

his general:
Abner...Patriarchy's-Lamplight (from AHB 'father/patriarch(y)' + NYR 'lamp')

Abner's father:
Ner...Lamplight (from NYR 'lamp')...Saul's beloved (either uncle/relative or lover...most likely uncle though we are left wondering)

Abner's grandfather:
Abiel...EL's-My-Patriarchy (from AHBY 'father/patriarch(y)' + *EL*)

Yahweh/Lord...YHWH...YAHWEH...from the verb 'to be'...say 'yahweh' out loud a few times and what does it sound like? the breeze? one's breath? what any ancient and hopefully modern person knows sustains life...the air!

Ancient Israel (with Benjamin) & Ancient Judah

Israel...YSRAHL...nation named after the hero who wrestled EL, got groped and penetrated, and topped EL to win!...AHL = *EL* + SRH = 'to top/to be in charge' . . . literally, Israel means On-Top-of-God...I have chosen to draw it back to that primal story from J in Genesis which surely was on the mind of anyone who heard it, the story being so wild. And perhaps true to life. Breathe in and the air — yahweh — penetrates you and gives you your being, your life — yahweh.

Judah...YHUDH...'Judah, the tribe known for throwing up their hands/penises in praise' from YDH 'to throw' and YD 'hand' and such throwing one's hands was associated with prayer, exaltation...though as we well know, YD can also mean 'penis' and Genesis 38 certainly makes you wonder about which is meant, if not both at the same time

Benjamin...BNYMYN...'Benjamin, the small tribe known for its powerful children' from BN 'son/child' + YMYN 'right'...'right' in most ancient cultures (including this one) has to do with power or strength and 'left' being sinister or wrong or at least unexpected. Ironically, Benjamin was also one of the smallest tribal lands.

Often Named Cities/Places
in Ancient Israel & Ancient Judah

Aphek...AHPQ...fortress/stronghold...AHPQ = 'fortress, stronghold, contained/controlled place'

Bethel...Divinity's-House...from BYT 'house' + AHL = *EL/divinity*

Bethlehem...YSHY   BYT-HLCHM...House-of-Feast-or-Fight... BYT 'house' + LCHM rather interestingly can mean 'bread' or 'to feast' or 'to fight'...and knowing something of David and his brothers, that all sounds about right

Carmel (the town in Ancient Judah)...CRML...Vineyard...CRM = 'vineyard'...and as for the L at the end, it very well could have been AHL/EL as in ELOHIM at one point

(the forest of) Chereth...(YAYR) CHRT...the honeycomb-like forest that's so thick it looks engraved, carved up, and thus full of hiding spots...YAYR = '(honey)combed' and CHRT = 'to engrave' and Strong's Exhaustive Concordance notes that forms of CHRT resemble forms of CHRSH = 'forest-thicket or wood' (note that like many of the place names in this fiction of 1 Samuel, this place-name is used only once in the Bible...lending me and others to think that it's more of a descriptor and not a place name)

Emek of Elah...AYMQ AHLH...valley with the big drunk tree...from AYMQ 'valley' and AHLH 'terebinth'...a type of tree from which turpentine and strong drink / liquor were made throughout the Mediterranean world

Endor...AYYN   DOR...Fountain-of-the-Generations...AYYN = 'eye or spring or fountain' and DOR = 'generation(s) or age(s)'

En-Gedi...AYYN GDY...Spring-on-the-River-Bank-Where-the-Young-Goats-Gather...AYYN = 'eye or spring or fountain' and GDY from GDH 'river-bank' (note that GDY can mean 'young goat' as well...and that's the play here, especially when in the story it's laid right next to Zoray-HaYaylim)

Gallim...GLYM...Heaps...from GLL/'to roll...on and on and on'... kind of like 'amber waves of grain' echoes in USA imaginations today

Gibeah (of Benjamin)...The Hill (in Benjamin, the small tribe known for its powerful children)...earlier in *The Naked Path of Prophet vol 1*, Saul has the hill named for himself...**Saul's Hill**... from GBAYH literally 'hill'

Gilboa...GLBAY...Rushing-and-Gushing-Over...GL = 'heap up or rush out in waves' and BAY from BAYH = 'to gush over, to swell, to boil over with questions'

Hill of Chakilah...GBAYT HCHCYLH...dark hill...GBAYH = 'hill' (GBAYT is in the construct state, meaning it joins the next word, with the next word as the modifier) and CHCLYL = 'dark'

Jabesh-Gilead...the city of dry ground and heaped up stones ... from YBSH/'to dry up, wither' + GL/ 'a heap, rollable' + AYOD/'to repeat, do again

Jeshimon...HYSHYMON...the wasteland...the verb YSHM = 'to be desolate, to lie waste'

Jezreel...YZRAYAHL...EL-Sows-Seeds...ZRAY/'sow seed' + AHL/'EL'

Jordan River...YRDN...Going-Down-River...from YRD = 'to go down'

Keilah...QAYYLH...the Citadel (in Ancient Judah)...probably from QLAY = 'to carve' or 'to sling'...which to say perhaps this city/citadel was carved out of rock and perhaps it was from its height that things could be thrown down upon invaders

Maon...MAYON...where married ones reside together...from AYONH/'cohabitation/marriage (rights)'

Mizpah...the watch-tower...participle form of TSPH 'to spy' or 'to look out/watch'

Naioth, sometimes translated in Bibles not as a specific place but as **'the sheds'...the shepherds' pen, the awe-inspiring home of the ecstatics, which can be anywhere and everywhere for such wanderers, bordercrossers....**NUH = 'home,' especially of wanderers like shepherds with their animals and all the breathtaking sights of the mountains and valleys and rivers and all in such a home without walls, a home perhaps with a roof for protection...NBAH = 'ecstatic/prophet'...it puts the story of 'Jesus being born in a stable' in a new light, and the writer/creator of that story — the writer we call 'Matthew' though we don't know their name — knew that a child being born in a shepherds' pen who will one day be a master of style (the parable) would resonate with his prophet-respecting Pharisee audience

Nob...NB...Fruitful...NB/NOB = 'to be fruitful, flourishing'

Ramah...RMH...The Heights...from RMH 'the high places' or 'heights'...where Samuel was born and where he makes his home with the other ecstatics

Rocks of the Wild Goats...TSURY HYAYLYM...Rocky-Cliffs-of-the-Wild-Mountain-Goats...TSURY = 'rocky-cliffs' and HYAYLYM = 'wild/mountain goats' and note that YAYL = 'to gain profit/benefit' which one could do by capturing/taming a wild goat...ancient wealth is animals

Seku...SCU...that sharp-place where only thorns grow, where wild phenomena happen, where all can be observed it's so high...used only once in the Bible, it's likely not a place on the Earth but a place within oneself and any kind of journey... probably from SUC = 'thorny-hedge' and SCVY = 'phenomenal'

Sela Hammachleqoth...SLAY HMCHLQOT...Rocky-Cliff-That-Divides...SLAY = 'crag, rock-cliff' and HMCHQOT from CHLQ = 'to divide, make a deal'

Shunem...SHUNM...Resting-Place...String's Exhaustive Concordance notes that Shunem derives from an unused word having to do with 'resting quietly' — which plays nicely as a contrast with Gilboa in 1 Sam 28 in describing the two soon-to-battle encampments

Stone of Ezel...HAHBN HAHZL...the stone where things slip through and disappear...AHBN = 'stone' + AHZL = 'go, evaporate, disappear' + H = 'the' and 'of the' depending on its position in the sentence...for that matter, could be 'disappearing stone'

Wilderness of Maon...MDBR MAYON...wilderness where married creatures/humans reside together (in Ancient Judah)...MDBR = 'wilderness' and M = 'from/where' and MAYON = 'residence' and its close relative AYONH = 'marriage'

Wilderness of Paran...MDBR PAHRN...Wilderness of Beauty-and-Self-Boasting (usually considered to be in the Sinai Peninsula)...MDBR = 'wilderness' and PAHRN from PAHR = 'to beautify or glorify oneself, to embellish, boast about oneself' and PAHRH = 'tree bough...often used ornamentally, for decoration'

Wilderness of Ziph...MDBR ZYP...wilderness of tar liquifying in the hot sun (in Ancient Judah)...ZYP probably from ZPT = 'tar or pitch used like tar in the ancient world'

> *Many of the cities named within 1 Samuel cannot be found today. Makes you wonder, yes? Perhaps the band of X was being very crafty with their fiction, especially when the city-name's <u>meaning</u> plays into the flow of the story. And it so often does, so I often translate it that way.*

Ancient Israel's 'Second-Cousins'
(technically, Ancient Judah is a 'second-cousin' too)

Moabites...From-My-Father-Inbreds-from-Moab people (Lot's son...Lot was Abraham's nephew)...MOAHB/'from my father'

Amelekites...The-Laborers, Ancient Israel's second-cousins (Esau's line...Esau was Jacob/Israel's twin brother)...AML means 'to labor'...Agag is their leader, a legendary bandit-warrior whom Samuel cut down with the sword in 1 Samuel 15 because Saul was protecting Agag despite YAHWEH asking Saul to kill Agag

Ammonites...From-My-Inbred-Kinfolk's   people...Ammon/'my people'...the Genesis story with Lot impregnating his daughters gives the name of the ancestor of the Ammonites as Ben-Ammi (BN-AYMY/'child of my people')...their leader Nahash...Snake from NCHSH/'snake, serpent'

Edomites...The-Reds' people (Esau's   nickname   Edom: AHDOM/'red'...Esau was Jacob/Israel's twin brother)

Kenites...Cain's-Kids (Cain's descendants...son of Adam and Eve)...their cities Chavilah (from CHUL/'to whirl around') and Shur (from SHUR/'wall')

Major Opponents of Ancient Israel
& Other Named Cities/Locales

Philistia/Philistines...PLSHTY...the   Dust-Rollers...from   PLSH 'to roll or wallow in the dust, as in mourning'

> *Of course some of these cities still exist today in Palestine and have been much in the news, tragically. Please note that in this translation I'm simply guessing what an Ancient Hebrew speaker might hear in these non-Hebrew city names. Non-Hebrews like the Philistines are always shown as having more faith in YAHWEH than Israelites in the band of YAH and band of X stories.*

the confederacy of the five major Philistine cities
mentioned throughout 1 Samuel:

Ashdod — one of its well-known, powerful cities known for its cruel violence and ravaging other civilizations (from SHADAD 'to deal violently with, spoil, ruin')

Gath — the city with the wine-press and their drunken concerts (see GAT 'winepress' and then see NAGAN 'to pluck the instrument's strings')...in 1 samuel 21 we are told it was ruled by Achish/'Sure-Man'

Ekron — city known for things pulled up by the roots, for childlessness...perhaps a city where DAGON was never able to get fertility going despite the people's prayer (from AYQR verb: 'to pluck up by the roots' noun: barren, having no children)

Gaza — city known for its strength (from AYTS 'strong')

Ashkelon — city known as the bank for weighing produce/wealth... (from SHQL 'to weigh' as in a 'shekel' = a weight/a value of wealth)
the city Sure-There-Achish gave to David:

Ziklag — TSQLG — A-Pint-of-What's-Squeezed/Oppressed — from TSUQ/'pressed or oppressed' and LG/'pint, as in measurement'

other peoples and places...

Beth Shahan...BT SH(AH)N...house of quiet and resting securely...BT = 'house' and SHN or SHAHN (as some texts seem to have it) = 'quiet, resting securely'

Addullam's cave — no known Hebrew cognate — a city not controlled by Ancient Israel or the Dust-Rolling-Philistines, maybe 20 miles away from Sure-There-Achish's city of Gath

Cherethites...CRTY...They-Who-Cut-People-Down...CRT = 'to cut off, to cut down' as in executioners...David will one day claim this foreign people as his personal bodyguard unit

Egypt...MTSRYM...Suffering-Egypt, same consonants as a singular word in Hebrew that means 'suffering'...who knows what an ancient Hebrew would first think of when they heard MTSRYM? To many Hebrew people though, Egypt was a place of suffering as the story says they were slaves there, a place with a significant hierarchical imagination, enough to use slaves to construct pyramids and great cities for their thought-to-be-divine Pharaoh. Egypt, of course, did not call itself "suffering"... that combination of sounds surely produced different meanings in the many languages used in Egypt but to Hebrew ears it was often "suffering" and far from the wandering-freedom of the ecstatics-prophets...Egypt referred to itself by many names, Masur being one name...notice the similarity between Masur and MTSR...in any case, the great irony is that Ancient Israel chooses a similar hierarchical and slave-holding system as their legendary enslavers — the Egyptians — for the form of government they would most like for themselves.

Geshurites...GSHURY...the people known for their bridge-building...*Strong's Exhaustive Concordance* notes that GSHUR is from a word that has to do with 'joining/bridging'

Gerizim...GRZY...the people who lived off by themselves by the rocks...*Strong's Exhaustive Concordance* notes that GRZ is from a root that means 'cut up or cut off, rocky'

Brook of Besor...NCHL BSOR...Cheerful-News Stream...NCHL = 'brook, stream' and BSR = 'glad tidings, good news, happy'

Jerahmeel...YRCHMAHL...EL-has-womblike-compassion... RCHL/'womblike-compassion' and AHL/'EL'

Shur...SHUR/'the wall'

Prophets-Ecstatics
...and their circular,
all-are-equal imagination
inviting people to
relationship with the
wind/YAHWEH...
all one needs is to feel
such ecstasy

Priests & Authorities
...and their hierarchical
mindset demanding that
God be worshipped
through their leadership
with the ark, temple &
613 laws of the Torah

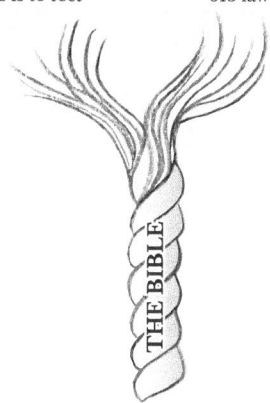

The Levitical priests and the political party called today "the Deuteronomists" twined the Bible together. While it's a gift to us all that they included the ecstatics'-prophets' stories and poems, the ways the Levites and Deuteronomists assembled the Bible usually has us readers today looking at the ecstatics-prophets through a priestly-lens or authoritarian-minded lens. The ecstatics-prophets were pointing out the ridiculousness of priestly-political attempts at control when YAHWEH gives life and freedom with a wind flowing over all human-made borders.

The word 'Hebrew' actually means 'bordercrosser'...someone who is flexible, can grow roots anywhere, can be in relationship with the wild wind anywhere and everywhere YAHWEH invites. The ecstatics-prophets told stories inviting people to breathe in this perspective and this wandering, nomadic experience their ancestors used to know well before they built cities and temples and joined empires, by choice or not.

The rivalry and family-quarrel between the ecstatics and the Levites/Deuteronomists is the entire purpose of the Bible with each camp speaking at each other and trying to sway each other through the many centuries of crafting the Bible.

One invites love
and flexibility...

today...groups who are curious about the deeper roots
and who seek to mine the gifts of the present moment
and all present...circles of deciders

the writer of the Gospel of Thomas, wisdom through
personal experience and 'study-through-play' of past wisdom
to create new wisdom

Paul and his all-are-equal-before-God imagination...Paul is the
first imaginer ever of democratic communities without slavery

Jesus and his clever, funny wisdom sayings and actions
inviting conversion within and love of enemies and relying
on God alone (not priests or kings or authorities)

wildly clever poems of the prophets...
Amos, the Isaiahs, Jeremiah, and others

the band of X, authors of 1 & 2 Samuel and (perhaps)
1 & 2 Kings and the inspiring stories about the prophets and
the foolishness of kings & priests

the band of YAH's Genesis stories that upset the
hierarchical & patriarchal apple-cart of Ancient Babylon

ecstatics' (prophets') mountaintop experiences of
YAHWEH, the wind...the playful, clever, spiraling, poetic
imagination reacting to Ancient Babylon's and Ancient Egypt's
royal/slave superpower imaginations

today…groups who still think one human being
is worth more than another (hierarchical, priestly,
royal/slave fascist imagination)

the writer of the Gospel of John and "belief"
as all you need (makes Thomas look like a fool)

Peter and his hierarchical camp that rejected Paul's vision of
equality and perhaps wrote Acts of the Apostles to reduce Paul's
power/prestige (they also change Paul's letters years later)

the military/royal title "**Christ**" and the king/redeemer
mythology inflicted upon Jesus, an imagination
cementing over Jesus' wisdom and lifestyle

Ezekiel, Nehemiah, Ezra and I/II Chronicles…
the priestly efforts to craft a priest-led religious
tradition and subvert the prophets

priestly imagination that assembled the **Torah**
and the character **Moses** as greatest of everything,
even greatest prophet…though he has little to no
ecstatic poetry/action like the prophets

the **Deuteronomist** "political party" who enabled
the royals and began the first written Bible during
King Josiah's reign

Ancient Babylon & its towers and metropolises
like Uruk…and **the hierarchical, royal/slave
imagination** required to build such things…
where one human is thought to be better than
another…the imagination of slavery/royalty

…one does not.

Bibliography

Jean-Louis Biget. *Les Cathares: albigeois et <<bon hommes>>*. France: Editions Gisserot...though I benefitted most from the exhibit where I bought the book in Toulouse at the Couvent des Jacobins: *Cathares: Toulouse dans la croisade,* visited 10 July 2024. This exhibit was very out front with saying that the Albigensian Crusade was essentially a partnership by the King of Paris and the Vatican to kill off most of the people of the southern French towns to steal their land and property to enrich Paris/France and the Vatican.

Walter Brueggemann. *The Prophetic Imagination*. Minneapolis: Fortress Press, 1978.

Reinier de Blois offered a workshop "Cognitive Linguistics in Biblical Interpretation" at the Society of Biblical Literature annual conference, San Antonio 2023. I was delighted to learn that other scholars are wondering about the many directions Ancient Hebrew words can move...and how few scholars in the room could play with such gray areas of meaning.

Arthur J. Dewey, Roy W. Hoover, Lane C. McGaughy, Daryl D. Schmidt. *The Authentic Letters of Paul: A New Reading of Paul's Rhetoric and Meaning*. Salem, OR: Polebridge, 2010.

Bryan Doerries (translator). *All That You've Seen Here Is God: New Versions of Sophocles & Aeschylus*. New York: Vintage, 2015.

Moshe Feldenkrais. *The Potent Self: A Study of Spontaneity and Compulsion*. Berkeley, CA: Somatic Resources & Frog Books, 1985/2002.

Israel Finkelstein. "A Great United Monarchy? Archeological and Historical Perspectives." (I read it via academia.edu...

originally published in *One God - One Cult - One Nation*. ed. by Reinhard G. Kratz and Hermann Spieckermann. Berlin: De Gruyter, 2010.)

Israel Finkelstein and Neil Asher Silberman. *The Bible Unearthed: Archaeology's New Vision of Ancient Israel and the Origin of Its Sacred Texts*. New York: Touchstone, 2001.

Robert W. Funk, Arthur J. Dewey, & the Jesus Seminar. *The Gospel of Jesus: According to the Jesus Seminar*. Salem, OR: Polebridge, 2015.

Hans-Georg Gadamer. *Truth and Method*. New York: Continuum, 1993.

Theodore W. Jennings, Jr. *Jacob's Wound: Homoerotic Narrative in the Literature of Ancient Israel*. New York: Continuum, 2005. This book flipped my world up-side down. I found a used copy at Strand Bookstore in New York City six years ago while there for Feldenkrais training. For the past year or so before that, I had been working on a book about the prophets and was flailing around with it. There were strange things in the Ancient Hebrew texts that I didn't think were palatable for modern audiences. I wondered if I had the courage and resolve to say out loud — or in writing — what was there. Dr. Jenning's book gave me the nudge to go with it, to let those ancient writings say now what they were trying to say then...hopefully with some ears in this 21st century that might wish to listen and ponder a YAHWEH that wants intimate relationship with you and me. Irony of ironies, a high school religion colleague took graduate school classes with Dr. Jennings at Chicago Theological Seminary! My only sadness is that Dr. Jennings died before I could meet him. My condolences and love to his wife and family and many students.

Carl Gustav Jung, edited by William McGuire and R.F.C. Hull. *C.G. Jung Speaking: Interviews and Encounters*. Princeton, NJ: Princeton (Bollingen Series), 1977.

Caleb K. King "What Sounding Alike Sounded Like: Understanding Sound Similarity in Biblical Poetics Through Close Consonance" at the Society of Biblical Literature annual conference, San Diego 2024. The most important paper I heard at the conference.

Stephen L. McKenzie. *King David: A Biography*. New York: Oxford, 2000.

Robert J. Miller, editor. *The Complete Gospels: Annotated Scholars Version*. Sonoma, CA: Polebridge, 1994.

William Armstrong Percy III. *Pederasty and Pedagogy in Archaic Greece*. Urbana/Chicago: University of Illinois Press, 1996. While it makes no mention of Ancient Israel as a potential place for military-pederasty, this book helped me to understand how that practice was used in Crete, Greece, and Sparta to create a very organized, vastly hierarchical military-system.

Thomas Römer. *L'Ancien Testament*. Paris: Que sais-je? / Humensis, 2019.

Thomas Römer. *The Invention of God*. (trans Raymond Geuss). Cambridge, MA: Harvard University Press, 2015.

Thomas Römer. *The So-Called Deuteronomistic History: A Sociological, Historical and Literary Introduction*. New York: T&T Clark/Continuum, 2007. This book began the paradigm shift in me that led to the second edition of *The Naked Path of Prophet* with all improved commentaries and a better understanding of how this wild text of 1 Samuel ended up in the Bible. My only hope is that scholars will begin to spend more time with my translation and wonder about it and return to the Hebrew text and wonder some more...and then come to notice even more deeply the supreme cleverness of the biblical authors I call 'X' and their playful ecstatic-prophetic style.

Thomas Römer, editor. *The Future of the Deuteronomistic History*. Leuven: Leuven University Press / Peeters, 2000.

Thomas Römer and Loyse Bonjour. *L'homosexualité dans le Proche-Orient ancien et la Bible*. Geneva: Editions Labor et Fides, 2016.

Indries Shah. *The Sufis*. New York: Anchor, 1971.

Jacob L. Wright. *David, King of Israel, and Caleb in Biblical Memory*. New York: Cambridge, 2014.

biblehub.com was very useful as well in helping to compare verb-form possibilities as well as an easy-to-use *Strong's Exhaustive Concordance*

> Please consult the Resources for Further Study in *A Wildly Sensual YAHWEH* for more.

about the translator/commentator

In addition to **The Naked Path of Prophet** series, Brian Shircliff is the poet of **winds of (r)evolution** (paintings by Matthew Klooster) and author of the graphic novel **YAHWEH IS THE WIND!** (illustrated by Sean K. Long). Having taught high school religion for seventeen years, he felt the need to swim away from the shipwreck of organized religion for a more inclusive perspective. He is a Bones for Life® Trainer, Guild Certified Feldenkrais Practitioner, Healing Touch Certified Practitioner, and thirty-year student of many styles of meditation. He co-founded and continues to direct VITALITY Cincinnati's donation-based holistic self-care programs.

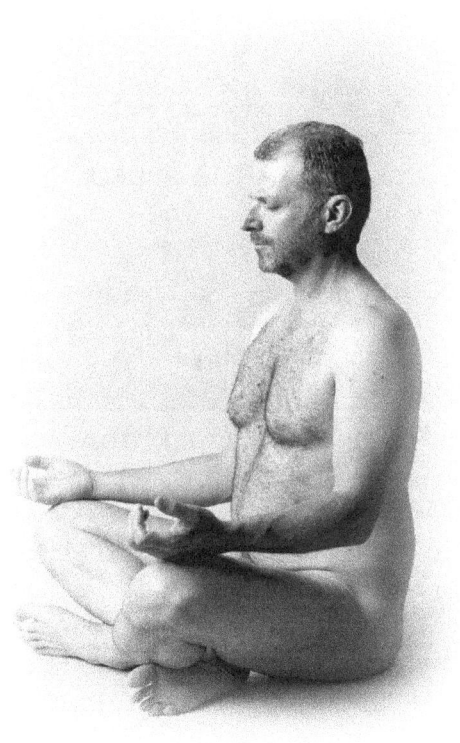

about the artists

Sean K. Long...cover image

Sean Long is a father and husband based in Cincinnati, Ohio. He is an accomplished artist, musician, poet, and writer. His creative works range from murals, portraits, sculptures, music, to cartoons, comics and so much more, including the graphic novel YAHWEH IS the Wind! with Brian Shircliff. Sean has a true dedication to his craft. He infuses his work with passion, creativity and life experience. Through his company "The Art Department" he brings his creative vision to clients. For collaborations, contact Sean at TheArtDepartmentCincy@gmail.com

Julie Lucas...all interior images, cover design, VITALITY's logos

Julie Lucas is a graphic designer, illustrator and meditator whose creative process draws from inquiry and deep listening into the heart of it all. See more of her work at withinwonder.com.

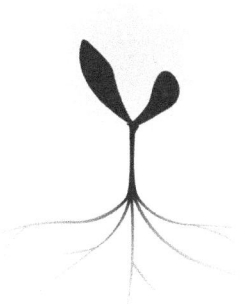

about VITALITY

VITALITY is a circle of friends welcoming all, awakening each other, and reminding each other that we are Whole. Our affordable self-care programs invite everyone to move, to breathe, to rest, to contemplate, to grow...wherever each person begins their self-care journey, wherever and however they want to become.

It's the power of a circle!

we invite you to explore with us through our

donation-based drop-in classes...in person & via Zoom
affordable trainings
individual sessions
volunteer opportunities

vitalitycincinnati.org

VITALITY
buzz, bliss + books

publishing books from VITALITY's circle of friends
inspiring love, creativity, + possibility

vitalitybuzz.org

a vignette to send us off with import

...if you were gathered at the family holiday table and everyone was sharing stories about a long-ago deceased relative, all these wonderful stories about him and you always notice there's a pause after the stories as if there's more to it than that but no one is saying and if they do say anything they say "such a wonderful man—" before rushing off to the next topic

— this "wonderful" relative after whom you've all been named —

and finally you ask more about him and the relative at the end of the table who has had just a bit too much to drink spits out, "—you mean about the 500 innocent human beings he killed?"

and everyone gets super quiet and hides their hands in their laps and avoids eye contact with each other

except the older relative who doesn't hear well says, "Wonderful man, all the philanthropy he did..." to the collective shock of everyone else at the table, at this hard-of-hearing relative's timing,

and the drunk-relative seems even more emboldened by the hard-hearing relative and sputters out, "—wonderful, wonderful, blah blah blah—in all his wonderfulness he slaughtered 500 people and took their wealth and that paid for this fine table around which we gather and all of our homes and all of our educations and—and—and—"

and now the story is out in the open — and everyone seems to have known it besides you and does not challenge the drunk relative's important addition — and ancestor-so-and-so after whom you are named just like everyone else at this feast just got way more complex for you...and your relatives just got way more complex too in that they'd been saying your whole life "what a wonderful man" about a relative who they had known killed 500 innocent people and got rich — even generationally rich — from it

and as the now very awkward meal begins breaking up, you find one relative you trust and ask that they tell you more and they do and you are (likely) shocked at the details and the gruesome nature of these crimes and at how for decades of your life you were led to believe that this ancestor was a "wonderful man" but indeed now you have to wonder at the incomplete image you had of him and at the silence of your family all these years...

and with this little vignette you and I might wonder together how humans have been perpetuating the *christ/messiah* myth all these generations — millennia — without evaluating it and all that goes with it...and wishing our "Merry Christmases" with reverence and raising up David with pride...all the while perpetuating a problematic story, even with our good intentions...

and in this pregnant moment of pause we can decide if we want to be silent any longer, or if we want to begin to peel away the razor-sharp barbed wire of a story from the goodness interwoven around the dangerous barbed wire...

peel them away from each other and then, in every interaction and with every generation, ask oneself and one another, "Out of which one do you want to live? What do you choose? More life/love for all or more killing to benefit a few?"

We have this choice.
If we all choose love, we just might make it.

www.ingramcontent.com/pod-product-compliance
Lightning Source LLC
Chambersburg PA
CBHW060759120626
46557CB00001B/29